the three day Nanny

I dedicate this book to my mother:

my mentor, my guide and my sounding board,

the major influence who made me what I am today.

With love and thanks

Kathryn x

the three day Nanny

Your toddler problems **solved**

Kathryn Mewes

Vermilion
LONDON

10 9 8 7 6 5 4 3 2 1

Vermilion, an imprint of Ebury Publishing,
20 Vauxhall Bridge Road,
London SW1V 2SA

Vermilion is part of the Penguin Random House group of companies whose
addresses can be found at global.penguinrandomhouse.com

Penguin
Random House
UK

Produced by **Bookworx**
Project editor Jo Godfrey Wood
Project designer Peggy Sadler

First published by Vermilion in 2015

www.eburypublishing.co.uk

A CIP catalogue record for this book is available from the British Library

ISBN 9781785040306

Printed and bound in Great Britain by Clays Ltd, St Ives PLC

Penguin Random House is committed to a sustainable future for our business,
our readers and our planet. This book is made from Forest Stewardship Council®
certified paper.

Contents

About the author

Kathryn Mewes was born in London in 1973 and she lived there for the first seven years of her life. Family moves took her first to Wiltshire and then to Hampshire, where she completed her education.

In 1992 Kathryn started studying at the Norland College in Hungerford and graduated from there with a Distinction in 1994. She also won The Gifford Hall Award for Excellence. From there she began her career as a Norland nanny, staying with families for extended periods and learning and growing alongside the parents. She soon developed a fascination for the dynamics of family life and it became an ongoing study.

After nine years as a nanny, Kathryn went to Australia, where she lived for three years and spent time with many families, helping to resolve concerns they had about their children's behaviour. Before long she realised that she only needed to be in a family's home for three days in order to bring about long-lasting change.

In 2007 Kathryn returned to London and launched her own business in the UK. Now based in Southwest London, she travels the country every week working with different families on their particular challenges. Her business is called Bespoke Nanny and her formula is to stay with the family for up to 72 hours and then carry on guiding them and advising for the next month via phone.

In her first book *The 3 Day Nanny*, Kathryn shared with parents the techniques she developed over the years in personal consultation, outlining her strategies for helping parents with problems with children from aged six months to six years. In 2013 she made the highly successful TV programme *The Three Day Nanny* and another series is planned for 2015 to coincide with this book.

Introduction

Make no mistake, parenting can be a tough job! The moment you think you've got something right, whether it's getting your child to stay in her own bed at night or learning not to use a loud voice in public, your child changes. The goalposts shift and all of a sudden you're looking at slightly different issues. You have to adapt to change quickly and many parents beat themselves up about not being able to do everything 'perfectly' every time.

'My process is 99.9 per cent guaranteed to work, with consistency as the key.'

What I am offering parents

Well, I have news! When it comes to parenting, there really is no such thing as 'perfection'. If you get it right half of the time, you'll be doing well. The other half of parenting is what is called 'life' and sometimes you will just have to roll with the punches. My aim is to help you, as a parent, feel guilt-free, confident and realistic in your approach to raising your child. It's a good idea not to set up overly high standards and expectations of your parenting skills, because you will have to make mistakes (and learn from them) sometimes. It may be reassuring to hear that it's also important for your child to witness you making mistakes and learning from them too – your behaviour (in all areas of your lives) will be reflected in your child's behaviour. That way they will feel able to make mistakes and learn from them in their future lives.

In my 20 years' experience of working with families as a Norland-trained nanny, I have developed my own three-day process for solving common problems and issues connected with children and raising them. My method is to spend three days staying with a family to help them understand and then sort out their family problem using the techniques that I have developed. My process is 99.9 per cent guaranteed to work – provided you follow my guidelines and remain consistent at all times.

It's not always obvious to parents how best to raise their child and children certainly don't come with instruction manuals attached! So often it's a steep learning curve for everyone. It's been my great pleasure to be able to help parents and guide their children towards a happier and more harmonious family life. This book has been designed to help you resolve any problem that might be holding your family back and get everyone back on track.

About the three-day process

My process relies on using specific Tools and Skills over a three-day period. The Tools are created by parents themselves, and sometimes the children too, from ordinary, everyday materials (improvisation and creativity can come into play here!). They are used during the three-day process, often as an incentive to learn and behave better (and that includes the parents too!). The Skills are devised from commonsense knowledge, which most parents already have but perhaps just need to know how to make use of. I also help parents alter the way they relate to their child by offering constructive speech patterns to help point the child in a more positive direction. This approach can move the child on from the unwanted behaviour and help him grow and develop in the way that everyone wants to see. With persistence, consistency and awareness of the child's needs, parents can use the Tools and Skills to guide the child forwards in life in a way that's good for everyone. The original problem or issue will soon become a distant memory.

'Emotions come to the fore at difficult times and sometimes it's hard to know what to do for the best.'

We all have different personalities and characters, including children, so it's not surprising that sometimes we clash with our children and find them hard to handle. The toddler age group is when we first notice our child asserting his will and perhaps refusing to go along with what we want, but if we can solve such clashes early, the way forward into childhood, the teen years and beyond will be much more happy and straightforward. Mutual respect is something that we need to find and then nurture with our children.

Emotions come to the fore at difficult times and sometimes it's hard to know what to do for the best – our minds become confused and we are unhappy. I offer a range of helpful personality archetypes to help parents understand their children and themselves – and suggest why sparks sometimes fly.

Life can be complex and the demands made on parents in their everyday lives can be huge. I understand that many parents have busy working lives and have to juggle the stresses of their jobs with the demands of home life. The Tools and Skills in this book are fuss- and guilt-free and can be returned to and adapted whenever you need. I hope that this book will help you not just resolve your family problems but also grow into a happy family unit – ready to launch your children into the world.

Kathryn Mewes

How to use this book

This book is divided into two main parts – Part 1 The three-day process: background and Part 2 The three-day process: tools, skills and scenarios.

Part 1 explains the three-day process and the theory behind it. In it you will find all the background information you need to prepare for using my advice. Included are nine detailed case studies to show you how the process can become a reality – to turn your lives around.

Part 2 begins with an alphabetical list of all the Tools and Skills used in the scenario section which follows, illustrating how you can use them and giving helpful examples. Then follow more than 100 real-life scenarios of common toddler problem areas connected with: Sleep, Eating, Behaviour and Potty Training. The final section, 'Out and About', explores situations that might arise when you and your child are outside the home.

'This book is designed to be dipped into or read from start to finish – whatever works best for you. '

The scenarios are designed to be a bit like recipes. You are presented with the issue or the problem and then offered 'ingredients' of Tools and/or Skills. The 'method' teaches you how to react, what to do, what to say to your child, how to use the Tools and Skills and how

Mums, dads – and everyone else!

You will see that throughout this book 'parents' are referred to as comprising one man and one woman. Mums, because they are often the main care-givers in the family, are usually the parent that is referred to in the text. But when it comes to being a parent, dads (and/or the other partner) are just as important! Many families have different parenting variations and combinations, and they are just as much parents as the conventional 'norm'. This decision had to be made for the sake of editorial convenience, so please don't be put off if you feel that your own situation has been overlooked or not reflected adequately. The situations described here are universal and are found in any family, whatever its make-up. Just take what you need and adapt it to your own situation.

What if the three-day process doesn't work?

All the processes described in this book have been tried and tested by the author and by many parents over the past 20 years. However, not everyone has succeeded in achieving what they set out to do the first time around. Perhaps the time wasn't right because of other family pressures or for health reasons. Perhaps the parents didn't remain fully consistent or started to adapt the process as the days went by. Or perhaps they failed to remain consistent with the idea that only one parent should be the one in charge of the process for the first three days.

For example, in relation to sleep issues, you have to have the same parent putting the child to bed and getting up in the night for between five and seven nights. If this doesn't happen, you might find that your child plays one parent off against the other, saying, 'Mummy said I could have the light on' or 'Daddy said I can have one more story'.

The process can easily break down if you don't remain completely consistent, doing EXACTLY the same things for three consecutive days at least. Then after the initial three days the consistency needs to continue. If you start to relax after a week you will slowly see your child taking back the control and recreating the problem that you so brilliantly solved only a week ago.

Even if you have not been consistent you can learn from your mistakes and start the process again. There is no need to give up, since making mistakes is often the best way to learn.

to persevere if the process doesn't seem to be working at first. Adapt the Tools and Skills to suit your own situation. Be as creative as you like and give your personality full flow. Get your child involved. For example, if you want to use the fill-it-up jar Incentive System with pasta, have fun painting pasta shells in different colours. Your child will feel involved and will enjoy a fun craft activity. You may not find the exact scenario to match your own predicament or difficulty, but you will be able to search through and find one that is similar, adjusting the advice for your own purposes.

PART 1

The three-day process: background

Don't despair! Before you start on the three-day process, take a few minutes to become familiar with some background information. It will give you a firm foundation to work on. Think over the 'big five' areas that commonly present problems: sleeping, eating, behaviour, potty training and going out and about. Then pause to think about what kind of parent you are and what kind of child yours is, followed by looking at the 'ground rules' of parenting. Lastly, discover how the three-day process can work to turn your family life around and read through some real-life case studies to see how parents have already used the process successfully.

1 Empowered parenting

Raising a child requires you to adjust and adapt your whole life. The three-day process will help to turn you into a parent who is truly empowered and in control. You'll soon find that by looking at the five key childcare issues (sleeping, eating, behaviour, potty training and being out and about), life with your child will become a whole lot easier – and more enjoyable too.

'Everything is new and there's a lot to get used to and integrate into your life.'

Life before parenthood

Having babies is a joyous time of life, but you may still be getting used to the many adjustments that having a child has led you to make. It could be that you never really had much contact with babies and children before you had one yourself, so you will have been through a steep learning curve – everything from handling a tiny baby, getting her changed to figuring out why she cries and how she feeds plus her initially unpredictable sleep patterns. Everything is new and there's a lot to get used to.

You might not be able to remember what 'life before children' was like, but you may look back fondly on an era of some, or all, of the following: educating yourself, working a job, spending time with your partner, friends and family, enjoying cultural and social activities and generally living your life the way you wanted. You were probably mostly in charge of your time, your day and how you spent it. It therefore may have come as a bit of a shock when you had your baby and found that your time was more or less governed by this little person, who demanded a lot of attention. In fact, it almost seemed as though your small one needed you 24 hours a day, at least at the beginning.

On top of all this, you may have had to move house, put your career on hold, drop some work days, arrange complex childcare arrangements and generally go through a massive adaptation to having a child. Not easy. You might still be feeling a bit overwhelmed by all the changes, but equally you might also feel challenged and empowered by what you need to do. Your life might seem a bit chaotic but mundane at the same time. But don't worry! You can bring it to order and make it a whole lot more enjoyable – and that, on its own, is supremely satisfying.

Another common scenario that might have affected you is becoming a step parent. You might have teamed up with a partner who already has children. Although this book doesn't tackle all the intricacies associated with that situation, you might well find that some of the parenting problems that come up are addressed in the Scenario chapter (see page 78). Hopefully these will help you.

We all have ideas about what being a parent might be like for us. The reality might be a little different. The good news is that you can really turn your life around in just three days. But you need a strategy – and this book can help!

How can you make change happen?

So maybe the time has come to make some changes. How can you do that? Perhaps you can take a look at the presenting 'problems' and isolate them. For example, your toddler might well be acting up because she is jealous of the new baby. She craves your attention around the clock, but she can't have it – nor does she really need it. She needs to grow up into a 'big girl' and feel happy in herself. She is not aware of being jealous; she can only express her feelings and these are not so surprising, really. How might you teach her to change, so that her impact on everyone else is more reasonable, so that you can have some space and slowly start to bring order to all your lives?

By learning some simple strategies and ways of talking to your child, you can identify a simple problem and set up an easy three-day process to help your child adjust her ways. You will learn about Tools and Skills you can use during the three days – some are commonsense reward systems that you can adapt to your own situation while others are skills

'You might still be feeling a bit overwhelmed by all the changes, but equally you might also feel challenged and empowered by what you need to do.'

you can cultivate yourself. For example, you can teach yourself to use a firm, authoritative voice (your Teacher Tone) and you will soon discover how effective this technique can be when dealing with your child.

'By solving every-day parenting problems, you can start to become a happy family group.'

Maybe you have already checked through some of the Tools (see page 54) and think that you aren't quite up to dreaming up suitable rewards, drawing up incentive charts or thinking up tools that your child will respond to. Rest assured! Most of these ideas are commonsense and the ones that require a bit of your creativity are incredibly simple to achieve. When you start getting a good response from your child, you'll soon feel encouraged to go further and dream up even more great ideas that your child will love to get involved with.

How things could, and will, be

By solving everyday parenting problems, you can start to become a happy family group, flourishing and enjoying being together. Your child will become more contented, developing as she should and becoming a joy to have around. You, in turn, will become contented parents, fulfilled in your parenting role, managing all aspects of your lives with ease. After three days of implementing the process 100 per cent of the time, the problem you have, or rather had, with your child should become a thing of the past. However, if, for some reason, things haven't improved, you simply have to persevere with the process until you do see results. And you will!

The five key areas that present problems

It's useful to think about your child's life as falling into five key areas that present problems requiring 'life skills', which you need to establish in your child early on – between six months and six years. Then she can move ahead with confidence. Each life-skill area affects another and they are, to a great extent, interconnected. Sleeping and eating are the two big issues, but also important are behavioural and social skills, without which your child cannot function effectively in the world. So parenting is not about you, the parent, merely 'bossing' the child to do your bidding, but more about encouraging her to think things through and then choose the right path. By using positive language, praise and rewards along the way, you can help guide your child through life smoothly and assist her in becoming a sensitive, aware and socialised human being. If, in the process, your child doesn't 'get' your suggestions and fails to do what you ask or develops bad habits that disrupt family life, you can create a bag, or shelf, of homemade Tools to help you, as well as a rich supply of useful, commonsense parenting Skills to draw on to help you achieve results.

> **THE FAMOUS FIVE!**
> • Sleep
> • Eating
> • Behaviour
> • Potty training
> • Out and about

Sleep

The most important subject, sleep, comes first because without good sleep patterns all other aspects of the child's (and yours) life can go off track. Think about it: if your child's sleep is constantly being interrupted, for whatever reason, she can become grumpy, pale and wan. On top of this she won't be able to concentrate on playing and learning. She might stop thriving and, in the long term, her growth might even be affected. So establishing good sleep patterns for your child is a top priority. Oh and don't forget yourself! You need sleep to be a good un-grumpy parent.

Eating

Eating comes a close second – it's a huge one and one which parents worry about constantly. Issues around food – especially if the child seems to have turned into a picky eater – are commonly heard about and it's not unknown for the child to dominate family mealtimes by insisting on only eating certain foods, ruining the occasion for everyone, not least themselves. No one likes a fussy eater, especially not in later years, and it's just not good for your child to be like this (nutritionally or socially), so this is an issue you want to crack – if at all possible.

Behaviour

Behaviour? Well, that's a big one too! This isn't just about your child remembering all her p's and q's or being able to share her toys with her friends – and for you to feel rightly proud of your little darling. It's more about the child feeling engaged with the people and the world, respectful and having a sense of belonging in it. Good behaviour all adds up to one thing, really – a child who is a pleasure to be with and who can flourish and learn.

Potty training

Potty training is a subject that exercises and exhausts a lot of parents. However, this is usually a simple issue. The decision to be nappy-free is one that your child makes, not you. Unfortunately if you turn it into a battle of wills your child will win. Potty training is all about the timing, but rest assured, it will happen! It's just a question of gauging when your child is ready and able to take on the challenge of going without nappies. And there are plenty of things that you can do to help make the process simple and straightforward.

Out and about

This is our final category – and an important one too. This is where you are out of the home, whether just walking down the road to the shops or visiting an elderly relative. Wherever you are when you are out of the house, you want to be with a child who is safe, who reflects well on you and your parenting and who is happy and a delight to be with. The last thing you want is for your toddler to throw a wobbly all over

'Good behaviour all adds up to one thing really – a child who is a pleasure to be with and who can flourish and learn.'

How this book can help

This book tackles the key areas that I've seen families struggle with time and again. It will help you delve into your own resources and find the skills you need to help sort out the commonest tricky annoyances. Perhaps you need help in gaining control over a situation that has slipped under the radar – without your noticing it.

For example, one day it dawns on you that you have been giving your toddler pasta, and only pasta, for a whole week. How did that happen? After all, you are a sensible parent who knows about what is 'good' and 'bad' food, who wants their child to eat a healthy balanced diet, but somehow this situation has become a reality. Don't panic. The processes, Tools and Skills described in this book will help to build your confidence and get you back on track.

the supermarket and for people to be looking at you and waiting for you to do something, while you lose your cool and shout at your child. If you do anything, you want to display your skills as an effective parent who can act calmly, do something about the situation and put things right.

You are your child's main role model

Your child learns from the world around her, and at the toddler age you, as parents, are her main role model. When you reflect, you might notice that your child's behaviour mirrors your own – for good or ill! The good news is that by understanding yourself as a parent, understanding your child and following the advice in these pages, you will learn how to turn your family life around and get everyone back on track in no time at all.

' You will learn how to turn your family life around and get everyone back on track in no time at all. '

2 What are our personalities?

We all come into this world with a different personality from the next person. How do your react to your child's personality and how does he react to yours? This will have major impact on the way you interact and engage with your child's behaviour. The first thing to do is decide what personality types are present in your family.

What type of parent are you?

'We are all different as individuals, and so it's no surprise to hear that everyone has their different ways of raising their child.'

Well, we're going to start with you – yes you, the parent. You may find this a bit surprising, as you're probably thinking that it's the child (and his behaviour) who needs to be looked at and 'improved' or 'corrected'. But you have to ask yourself – how did my child get to be the way he is? He can only have learned his behaviour from one or two people thus far in his short life, and those people were probably you...

In my work as Bespoke Nanny, I spend a few days with parents who believe their child has a problem that I could help with. Whenever I see new clients I always get the ball rolling by asking them about their own lives, how they deal with and balance everything and how they go about parenting their child. We are all individuals, so it's no surprise to hear that everyone has their different ways of raising their child, according to their own personalities and the kinds of upbringing they've had themselves. It's vital for me to find out what their parenting style is, so that as we pursue my three-day plan I can work with them to use their strengths to the full while bolstering weaker aspects. It's not my role to tell them whether they are 'right' or 'wrong' – they are who they are – so I have identified three typical styles of parent:

- Orderly and organised
- Mindful and attentive
- Relaxed and adaptable

Perhaps you can identify with one of these categories.

The orderly and organised parent

You are the kind of person who gravitates naturally towards rules and regulations, helpful guidelines and established procedures. You like to have things set down in black and white, you love to have your life under control and you favour structure and order. For example, you always put your appointments in your diary (and then you remember to look at it frequently!). To-do lists – well, you practically invented them! The impact your personality has on being a parent? Well, you are a dab hand at organising your home life and 'efficiency' is your second name. This is all good, since children love order and routine and thrive on it, as we shall see. However, sometimes you get thrown when your plans have to change. For example, doing the three-day plan might irritate you at first because it might mean you have to alter your carefully worked-out routine. Not to worry, though. You can get back on track by studying all the information and planning the time in detail. For example, stocking up your fridge in advance of starting the three-day plan will put you straight back into your comfort zone.

'Keep things light and you will soon see positive results.'

You may be used to being completely in charge of handling your child, and it could be that he feels a lack of power as a result. It's good to remember that you won't be implementing the ideas in the three-day plan just by dishing out instructions (but you do need to explain how it will work to your child in a challenging, exciting way) as something that everyone in the family is going to be involved in. Keep things light and you will soon see great results. If the process is presented in the right way, your child will feel involved and empowered in it.

The mindful and attentive parent

If you feel that this is 'you', you are very likely to be a first-time parent and you may feel pretty unsure about things, which is quite normal. You are open to receiving advice and differing views and you have read a lot of books about how to be a good parent. Before making up your mind about any issue, you like to gather as much information together as possible. You tend not to take an instinctive approach but base your actions on carefully weighed up information. You may be a bit of a worrier because you tend to err on the cautious side and this can be very tiring for you – and for your children too – when they pick up on your worry and perhaps misbehave more. If only you could stop doubting your own parenting capabilities, in the long run your child's behaviour would improve.

The relaxed and adaptable parent

You will relate to this category if you are a calm kind of person who takes things as they come. Your biggest downfall with regard to looking after children is that you are super-aware of everything around you and you are likely to be highly involved in many aspects of life – you may find it hard to focus on what really needs to be done now. You have a lot of distractions in your life and you are not good at sticking to routines and meeting deadlines. This can make things hard when tasks fail to be completed and projects that need finishing back up behind you. You probably have a calm, relaxed approach to looking after your child, which is great, but sometimes this might result in your child lacking good boundaries and trying to put himself in charge, leading to challenges with discipline and difficulties in following set routines such as the three-day plan.

What type of child do you have?

'If you study your child's behaviour for long enough you will see yourself – or your partner – or both!'

Just as there are different types of parents, so there are different types of child (in terms of exerting their own power and getting their own way) – their personality and disposition – and the way they react to the world around them. Of course, your child might be a mixture of these types, but there tends to be a pattern to the more common problems and it is these three that seem to be typical, seeming to try to gain control in the household and in need of the three-day process. If your child has an easy-going and sunny outlook and is easy to manage he is probably not in need of the three-day process in the first place. You will probably know straight away which category your child is in:

- The Negotiator
- The Fighter
- The Drama Queen/King

Child types

The Negotiator This child, no matter what you do, always wants a bit more, or something a little different from what's on offer. Or he wants the next thing that's going to happen. For example, he will insist on only eating certain foods and before you know it you always seem to be serving him his favourites – not good when you are aiming to give him a balanced diet and if you have other children this can create problems. They might decide they all want to eat something different.

The Negotiator gets his own way by using charm – so even a tiny babe might flash you a disarming grin while insisting that you fetch him his preferred dish instead of the new foods you are trying him on. Later, when your child learns to speak he will use words to argue with you and to try to get his own way. It doesn't matter what you do, he will always want something different and you can easily find yourself being pushed around by this tiny tyrant. When you are this child's parent, you need to adapt your parenting style, gather your confidence and strength and exert your own will. You have to remain in charge.

The Fighter This individual sees life as something that challenges him and he is always adamant about getting his own way. So if he thinks he's 'losing', he may well become very upset – shouting and perhaps even hitting out. You might feel that you have to give in to him – just for the sake of an easy life. But this approach is really not going to do anyone any favours long term. The Fighter can make his personality traits felt right from the get-go – so a tiny baby will tend to fight with you whenever you, for example, put him into his car seat. Even if he understands what the plan is, he will tend to resist you every inch of the way. As a parent, your best plan is to stay cool and calm, but you may well find that this is a challenge that's hard to deal with. Your best plan is to pick off one tricky issue at a time, solve it using the three-day process and then move on. You won't get anywhere by fighting with your Fighter child.

The Drama Queen/King Life is never dull being the parent of a Drama Queen/King. The slightest reverse and your Drama child will start to whine and shout, using tears to make his feelings heard. The best way of parenting such a child is to always stay consistent and never cave in to his wishes. You may be sucked in by his dramatic 'performances' but be aware that he loves an audience and if you remove that, you will be moving in the right direction. He will probably calm down straight away. He needs to get his emotions out, so the best parenting tactic is to guide him somewhere calm and quiet and let him soothe himself. Then you can move on with the day.

Adapting your parenting styles to suit your child

Here are some general tips for dealing with different types of child.

- Try 'going against' your instinct (if this has not been working). So start by stopping and thinking before you react.
- If your child won't accept the word 'no' and continually negotiates, try to find a firmer voice (your Teacher Tone – see page 75).
- If the Drama Queen/King is regularly having tantrums, maybe you need to walk away from the situation more and give him space.
- If the Fighter is shouting at you, you might want to approach him more calmly in the first place – he will fight fire with fire.
- Adopt different tones of voice. Try: a reassuring tone, a praising tone and a Teacher Tone.
- If your child ignores you, make eye contact and use Teacher Tone.

Try these practical ideas and examples

If you are tempted to revert to your old ways, stop, think and correct yourself. Remember, if you start talking to your child differently you will soon start seeing changes. If, after using these approaches you need more backup, try the Ask, Tell, Warn, Act skill (see page 72)

'Practise saying negative things in a positive way.'

The Negotiator needs the following approaches from you (to practise these, stand in front of a mirror and talk to your reflection):

- Use a strong, firm voice, 'I have made my decision. I am NOT changing my mind. We do not need to talk about this any more.' Then turn and walk away (using The Back skill – see page 75).
- Practise lowering your voice. Think of speaking in a more 'masculine' way. The deeper your voice, the more your child will listen.
- Look into the mirror, say, 'No means no. I'm not changing my mind.'

The Fighter needs to be spoken to differently. If you were to speak to this child in the same way as for the Negotiator, he would become furious. He needs a firm approach with a positive edge.

- Practise saying negative things in a positive way. Listen to the negative statements you make and see how you could make them more positive. Try following your instruction with a good thing that's going to happen and make sure you remain calm. For example, 'We aren't going to have a biscuit now. We will have one after dinner.'

The Drama Queen/King needs the following approaches from you:

- State that your answer is 'no' but don't be nervous about the dramatics that you know will follow.
- Let your child know that it's okay to shout and moan and throw himself on the floor – away from everyone else. Nobody wants to see him. Also your child doesn't want anyone to see him behaving badly.
- Find a place for the Shout Spot (see page 68) and tell your child, 'When you shout make all the noise you want. When you calm down I'll open the door and you can come in.' Practise this speech in front of the mirror and then try it out.
- When he is on the Shout Spot and the 'drama' is beginning, walk away (use The Back skill). He needs you to show strong resolve.

Using the word 'no' with different personality types

You will need to adapt the way you say 'no' according to the type of child you have. Here are some suggestions to get the best results. Answer 'no' without injecting forcefulness into your voice. For example use, 'I know you love those biscuits. We will choose one after lunch' rather than 'NO. You can't have a biscuit.'

The Negotiator needs to hear the word 'no' as a finite response from you, otherwise he will continue to moan and negotiate. Use eye contact and a firm phrase, such as 'I am NOT changing my mind'. Then walk away, showing your back. The discussion is over.

The Fighter needs his parent to remain calm and consistent. If you use harsh 'no' language the Fighter can take your reprimands personally and become defensive and retaliate or regress in his behaviour. If you use a softer 'no' and move the child on positively you can talk about how what he was doing made you feel sad. Talk things through with the Fighter when you are both calm.

The Drama Queen/King The chances are you can be direct with your 'no' and walk away or take the gentle, calm approach with your Drama Queen/King and still have them do as you ask. However, it's not good to suppress their emotions, so if they need to throw themselves on the floor – let them. Find a space where they can do this alone, in safety, and leave them to it. Some Drama Queens/Kings can calm themselves and come back as if nothing has happened. Others need to be taken back to the Spot a few times to get rid of their frustrations first.

3 The ground rules of parenting

This chapter details the most important elements of parenting and how to use them, explaining how they can affect parent–child relationships. Communication is the single most important element in human relationships – especially between parents and children – and you will need to draw on all your skills in this area to implement some good ground rules and benefit from them.

'There is nothing more confusing for a child than to be told one thing by one parent and something else by the other.'

Boundaries

An important tool you can use in raising your child to be a happy, balanced individual is the good use of 'boundaries'. These are guidelines you can agree on as parents for how you want your life to be – you want your child to follow them so that everyone knows where they are. Your child will feel more secure if she understands what the boundaries are, too. It's vital that you, the parents, agree boundaries between you, so you are both singing from the same page and know what you have agreed. There is nothing more confusing for a child than to be told one thing by one parent and something else by the other. When it comes to doing a three-day process, one parent only should be 'in charge' of the process for the first three days – backed up and supported by the other. That way there is no confusion for the child (or you).

Another way to save confusion is to write up your list of agreed boundaries and post them where everyone in the family can see them. It might be useful to discuss a few issues from your own childhood – there may be things you want to avoid perpetuating, or other things that you really approve of and want to continue with your child.

Here is a sample list of boundaries – you may choose different things that are important to you. You can work on them and give your child rewards whenever they are followed. We all need little incentives to do things correctly – children are no different.

- We listen and do as Mummy and Daddy ask.
- We do not shout at one another.
- We do not take food from the kitchen without asking first.
- If we want to moan/groan and shout, we do it on the Shout Spot.
- We sit down nicely at the table together and ask to get down after.
- We go to bed without any fuss and stay there until Mummy or Daddy calls us in the morning.
- We share our toys.
- We NEVER hit or hurt one another.

Praise and reward

Your child is moulded by you – this is no exaggeration – and you can achieve a great deal of positive moulding just by giving her praise and little rewards, when these are due. It's important to tell her she is doing well and that you are pleased with her. She is likely to want to please you even more because she likes positive attention. If you continually tell her what she is doing is wrong, this will knock her confidence and self-belief. A balance is the best position to aim for as too much praise can give your child the idea that she always does things perfectly.

Listening

Always speak directly to your child on her own. She won't pay you much attention if you seem to be talking while facing away from her or doing something else. She will just assume you are talking to yourself. Bend down to her level and make direct eye contact. If she won't look at you, perhaps if she is occupied with a toy, she won't be listening to you either. By the same token, it is important to make the time to listen to her. Sometimes this happens during quiet times when she is playing. You don't need to fill these times with chatter – she may want to tell you something. Find the time and be happy to listen.

'Bend down to her level and make direct eye contact.'

A united front

It is important that everyone involved in raising your child is carrying out things in the same way and presenting a united front. Children take adult relationships very seriously – they are a pattern on which they model themselves: a huge life lesson. So to be able to witness adults respecting one another is extremely important. If a child sees two adults constantly bickering, she is being taught that this is a norm in adult communication. A confused child might try to take the control away from you or perhaps refuse to listen to you because she will stop believing in the system – not everyone is following it. If several people (such as childminders and grandparents) are caring for your child, ensure everyone knows the agreed ground rules and boundaries.

If parents don't agree and fail to act as a unit, then one parent might be giving the child a different set of instructions from the other. This sets up mixed messages and a great deal of confusion in the child's mind. You might then get into the situation whereby the child realises that her parents aren't united in their thoughts and actions and she will try to play one parent off against the other.

Teamwork

Responsibility within the family is a vital part of your child's development. She needs to see compatible teamwork in the family group to be able to understand that she is part of the bigger picture of life. She starts to see that everyone has responsibilities to help and look after one another in the group – and eventually in the world. The sooner you foster this idea at home the better it will be.

'She needs to see compatible teamwork in the family to be able to understand that she is part of the bigger picture of life.'

Positive language

Your child needs to be able to respond to positivity in the world, since negativity can lead to a downward spiral in mood and behaviour. So if you need to say something that you need your child to act on, try to give it a positive spin. See opposite for a list of positive ways of saying 'no'. The key to all these statements is to say them with a confident Teacher Tone and then walk away. By showing your child your back as you walk away, your body language tells her you have made up your mind. From this moment on ignore her and if her behaviour starts to aggravate you, then give her the choice 'Stop or Spot'. At this point she knows she has to find something to do or spend time shouting on the

Shout Spot. Here are some examples to try: note that each phrase has a positive spin and moves the action forward or away from the problem.

- 'Let's not do that right now.' This is followed by distraction, removing the object in question or walking away.
- 'I don't want that to happen. Thank you.' Use your firm Teacher Tone, showing that you are serious.
- 'We are not doing that. Let's ...' (then make another suggestion).
- 'Stop that, please.'
- 'I am going to count to three. Stop or Spot?' This must then be followed through.

- 'Come here and find something to do with me.'
- 'Put it back or I put it back. One, two, three.' Then act on this.
- 'No more, thank you.'
- 'I am tired of watching this. Stop now.'
- 'That is boring to watch. Enough, thank you.'

When answering a request:

- 'We are not having that right now. We are having it (state when).' Then confidently walk away. Ignore her moans!
- 'We cannot do that now. Let's think about when we can do it.'
- 'We are not having more TV. It needs to rest, ready for tomorrow!' Turn if off and walk away, first ensuring she cannot turn it back on.
- 'Good idea, but that needs to be saved for later.'
- 'I am going to think about that and let you know in a minute'. Bide your time to think before you answer.
- 'Not today, miss, it is too late now.'
- 'I don't want us to do that now. We are saving that for tomorrow.'
- 'That is a great idea for something to do with Daddy at the weekend. Let's text him to tell him about it!'
- 'We are saving that until Tom comes to play next week. Let's find something else to do now.'
- 'Not now. This isn't the right time. Let's plan when we can do it.'

Routine

It's vital to get a good routine going in your home. That way your child will feel secure, knowing that you lead the way through the day and control what happens next. New experiences can be brought in one at a time and your child will be able to get used to them in the context of what she is already familiar with at home. If you are bringing in new ideas, then you have the chance to explain what you are doing and why, using clear, positive language – and your firm Teacher Tone if necessary.

If you don't establish a good routine you might find that your child starts to become uncertain and unconfident – she doesn't know what to expect next. To give an illustration, it's easy to imagine how a child might feel if she doesn't know when to expect her next meal; she will become anxious as well as hungry, grumpy and hard to manage. The same applies to missing her bedtime. You will miss the moment when she feels ready to settle naturally (the Window of Tiredness) and she will become crankily tired, hyper and harder to settle when the next Window does come round.

Routine might sound like a 'stuffy' concept, but do remember that it's good for parents too. You like your free time; in fact you love it! So to be able to look forward to putting your feet up in front of your favourite TV show with a glass of wine when your child has gone to bed is something that you need for your own sake, not just for your child's. If you can switch off from parenting mode for twelve hours you will enjoy it far more.

Consistency

The key to changing an undesirable behaviour is to repeat your new version three times in exactly the same way – your child will slowly start to understand how you want things to be done from now on. Before long, she will know what to expect and do it automatically. If you seriously want to alter your child's behaviour it normally takes three days to make a fundamental change – you need to reinforce what you want in order for the behaviour change to sink in and become habitual. However, it can take only one day of *not* following the new plan for all your hard work to come undone! This means that if you 'fall off the wagon' and lapse in your reinforcement of the new habit, you must be sure not to leave it too long before you resume the desired behaviour.

Things to remember

Adopt a positive approach
If you are always telling your child that what she is doing is wrong, she will continue to do it. However, a positive approach will give you positive behaviour back because children crave attention and they'll get it however they can.

Focus on positive behaviour
Praise positive behaviour and try to alter negative behaviour. Then move on. It's important not to hold grudges, so after you've dished out the discipline – move on.

Don't talk about your children negatively
Resist the temptation to talk about your children in front of them, especially negatively, even if you think they can't understand. On some level they can.

The importance of change
Change is important – for all the family. So if you don't like the way things are working in your home, you know you need change. Go ahead and do it!

Don't procrastinate
The longer you leave bad behaviour untackled, the harder it will be to change.

The effects of improvements
Improving things lifts the spirit of the family and brings adults closer, forming a team bond. You are more united.

Make sure the time is right for change
The time has to be right for you – you need to be 100% engaged and 100% ready. Don't try to create change if you aren't completely ready for it.

Apology

Sometimes you need to apologise to your child as well as have her apologise to you. It is important that your child sees that you are not perfect. You make mistakes – as does she. If she sees and hears you apologising to her, this is a vital life lesson that she should imitate. It also helps you to apologise – you can shed some guilt. Perhaps you weren't listening to her. Such is life! Be aware that before the age of five, a child doesn't really understand the true meaning of the word 'sorry' and if you push her to use it she might view it as a 'get out of jail free' card. The word will start to roll off her tongue casually because she thinks this will stop you telling her off. So after you have disciplined your child and explained why you didn't like her behaviour, don't force her to say 'sorry'. Say instead, 'Let's hug to say sorry and go and find something to play with'. When you are playing with her, briefly mention the word 'sorry'. Perhaps try, 'Remember, it is good to say sorry after you have done something you shouldn't. It shows me you are going to try harder next time not to (state incident).'

'It is important that your child sees that you are not perfect.'

4 Turn your family life around in three days

Now you are ready to try out the three-day process for yourself. Take a few moments to read about how it works and how to plan it.

So the time has come to seriously think about trying the three-day process. Maybe you have realised just how much one of your child's habits is not just annoying but quite destructive and you have decided to do something about it. For example, perhaps your child wakes up shouting in the night or maybe you have realised he hasn't eaten a single green leaf for months and you are seriously worried about his diet. It's time to use the three-day process! First things first: make sure that you, your partner and your support network are all on board because everyone who cares for your child will need to be involved.

'Do make sure that you, your partner and your support network are all on board with the three-day process.'

How the three-day process works

You may be wondering why the process takes three days to be effective. Good question! Well, this is because on the first day you need to absorb information and new ways of doing things. You need to get used to the new regime – this means both you and your child (only one parent should be involved in carrying out the process – the other parent takes a supportive role at this point). This can be very tiring. But you need to persevere. On the second day you know roughly what you are doing and what to expect, but there is still more new stuff coming at you. By the time you get to the third day, you feel more familiar with what you are doing. Your confidence starts to grow as you begin to see positive results in your child's behaviour. With just a little more staying power you will start to see big changes.

Total commitment
You may have been struggling with a problem with your child for some weeks, or even months, and find it hard to believe that you really can turn things around in just three days. Rest assured – if you can really

apply yourself 100 per cent to the task at hand and give it all your attention, making it a priority, you will succeed. This means that you will have to make plans. If you work full time, you may need to take holiday or rearrange social events. But, it will be worth it!

Believe in yourself
Part of the secret of the success of the three-day process is self-belief. You really do have to believe it will work. You don't just read the words and go through the motions. You have to take the whole message on board and believe that you can make a change for the better. Try looking in the mirror and repeat the words, 'I know I can do this. I really want to do this and I am determined to make the necessary changes.'

'You must believe in yourself and your abilities one 100 per cent.'

Believe in others who are involved
The next step is to believe wholeheartedly in all the other people who need to be involved in implementing the three-day process – or at least continuing with it and reinforcing it after the three days are over. This may include your partner, grandparents, relatives and carers. They all need to be aware of the details and be prepared to support you in following them through.

Believe in your child
Last, but not least, you absolutely must believe in your child. You may have found yourself not able to believe in him recently. Things have gone a little wrong and you may be feeling that this is the way things will always be. However, for this process to work, you have to change your thinking and feel positive about how you can influence your child for the better. You will find that once he senses your new-found confidence in him he will start to think he can change – and he will.

Three consecutive days
Be sure to plan for three days – one after the other – not one and then a gap or two and then a gap. If you leave gaps you will find that all the good work you do on the first day comes unravelled on the second. Then you will have to start the process all over again.

Consistency is everything
Consistency is one of the most important concepts to understand to make the three-day process work. You must always behave with consistency towards your child. Always do the same thing, with confidence, and do not waver. You will soon see positive results.

Make a shift for life

Once you have made a change, that's it! There's no going back to bad old ways. You have changed and so has your child and his behaviour. You just need to carry on applying the process, day in, day out, without wavering, and all will be well. Job done! However, it's important to be realistic. You may slip up or waver, but you can always get back on track.

Planning the three-day process

Plan ahead. You will need to earmark three days when you are not committed to anything else (such as work, holiday or appointments) because you will need to mostly be focusing on, and be sticking closely to, the process (which includes your ordinary family routine at home). You have to put your child first. This doesn't mean that you have to cancel your normal life; you just need to avoid overfilling it with other commitments. Take care to choose a suitable slot – for example, Granny coming to stay is probably not good a time.

'You need to fully commit to three days of consistent behaviour from you both.'

One person is in charge

Although both parents need to be united and in agreement about the three-day process, it's best if only one of you remains on the spot to implement the regime. So decide who is going to be in charge for the three days and then establish that the other partner keeps a low profile when it comes to discipline. Obviously the absent partner has to give the one in charge their full backup and support – albeit remotely. Any intervention on their part could confuse your child because what he needs at this time is full consistency from one person. You are both learning about how to carry out the process – mistakes will be made. But keep on practising. You will need to back one another up as a team and save any heated discussions for when the children are asleep. If you need to talk 'discipline' while your child is around, instigate a 'communication note book' and write things down for each other.

Explain the changes

Devise a plan of the changes you are going to make and sit with your child to explain them to him. The moment you hear yourself saying this out loud you HAVE TO follow it through. So, for example, you could say, 'Now Daddy and I have decided that we need to have some house rules'. Show the written rules to your child, read them out, then sit down with him and decorate them before you display them (stick them on the fridge, for example). He can embellish them with stickers or felt-tip pens, depending on his age. Alternatively, try this incentive, 'We are going to build a very tall Lego tower as a family. Every time someone follows the house rules we will give them a brick to add to it. Fifty bricks and we will have a family reward.'

Follow my leader
As the three days of the process go by your child will begin to notice a positive attitude and determination in you – he will follow your lead. This is because you have changed and so will he. All you need to do is be consistent and the three-day process will work.

Beyond the three days
After the three days are over and the process seems to have worked, you may find that things slip a little. There may well be difficult moments to contend with still, but this doesn't mean that you are going backwards or that the process has failed. If you feel you might have made mistakes, just notice them and learn from them – don't write the day off as a disaster. Aim to get things right 50 per cent of the time – the other 50 per cent is called 'life'! Don't forget to enjoy your child during the process – there's a danger in being so intent on fixing your family problem that you lose your lighter touch. It's not meant to be like that – so lighten up occasionally. Life will get in the way of even your best-laid plans and your consistency might have to be put on hold now and again. But remember, if you have made changes once, you can do it again and you can always get back on track.

Take time for yourself
Remember to do things for yourself occasionally – and make sure that your child witnesses you doing so. It's not all about him! However it takes some children a long time to realise this – as far as they're concerned, they're the centre of the universe! But you can influence his way of thinking. For example, if your child is happily playing on his own, state firmly that you need to go and send an email, order the groceries online or even paint your fingernails.

'Keep calm and carry on – it will be worth all the effort.'

Feel encouraged
When you start to notice positive results, the process is starting to work. Keep calm and carry on – it will be worth all the effort.

5 Case studies

The next few pages give you a selection of real-life case studies in which parents have successfully used the three-day process to solve a variety of problems. They illustrate how they used the process in their lives, adapting it to their own needs and, even though they sometimes made mistakes, learnt from them and persevered to make the whole experience a success. Some problems are practical, but others involve a clash of personalities that had to be unravelled before things started to gel better. Perhaps, in reading these, you will be able to relate to what these families have gone through and use their experiences in your own life. (See Tools on pages 54–71 and Skills on pages 72–77.)

CASE STUDY 1
'All I do is shout!'

Family scenario

Susan and Paul have three children and both parents work full time. The children are aged between four and seven years old and they all attend school. Paul leaves for work before the rest of the family wakes and Susan gets all the children up and ready for school. They have to leave the house by 08.00.

Susan is very Orderly and Organised in her approach (see page 15) and she prides herself in juggling between work, children and managing the house. She never seems to slow down or relax as there is always something that needs to be done. Because of this she feels she is constantly up against time pressure, especially on weekday mornings.

The children are all lively characters and they get themselves dressed in the mornings – but only after being asked again and again and then shouted at! They eat well, but usually only after being told to 'eat up! eat up!' and then being shouted at again (by Susan). They eventually all get their coats and shoes on for school – after being shouted at, yet again.

Susan's feelings

By the time everyone is in the car, Susan feels as though she has run a vocal marathon and can't wait to get to work just to get some peace and quiet. She admits that she would sometimes rather be at work than at home because she at least feels listened to there.

Susan is not alone in feeling like this. So many families go through a mad rush in the mornings, but Susan has got to the stage where she can't cope with it any longer and she wants to change the way things are.

How the children are affected

The children are, overall, very happy and contented and are doing well at school, but their home life is very noisy. They are now at a stage where they don't talk to one another, they shout. They bark orders at each other without allowing time for the other to respond and they see being loud as the norm. When they are spoken to at a 'normal' volume they don't always respond because they don't take it seriously, so they have fallen into the habit of only answering when they are shouted at.

Unfortunately the oldest child has reached a stage where she has started to answer by shouting back at her mother and she reacts like this immediately her mother shouts at her to do something.

Susan feels very frustrated that the children never listen to her and do

'Before I had children, I swore I'd never become a shouting mum, but, sadly, I have.'

as they are asked without her resorting to shouting. The fact that she has to ask them over and over again and eventually resort to shouting before they respond exhausts her.

Tools needed
- Incentive System (fill-it-up pasta jar)
- Get-Dressed Stencil
- Timer

Skills needed
- Teacher Tone

Making the change
Susan and Paul sit down one evening and Susan explains that she feels awful – her only interaction with the children is to shout at them.

They make the decision together that at the weekends Susan will spend one-to-one time with each child. This could be reading a story, walking the dog, baking a cake or doing homework together. Susan also decides to use an Incentive System (tool) to help the children improve their listening.

The next Sunday Paul makes Get-Dressed Stencils (tool) with the children ready for Monday morning and he explains to them that they need to listen to Mummy when she speaks to them because she is trying very hard not to shout any more because it is making her sad.

Susan and Paul sit together with the children and explain how the fill-it-up jar Incentive System with pasta works. The jar is a very large one that Granny used to use for bottling fruit and they find a box full of pasta on the top shelf in the store cupboard. They explain, 'Every time we ask you to do something and you do it, you get to choose a piece of pasta and put it in the jar.' PAUSE. 'We want to have this jar filled by next Sunday and then we will have a family reward.'

They sit and discuss, as a family, what they might like to do as a reward. Paul then says, 'We are going to try to fill the jar every week and then have a family reward every week, too!'

That night, when the children are going to bed, Susan lays their clothes out for the following morning on the Get-Dressed Stencils. She takes the teeth-brushing things downstairs ready for the morning. The shoes are lined up at the door and the coats are all hanging by the front door with the school bags. Susan feels so much more organised and in control and finds she's actually looking forward to the next morning.

Paul asks her what she has to do each morning that causes her to rush around and get so stressed. They then find a way of sharing these tasks

'We are going to try to fill the pasta jar every week and then have a family reward every week too!'

so that Susan is not trying to tackle them all when there's so much else going on. That evening Susan sits in front of the mirror and practises her Teacher Tone (skill) – a firm, low voice that the children will listen to and respond to without her having to shout.

The following morning the children are awake when Susan goes into their bedrooms. She bends down and makes eye contact with each child. She says, 'I need you to get dressed now and meet me downstairs for breakfast. Come and see what I have laid out to eat – it's yummy!' Susan goes into the kitchen and has to bite her tongue to stop herself shouting out, 'Get dressed!' She has to trust the children. She unloads the dishwasher and lays the table. The new regime involves Susan eating with the children so that they all have some family time. She cannot remember the last time she even had breakfast herself, let alone with the children.

'I cannot remember the last time I even had breakfast, let alone with the children.'

The children come down dressed after Susan calls cheerfully up the stairs, 'Breakfast is on the table!' She sits peacefully nursing her cup of coffee. They all have breakfast and Susan thanks them for getting dressed without her shouting. She says, 'We will put pasta in the jar for getting dressed after we have brushed our teeth.'

The fill-it-up pasta jar is on the kitchen table and every time one of the children does as he or she is asked they get a piece of pasta to put in it.

Teeth get brushed, one child at a time, and everyone clears the table together. There are now 15 minutes to go before the school run and the children are ready. Susan says, 'Go and put a piece of pasta in the jar and I will make the beds.' This happens without her shouting. Susan now sets a Timer (tool) for five minutes and says to everyone (eye contact and Teacher Tone), 'When the timer goes off, it's time to put your shoes on'.

She gets herself ready and the timer rings. She says, 'Okay, let's go. Front door, everyone.' Susan goes to the door ready for school and the children trickle towards the door. 'I will meet you in the car,' Susan says. 'Last one out, shut the door.' Walking away from them gives the children responsibility and independence. They come to the car, bickering as children do, but Susan has done it. She has remained calm and not shouted once. When they are all in the car, she says, 'Thank you, everyone. We managed to work as a team and I didn't have to shout once. We are all going to have a great day. I can't wait to show Dad how much pasta there is in the jar!' Paul and Susan talk that night about the success of the morning and Paul encourages Susan to remain consistent. He says, 'After managing a week of calm school runs, you should have a lie-in on Saturday mornings. I'll do the morning shift!'

CASE STUDY 2
Teacher tone

Family scenario

Claire and John married four years ago and they have a three-year-old son, Griff. They thought they could never have children and Griff is a 'miracle' of IVF. He is likely to be an only child and both parents simply dote on him.

John works full time, but gets home at night in time for Griff's bath. Claire is relieved by this stage as John takes over and finishes Griff's day. She feels quite drained at the end of the day.

Griff is a healthy and intelligent boy and is a great Negotiator (see page 16). Claire is Mindful and Attentive (see page 15) as a mother but feels that Griff gets his own way all day long – right from waking up to closing his eyes at night.

Claire admits that she starts off saying 'no' to Griff, but he persists and persists until she gives in. She isn't happy to admit that she is a parent whose 'no' always seems to turn into a 'yes'.

John has a very different approach with Griff: he stops the negotiation before it even starts. This can cause Griff to moan and groan and sometimes throw a tantrum, but John lets this behaviour take its course – he doesn't back down on what he says. Claire finds this hard to watch and doesn't like to see Griff getting upset, but she knows it is the right way to manage him.

'I want to be a parent in control rather than have my child in control of me.'

Claire sits with John and explains how she feels she wants to make a change and be stronger and more consistent with Griff.

Claire's feelings

Claire is honest with John and says she is nervous of saying 'no' to Griff – he starts to moan and as soon as he shouts, she gives in. She explains how she wants to feel confident around him and be a parent in control rather than let her child control her.

How Griff is affected

Griff has reached a stage where he thinks he can be in charge of all the decisions in the house. He will instantly get cross at having to wait or compromise, which can cause him to shout and tantrum. Griff is a very intelligent child but emotionally he is younger than his age and he has arrived at a point where he needs to realise that the world does not revolve around him. Griff is going to start school the next academic year, but he finds it hard to follow instructions without always questioning why and trying to get Claire to change her mind. This isn't going to go down well at school, so the sooner he learns to change his ways at home the better.

Tools needed
- Incentive System (fill-it-up jar)
- Shout Spot

Skills needed
- Teacher Tone
- You Choose
- The Back

Making the change
Claire and John sit down and talk about how Claire is going to make some changes. They decide to do this over a weekend, when John is at home, so that he can help her stay strong and consistent in the background. They both accept that things have to change and they are ready to support one another. This is now Claire's main focus in her parenting activities.

'We both accept that things have to change and we are ready to support one another.'

They decide together on an Incentive System (tool). This is going to be using the fill-it up jar (putting tiny rubber animals into a big glass jar). Griff loves animals, so Claire and John are both pretty sure he will enjoy this part of the process. Griff gets an animal each time he does as he is asked. He might moan and groan, but when he quietens down he gets an animal. He doesn't get rewarded if he starts to scream and shout and if he does so he will be taken to the Shout Spot (tool) in the hallway.

The weekend begins with Griff refusing to get dressed. Claire usually lets him come downstairs in his pyjamas and he then doesn't get dressed until they need to leave the house, which sometimes is much later on.

Claire explained to Griff the night before that everyone is going to get dressed before leaving their bedroom in the morning and in this she is already thinking of the school run that will start in September.

Griff starts to shout. John is close at hand, but Claire is determined to start the day by showing Griff that things are changing. She stops what she is doing and reminds herself of her Teacher Tone (skill). This is something she has had to practise hard as it doesn't come naturally to her. She says, 'Right, Griff. You don't have to get dressed yet. Play in your room. I am going back to my room. Knock on the door when you are ready.' Claire leaves the room and closes the door behind her.

Griff instantly starts to shout and John is immediately by Claire's side, reassuring her that she is doing the right thing. They wait until all is calm in Griff's bedroom, which takes about 15 minutes. Claire walks in and says, 'Let's go and see what we are having for breakfast. I might just make some weekend pancakes.' She starts to help him dress, but he kicks up a fuss.

Claire looks him in the eye and says in her best Teacher Tone, 'You Choose (skill). Get dressed or stay here!' Griff is now seeing a shift in control and he doesn't like it.

He ignores her, so she leaves the room again, saying, 'Knock on my door when you are ready.'

This process goes on for 45 minutes, with Claire going to him three times and each time him refusing to get dressed. Only on the fourth attempt does he start to dress with her.

Claire doesn't mention clothes at all because she wants to move things on positively. She busily talks about the ingredients needed to make the breakfast pancakes. John is downstairs already making the pancakes and waiting for Claire with a strong cup of her favourite blend of coffee!

The day continues and there are times when Griff tries to negotiate. Claire has learnt that the Teacher Tone really does work and it is becoming more natural as she starts to see results. When he demands a biscuit, she says, 'Griff. I have made up my mind that we are not having a biscuit now. Apple or banana?' She puts the two fruit options on the table and walks away to boil the kettle using The Back (skill). She is learning the power of closing a discussion and walking away.

Each time Claire needs to discipline Griff John leaves the room. If Griff tries to go to his dad, John simply says, 'I'm busy. Listen to Mummy. I will come back in a minute.' He walks away, closing the door behind him. This is something Claire and John had agreed on when they were planning the three-day process.

Griff does have a few meltdowns during the day and ends up on the Shout Spot, but, equally, he is filling his jar with little animals as he is gradually learning to listen and accept what Claire says. John, as the spectator, is very impressed by how Claire is staying true to her word.

John does the bath and bedtime routine, as he always does, and Griff's clothes are laid out for the following day. He says, 'Remember, Griff. Get dressed quickly in the morning. Let's not have all that shouting again.'

That evening, Claire explains how she is still fighting her instinct to give in to Griff and she feels drained, but she is so proud of herself that she didn't allow herself to give in once. She knows that this is the right thing to do and she is going to continue with the process.

'I'm so proud of myself that I didn't 'give in' to Griff once.'

CASE STUDY 3
Calm approach

Family scenario

Emma is an Orderly and Organised person (see page 15), while her daughter, May, who is four years old, is a Drama Queen (see page 17). They come head to head on a regular basis, which Emma finds very difficult to deal with, especially when they are out and about and socialising with friends.

Emma is a single mum and she and her partner separated when May was two years old. May's dad doesn't have any involvement with his daughter now. Emma works full time and her parents collect May from school, so Emma spends one hour with May in the mornings and two hours with her in the evenings. They spend weekends together.

May is a true Drama Queen and when she doesn't get her own way she will cause a scene, which is something Emma finds really hard to deal with, especially in social situations. This means she will often give in when they are out socially – just to avoid causing a scene. However when they are at home Emma is able to be very firm and she won't back down. She uses the Shout Spot (tool) at home when May starts to throw a tantrum. This tool works well and has been implemented since she was two years old. Emma is keen to maintain a social life at weekends and she and May are rarely at home. Many of Emma's friends don't have children, but they still like to see her and she takes May along too.

Emma's feelings

When mother and daughter are out of the house together, Emma feels as though she is constantly treading on eggshells. She is in fear of having to say 'no' to May about anything as she knows there is bound to be a scene.

Emma sometimes feels watched and judged by her friends because she often appears to be giving May whatever she wants. Emma knows this is wrong but is afraid of correcting it.

May has reached the age where she can read how her mother feels and is using this to her advantage. She now expects new toys and treats whenever they go out and Emma cannot afford to do this, nor does she think it is good for her.

'When I am out of the house with May, I feel as though I'm constantly treading on eggshells.'

How May is affected

May is very well behaved when she is with her grandparents and also when she is at school.

She listens to her mother when they are at home and if she shouts she is ignored. However, when they are out of the house, May is learning how to be manipulative, which is not a nice characteristic. There is an element, here, of May striving to get her mother's attention. They spend very little time together during the normal busy week and May has little one-to-one time with her mum. She is attention-seeking and constantly trying to take control of her mother when they are out.

Tools needed
● Shout Spot

Skills needed
● Teacher Tone

Making the change

Emma has a very honest and open friend, who has seen how Emma parents May both in her house and out of it. She makes Emma aware of how she is creating a manipulative daughter, but also that May needs some one-to-one time.

Emma confesses how nervous she is when she is out socialising with May. She reveals how she believes that if she doesn't give her what she wants, she will scream and shout and show Emma up.

Emma's friend says that she should just let her shout. 'We will support you. But you also need to understand that you need to have some time where it's just the two of you.'

Emma decides to make some changes the following weekend. She sits down with May on Saturday morning over breakfast and explains, 'Now, May. We are going to do things a little differently at weekends from now on.' PAUSE. 'On Saturdays we will go to the supermarket together to get the weekend food and come home and make lunch together.' PAUSE. 'After lunch we will see my friends and in the evening we will watch a film at home together.'

Emma is cutting down her time with her friends, but she knows that this is the right thing to do and that her friends will understand. She carries on explaining, 'On Sunday we are going to have a day that is just us! We can think of what we would like to do together.' They discuss some ideas and write them down in the form of a list.

Emma now uses her firm Teacher Tone (skill), 'Now May, when we go out I am not going to be buying you everything you see and want. When we go to the supermarket you can choose us a treat for after lunch, but nothing more.' PAUSE. 'If you decide to scream and shout, this is fine. I will stand you in the corner in the supermarket. This will be your temporary Shout Spot (tool). Everyone will be looking at you, not me. Then, when you have finished your shouting we can carry on with the shopping.' PAUSE. 'It is the same when we are out with our friends. If you shout because I say "no" to something you will end up standing or sitting on your own in another temporary Shout Spot until you are quiet.' PAUSE. 'In some places you might be asked to leave and we don't want that to happen do we?' PAUSE. 'Now. I would like us to have a nice day today and then we will have the reward of a great day with just us two tomorrow.'

Emma finds that a tantrum does takes place in the supermarket and also with her friends, but she does as she said she would (she is being consistent, which is very important) and May has become quieter sooner than she thought she would. Emma can see that if she remains consistent with this approach May will soon realise what she can and cannot have and will behave better because she realises that Emma will be spending time with just her.

> *On Sunday May and I are going to have a day that is just us! We can think of what we would like to do together.*

CASE STUDY 4
Avoiding the word 'no'

Family scenario

Fran and Clive have two children, Florrie and Isaac. Florrie is six years old and very well behaved. She likes to please people and is very popular with her friends at school. Isaac is three and a half years old and attends nursery school five mornings a week. He behaves well at school but is described as being 'headstrong'. At home he is very determined to get his own way and he hates to hear the word 'no' – he immediately starts to shout and throw things around in fury and frustration.

Clive works full time and usually only gets home once the children are in bed. Fran works part time three days a week and the children have a nanny on those days. The children both behave well for the nanny and Isaac gets on very well with her. The main challenge occurs in the house when Fran says 'no' to Isaac. Fran is very strong-minded and won't back down and neither will Isaac and this situation usually ends in shouting from them both and then tears. Fran does stay true to her word and doesn't back down to Isaac, but equally she wishes that they didn't have to have these regular battles.

> *I stay true to my word and I don't back down, but I do wish we didn't have these regular battles.*

Fran's feelings

Fran feels very frustrated because she sees Clive having fun and games with Isaac at the weekends and he never really needs to say 'no' to him. Fran feels as if she is the 'bad cop' while Clive is the 'good cop'. Clive will often say, 'Let him have what he wants' to Fran, but she doesn't agree with giving in.

Florrie can often get lost in the midst of all the shouting, but she is very happy and content in socialising with her friends and staying out of the way when the shouting starts.

Clive and Florrie have similar calm personalities while Fran and Isaac are the more fiery ones in the family. Fran doesn't feel that she likes her son very much as he is continually battling with her, but she knows things have to change and she is willing to try anything.

How the children are affected

Isaac seems to either be very content or is suddenly raging at his mother. He hasn't learnt how to accept and manage his emotions. There is frustration in him as he doesn't like to get angry and doesn't understand why it is happening. He is now at the stage where he thinks it is the norm for him and his mother to communicate by shouting at one another.

Florrie is a well-balanced and laid-back little girl. She is aware that Isaac is a 'handful' for Mummy and she thrives on knowing she is 'the good girl'.

Tools needed

- Shout Spot
- Incentive System (fill-it-up marble jar)

Skills needed

- Ask, Tell, Warn, Act

Making the change

Fran and Clive sit down one night and discuss how things can change. They decide on the following:

- House rules are needed.
- Isaac should be guided to his bedroom, which is his Shout Spot (tool) when he is becoming cross. He is to be told, 'Go and get your shouts out in your bedroom and come down when you are quiet and calm.'
- Fran and Clive need to ensure that Isaac's room is safe and that there is nothing precious and breakable in there.
- A lock is going to be put on the master-bedroom door.
- Clive, as well as Fran, is going to discipline Isaac. This will be done

by using Ask, Tell, Warn, Act (skill), followed by Isaac being put in his bedroom (his Shout Spot).

- An Incentive System (tool) is going to be introduced (the fill-it-up marble jar) for following the rules.
- Fran is going to avoid the word 'no' and think of alternatives to use instead. She is going to be calmer in her approach.

At the start of the weekend the family sit together and have breakfast. The house rules and fill-it-up marble jar Incentive System are explained, 'Every time you are able to listen and do as you are asked a marble goes in the jar. We are going to do this all week and next weekend, if the jar is full, we will have a family reward.'

Fran then explains to Isaac how she is going to stop shouting, 'I am going to try very hard. Now, if anyone starts to shout or scream they will have to spend time in their bedroom on their own until they feel calm. You then come downstairs when you are ready and we won't talk about it any more.' PAUSE. 'Does everyone understand this?' Fran hopes for a reply at this point, but there is a deathly silence. She carries on anyway, 'Okay, let's start now. Please can you help clear the table, Florrie and Isaac?' As soon as they do as they are asked they both get a marble to go in the fill-it-up jar. Florrie responds first and Isaac follows, motivated by the need to get a marble if Florrie is having one!

The day continues, with marbles being given out and Isaac being taken to his room twice by Clive and three times by Fran. However, they both notice how his rages calm down quicker each time.

At one stage in the day Fran takes herself off to her room and makes everyone aware that she doesn't want to shout (so she needs to disappear for a few moments). She is working very hard to fight her instinct to shout at Isaac. He does push the boundaries, but in general if Fran is focused and patient he does do as he is asked. Fran just has to find her calm and patient place.

At the end of the day, Clive and Fran feel far more united as a couple. Fran loves the fact that Clive has stepped up and is disciplining Isaac and Clive likes the fact that Fran is doing so well at being patient with Isaac and not shouting.

One step at a time, but after a good first day the parents are willing to continue with this new approach. It beats all the shouting!

'At the end of the day, Clive and I feel far more united as a couple.'

CASE STUDY 5
Positive speaking

Family scenario

Becky and John have twin boys, Ben and Laurie, aged three. Becky is a stay-at-home mum while John works very long hours in the week but is always around at the weekends.

The two boys are very energetic and like to be entertained. They can play alone, but only after being ignored for a period. They would much rather their parents played with them.

Becky is with the boys all week, so she feels the need for some help and support from John at the weekends. John is very willing to help, but he also needs to relax after a busy week at work.

The tension mainly mounts at the weekends. This is because the boys demand John's attention and he will give it to them, but then they will not give him the space he needs to unwind. He ends up shouting at them and telling them to go away and the boys frequently end up in tears.

John feels awful as a result and Becky feels very cross at how John has handled the situation. This tends to happen two or three times each day of the weekend. At the end of the day, when the boys are sleeping, Becky and John argue about how they have managed the boys during the day.

'I'm with the boys all week so I feel the need for some help and support from John at the weekends.'

Becky's feelings

Becky is very frustrated as she now sees her weekdays as being more enjoyable than the family weekends. She understands John's exhaustion from the week, but she has got to the stage of saying that things have to change or John may as well stay in bed all day – out of her and the boys' way.

John's feelings

John is frustrated because he doesn't know how to make the situation better. He wants to play with his sons, but he doesn't want to feel trapped and suffocated by them. He needs relaxation time after his busy week.

He hates the guilt he feels after shouting at them and can see how the entire family is disappointed and angry with him.

How the children are affected

The boys tend to be more balanced and calm during the week. This is due to Becky being consistent with them. They have their routine, know right from wrong and have the Shout Spot (tool) at home.

During the weekends the boys end up being more cautious around their father. They don't seem to be able to gauge when he is going to shout. They love playing with their dad but become genuinely upset when he does shout at them. They are confused as to why this happens – they don't see themselves as doing anything wrong. All they want to do is to continue playing – with his involvement.

Tools needed
- Shout Spot
- Incentive System (string and pegs)
- Timer

Making the change
Becky comes up with the idea of the boys filling up a washing line with pegs – to be used as an Incentive System (tool). Each time the boys listen and do as they are asked they get to add a peg to the line. When the line is full, after a week, they get a prize. John is willing to go along with this and is fully on board with changing his ways.

Becky states that she will start the process the following morning (Saturday) and John is to follow her lead. In the morning, when they are all at the breakfast table, Becky explains about the washing line hanging in the kitchen. She says, 'Every time you listen and do as you are asked, you will get a peg! Now if you don't listen and Daddy is saying, "teeth-brushing time" or "shoes on" or something like that we will be counting to three. After three you will be sitting on the Shout Spot. We do this in the week, but now Daddy is going to be doing it at the weekend, too. This will stop Daddy shouting.'

John now shows the boys a Timer (tool), saying, 'Now boys, when we are playing together I am going to set the Timer and when it makes this sound (sets off buzzer) that means I am going to ask you to carry on playing without me because I need a little rest. Do you understand? We are going to do this straight after breakfast.'

Becky now feels confident that John is going to really try. John says, 'If you then play on your own you each get two pegs for being so understanding.'

'I feel confident that John is going to really try.'

The day continues and the Timer works very well. John sets it for 20 minutes and then sets it for a period of time until he is ready to play again. The boys understand that they hear a buzz to stop play and a buzz to start play.

John prevents himself from shouting, but he has to take one of the boys to the Shout Spot for not listening. He is slightly abrupt about it and you can tell this is because of tiredness, however the reason for the child going on the Shout Spot was the right one.

At the end of the day, when Becky and John are talking, Becky suggests that when John wants to rest he leaves the living area. It is too much for the boys to understand that they have to be quiet while Daddy rests.

Together they decide that they are both going to take 90 minutes out of the day to rest upstairs and they will take it in turns. John is also learning that setting up play and walking away is important as well as playing intensely with the children.

Now, with his Timer, the Shout Spot and the Incentive System (string and pegs) John is ready to do this all the time and the added bonus of a 90-minute rest during the day makes the play all worthwhile!

CASE STUDY 6
United front

Family scenario

Ruth and Mark have two children: Honey, aged five, and Rupert aged two and a half.

The parents both work part time and share the childcare between them. Honey is at school from 09.00 to 15.00 five days a week. Rupert goes to nursery every morning until 12.00.

The children are both happy and content, but they are very spirited. Honey is a Drama Queen (see page 17) and will moan and whine until she gets her own way, a tactic that tends to work with Mum but not with Dad. Rupert has high energy levels and doesn't like hearing the word 'no'. He will scream and shout and tantrum when he doesn't get his own way.

Ruth is very honest in saying that she does 'give in' if the children are whining and shouting. She says that they won't stay on the Shout Spot and it is easier to give them what they want than persevere with saying 'no'. The children are not demanding all day – it is usually more in the afternoon, when everyone is becoming tired.

Mark had a strict upbringing and he believes that 'no' should mean 'no' and remain so. The children accept this from him and if they whine or shout, Mark can ignore the noise, knowing that it will defuse quickly as they realise that it is a waste of their time.

'At the weekend the children play one parent off against the other and then Mark and I start to argue.'

The strain can come at the weekend when both Ruth and Mark are with the children. The children play one parent off against the other and then Ruth and Mark start to argue with each other. If Mark says 'no' and ignores them, Ruth intervenes and 'gives in'. But when Ruth 'gives in' this infuriates Mark.

Ruth's feelings

Ruth sees Mark as being overly firm – so much so that she feels she has to compensate and be 'nice'. She doesn't like to see the children unhappy and would rather give them what they want. She knows that this is the 'wrong' way for her to be parenting and it scares her to think of what the children will be demanding from her when they are seven and ten years old, let alone teenagers. She knows she has to be firmer and more consistent, but she just doesn't feel she is capable.

Mark's feelings

Mark simply feels frustrated at how well the children behave when he is alone with them and it infuriates him to see how terribly they treat his wife. They whine and moan rather than talk at the weekends and Mark just feels very angry.

'I have practised my firm Teacher Tone in front of Mark and he has praised me for it.'

How the children are affected

The children stand and watch their parents argue. At times Ruth and Mark say some hurtful things to one another and this is witnessed by the children. This is not good, since the way we behave as parents shows our children how to treat and respect (or not) their future partners.

The children have learnt how to manipulate their mother. This is not a nice trait and the sooner it is resolved the better.

The lesson the children need in this home is 'respect'. They need to respect their parents and the parents need to respect one another.

Tools needed

- Incentive System (fill-it-up pasta jar)
- Shout Spot

Skills needed

- Teacher Tone

Making the change

Ruth makes the decision that she is going to remain consistent about saying 'no'. She has practised her firm Teacher Tone (skill) in front of Mark and he has praised her for it.

The following day they sit down as a family and Ruth explains the Incentive System fill-it-up pasta jar (tool). She says, 'You will be given a piece of pasta to put in the jar each time you listen and do as you are asked.' PAUSE. 'If you hear me or Daddy say "no" to something and you start to whine or shout, you are going to be taken to the Shout Spot (tool).' PAUSE. 'When you are there we are going to shut the kitchen door

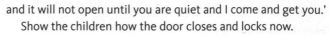

and it will not open until you are quiet and I come and get you.'
Show the children how the door closes and locks now.

The day proceeds and it isn't long before Rupert wants the ipad. He is told that he can play with playdough but Mummy is using the ipad to do the shopping. He shouts and Ruth says, 'Playdough or Shout Spot! – no shouting.' He continues to shout and is taken to the hallway. He shouts and kicks the door for 20 minutes and all goes quiet. Ruth opens the door and says, 'You can come in when you are ready.'

Ruth is surprised at how much she feels pleased with herself and that she doesn't feel bad for Rupert. She is pleased that she remained true to her word. She turns around to see Mark with a smile on his face handing her a cup of tea!

Mark and Ruth form a pact. When one disciplines one child the other removes the second child and stays out of the way. They can see that things are changing and this improves their relationship, not only with the children but with each other.

That night, when Honey is in the bath, she says, 'You didn't argue all day.'

This comment made all the hard work and the promise to remain consistent worthwhile!

CASE STUDY 7
Team work

Family scenario

Janey and Tom have three children and they are a very busy household. The children are Mason, aged three, Lexi, five, and Gracie, aged seven.

Janey is a full-time mum and Tom works from 08.00 to 18.00, five days a week. Janey spends her time tidying up after everyone, driving the children from ballet to football practice, to Kumon maths and to gym club. She is 100 per cent dedicated to her family.

The children are all well behaved, but they do very little for themselves. Janey dresses them in the morning, fetches and carries for them and tidies up after them.

'I have reached the stage where I know I have made a rod for my own back.'

Janey's feelings

Janey has now reached a stage where she knows she has made a rod for her own back. She feels very much alone in doing everything for everyone and she now wants this to change so that she feels she has some time each day to spend on herself.

How the children are affected
By doing everything for the children, Janey is stopping them from developing their independence, which leads to confidence.

No child wants to feel that they cannot do something for themselves and has to ask an adult each time. Something must be done!

Tools needed
- Incentive System (fill-it-up pasta jar)
- Shout Spot

Skills needed
- Teacher Tone

Making the change
Janey devises a responsibilities list as follows:

- Everyone gets themselves dressed in the morning. Clothes are laid out the night before by Mummy.
- Everyone waits at the table until everyone has finished. You take your own plate and cup to the sink.
- Everyone puts their own clothes in the laundry basket at the end of each day.
- Everyone takes their own bag from the car to the house after school.
- Everyone hangs their own coat up when they get home and puts their shoes in the shoebox.
- If anyone needs something in the house, they get it themselves. You don't ask someone else to get it.
- If you need some help with something, ask your brother or sister before coming to Mummy or Daddy.
- Everyone works as a team.

Janey and Tom discuss the Incentive System (tool) and what the reward will be next weekend. This will be kept as a surprise for the children. The children have to follow the responsibilities list to get a pasta piece for the jar. If someone doesn't carry out their own responsibility they sit on the Shout Spot (tool) until they are ready to do it. If they leave the Spot without carrying out the responsibility they are taken back to it.

Most children want to test boundaries and will be on the Shout Spot before they carry out some of their responsibilities.

> *'By doing everything for my children, I am stopping them from developing their independence.'*

The following morning Janey talks to the family about the rules and the Incentive System and everyone agrees that they are going to work as a team from now on.

However, the day progresses and as Janey goes into the bedrooms to make the beds, she sees dirty laundry scattered about. It would be only too easy for her to pick it all up, but she leaves it until later when the children are upstairs. One of the children shouts up the stairs, 'Can you bring my pencil case down?' Janey would usually bring it down, but instead she says using her Teacher Tone (skill), 'I am busy. You are going to have to come and get it yourself.'

'When a child can do something for him or herself I no longer need do it for them!'

The child moans and groans, but Janey ignores this and smiles to herself.

Janey realises that the only way the family are going to help is if they are told to. Children don't tend to offer to help, but they start to learn to do it the moment you ask them to do things for you. Janey decides to write down a simple rule and put it on the fridge: 'When a child can do something for him or herself you no longer need do it for them!'

CASE STUDY 8
Apology

Family scenario

Joss and David have two children, Lizzie and Imogen, aged three and four years. Joss works part time while the children are at nursery school.

David has a very stressful job and works long hours, so at the weekend he likes to be able to relax. The girls are very good at playing together and have wonderful imaginations. The stress starts when the girls decide to make dens, get all of their toys out and start becoming noisy.

David objects to mess, whereas Joss just sees them as 'playing' – the things can be tidied up later. However, David tends to shout at the girls, making them tidy everything away all the time and also telling them to be quiet and play in their bedroom.

After one episode like this, the girls cry and Joss soothes them, explaining how tired Daddy is from a busy week at work. David then becomes very closed, clearly feeling awful for the way he has behaved. He then over-compensates by taking the girls to a toy shop and buying them whatever they want. This behaviour really upsets Joss as it is not how she wants the girls to be parented.

Joss's feelings

Joss thinks about these episodes, which tend to take place whenever David is with the girls. They seem to be a form of manipulation because of the way he gives them material things rather than apologising and this really upsets Joss. She wants to approach David about it, but she doesn't want to upset him.

How the children are affected

The mixed message that David is giving the girls is very confusing. They connect the fact that he shouts with going to the shops and buying nice things. In time, the girls will see it as 'normal' to be shouted at by their father, but this is not what we want the girls to think that people are allowed to do.

Making the change

Joss sits down with David and explains how it upsets the girls when he shouts at them and makes them tidy up their games. 'I understand it, David, but they don't.' Joss explains that she wants him to apologise to the girls when he has an outburst, rather than buying them things to make himself feel less guilty. 'They are old enough, David, to understand that you are tired, worried about work and like things to be tidy.' They need to accept that you 'got it wrong' and understand that you are sorry.

David talks about how he hates the mess and they make a joint decision that when the girls become 'imaginative' and make a mess he leaves the room. He can choose to relax on the bed, have a bath or stroll in the garden.

Joss reassures him that before lunch and dinner the house will be tidied.

The following day Joss explains to the girls, with David, how the toys are going to be organised and that only two things can be taken out at any one time. They declutter the toys and take all those that are now too young for the children to the local charity shop.

'I took the girls to one side and apologised for shouting.'

David takes the girls to one side and apologises to them for shouting. He explains himself and says that he is going to try very hard not to shout. He says if things get too messy he will leave the room to stop his shout coming out. Things progress from here and Joss and David agree to meet in the middle about noise and mess. The toy-buying continues, but it is not linked to shouting and David understands that children and play involve making a bit of mess!

CASE STUDY 9
Time share

Family scenario

Charlotte and Neil have a son, Sebastian. Charlotte is a full-time mum and Sebastian is two years old. Neil doesn't get home until after Sebastian is in bed.

'I feel completely dominated by Sebastian and can't do anything around the house without him demanding my attention.'

Sebastian is a well-behaved little boy, but he does tend to think that he is the one who is in control in the house. He insists that Charlotte plays with him all the time.

This situation was initiated by Charlotte, who gave Sebastian 100 per cent of her attention from the moment he was born. She couldn't bear him to cry and she saw to his every need.

This situation hasn't changed, but as Sebastian has got older and can now talk, he demands that Charlotte plays with him, tells Charlotte what to do and even what he is going to eat each day.

Charlotte feels dominated by Sebastian and she cannot do anything around the house without him demanding that she plays with him.

Charlotte's feelings

Charlotte is exhausted by parenting and would love to see Sebastian play alone for short periods and let her get her own things done.

The only respite Charlotte has is at the weekend, when Neil is home. He plays with Sebastian all the time while Charlotte gets the chores done – something she would have liked to have achieved during the week.

How Sebastian is affected

Sebastian is still at the stage where he thinks the world revolves around him. He hasn't yet realised that at times you have to wait and you cannot have everything on your own terms.

It is clear to see that he is very demanding. He needs to learn before he starts going to school that he is part of the bigger picture.

Tools needed
- Timer
- Incentive System (fill-it-up jar)
- Shout Spot

Skills needed
- Teacher Tone
- You Choose

Making the change

Charlotte sits down with Neil and explains how she is going to use a Timer so that Sebastian can start playing on his own. She is going to set up activities for him and then set the Timer (tool) and not play with him until it buzzes. During this time (five minutes to start with) she will get something done for herself. Every time Sebastian is able to play alone he gets to fill the Incentive System jar (tool) with some coloured water. When the jar is full he will get a prize.

Neil thinks this is a great idea and supports her. She explains about the Shout Spot (tool) so that if Sebastian doesn't play alone and let her get something done he waits there with the door shut until she is ready.

Neil instantly says he is willing to do the same at the weekend as he finds the continual play exhausting.

Charlotte practises her firm Teacher Tone (skill) and explains the system to Sebastian the following day. He loves the fill-it-up jar idea and Charlotte aims to set up as many activities as possible and have him play while she works around the house.

He ends up having to visit the Shout Spot five times due to continually interrupting Charlotte when the Timer is on. She says, 'Two minutes to go. Get busy and let me finish my job.' When he starts shouting for her, she goes to him and uses the You Choose skill, 'Play or Spot?' The shouting continues, so he has to go and sit in the hallway on the Shout Spot.

'I still play with Sebastian but on my terms, when I want to.'

As the day progresses, Charlotte notices that he calms quickly when he is in the hallway and does then let her get things done when he returns to the kitchen. Charlotte still plays with Sebastian, but it is on her terms, when she wants to.

Charlotte can see that there has been improvement throughout the day and after three consecutive days she feels that she will be in a different place. The jar is filling up and the Shout Spot visits are lessening, so the process must be working!

PART 2

The three-day process: tools, skills and scenarios

So you are ready to start, but you need a little more information. This part of the book first lists the Tools and Skills used in the Scenario section. They are in alphabetical order so that you can find them easily. Next check through the Scenarios and when one springs out at you because it sounds familiar, read through and see which Tools and Skills can be applied and what you should do. Don't forget, use your own creativity and imagination to dream up bespoke Tools and Skills to suit you and your family.

1 Your tools

Here is a list of physical tools (props) to help you carry out the three-day process. Be creative and invent your own versions – adapt them according to your taste, what might interest and motivate your child and the materials you have to hand. Use what you have around your home – there's no need to spend a lot of money. Your recycling box or the kitchen shelves might be good places to start looking for suitable bits and pieces to use. The tools are listed in alphabetical order.

BAG OF TRICKS

There are many occasions when a Bag of Tricks might come into its own. Keep it under the buggy for when your child has to get back into it quickly. In the bag place a range of small, interesting things that your child might not normally play with at home, such as an old mobile phone, a bouncy ball and a bunch of keys. Rotate the items so your child doesn't get bored with them and can expect to find something fresh each time. The aim is that when it is time to leave the park or a friend's house simply say, 'Choose one last thing to play on/with and then we are going to go and see what is in your Bag of Tricks. I have put some new things in there!' The new thing can be something simple such as a clementine she has to peel. Then bring the buggy to your child and give her the bag to hold. Now sit her in the buggy and as you strap her in say, 'Now, here is the bag. I wonder what you are going to pull out first today!' Ensure that the bag is a size your child can manage by herself. Here is a list of suggestions of things to put in the bag.

An old calculator	A ribbon with lots of pegs clipped to it
A fabric retractable tape measure	A slinky
A notebook and biro	A bunch of old keys
A lump of silly putty or playdough	A compact mirror
An apple	A chap stick

BEAT THE BALLOON

This is a fun tool and there are many ways you can use it. It's good to have at mealtimes to encourage your child to eat, for example. You could associate Beat the Balloon with a certain day of the week or a certain meal, but you should dictate when it is used, NOT your child. You hold a balloon, deflated, and every time your child eats a mouthful of food (for example) you blow the balloon up a little bit more. When she has finished her meal and the balloon is fully inflated you give it to her to let go of to buzz around the room. It can be an enjoyable way of breaking the negative pattern of a child saying, 'I don't want to eat that!'

BOOK OF THOUGHTS

Many children say they cannot get to sleep and feel frustrated when parents say, 'Just close your eyes and go to sleep'. Create a book or a selection of cards with ideas of things she can think about as she is lying in bed waiting for sleep to find her. These thoughts can be shown either as pictures or words. Here is a list of examples:

Listen to your breathing while placing your hand on your stomach	Chat to your teddy bear about what you are doing tomorrow
Our family holiday at the beach	List all the animals you can think of
Your last birthday party	Say the alphabet three times
The school play	Say all the names of the children in your class
What you want for your next birthday	Sing your favourite songs
The day at the park	The last playdate you went on
List all the foods you can think of	Count backwards from ten

BOOK OF JUNK FOOD

This is a book containing all the 'junk' food items likely to be offered at parties or on playdates that you might not want your child to eat too much of. Cut pictures out of magazines and stick them into the book. Before the party, tell your child she can choose two items. Say that on a playdate she can have what her friend is having if she wants it, but to remember to stop and think of her body and not eat too much.

BOTTOM-STAIR SONG

Some children don't like to go upstairs on their own. To start breaking this habit, the next time she wants you to go up with her, sit on the bottom step and sing a cheerful song she can hear from upstairs. Build on this to singing in the kitchen (further away) to not singing at all. The more you do it, the faster she will overcome this anxiety.

BOX OF ACTIVITIES

This is a special box to keep at a house you frequently visit (such as a grandparent's) – to prevent feelings of boredom and to save awkward questions popping up such as, 'Can we go home now? There's nothing to do.' The box should contain activities that you can do at the kitchen table (for example, painting your own mini teaset, decorating hair-bands, bead-threading, painting your own moneybox, biscuit-decorating kit or playdough). This box should not be taken home.

BRUSH SONG

Children can often protest over teeth- or hair-brushing because they don't know how long it is going to last and they don't want to stand still. Find a song to associate with brushing. Say, 'As soon as I have finished singing "Animal Fair" the job will be done. Let's go.'

CUDDLY BOX

Keep a box reserved for your child's 'cuddly' (whether it's a blanket or a soft toy, or similar) on a shelf in your child's bedroom. She can take it out when she is alone in her room and then put it back after her rest times or after a night's sleep. That way it doesn't get dragged all over the home and outside and you get a chance to wash it sometimes.

DISSOLVING DUST

Some children talk about 'monsters' and 'baddies' coming into their bedrooms and use this as a reason for not going to sleep. Make a 'dissolving dust'. Find a glass jar and put a selection of harmless powders in it (such as flour, talc, baking powder, salt). With your child, sprinkle the 'dust' around the window sill and the door. The dust makes the monster sneeze and then he quietly dissolves, never to be seen again.

DON'T BE SHY PROP

This is a 'prop' that your child feels proud of. It could be a certificate, a special toy, something she's made on her own – anything that she wants to show off to other people or talk to people about. It helps her to break the ice in social situations, when she might feel a bit shy, and it gives her something to focus on rather than on other children. She may want to hold the prop in her hand as she walks around, and this helps her confidence too.

DRY-NIGHT WHEEL

There is no set age at which a child should be dry throughout the night. But if your child is wetting the bed, don't give her any drinks after 17.30 and take her to the loo before you go to bed (around 22.30/23.00). Walk her to the loo. She needs to be awake and completely aware of what she is doing. Create a wheel/clock, numbered one to seven, with pictures, on it. Each night that she has a dry night move the arrow on to the next number. After three consecutive nights of being dry, the job is done. If after two dry nights there is a wet one, you need to move the arrow back to the beginning of the wheel. You don't want to continually be doing this as it puts pressure on your child, so if she hasn't had three consecutive dry nights after seven nights, her bladder is not yet ready.

DUMMY BOX

Find an old shoe box, or similar, and decorate it with your child in whatever way you like. Encourage her to be creative. Use stickers, paints, felt-tip pens and brightly coloured tissue paper. Say, 'This is where the Dummy Fairy lives'. Encourage your child to keep her dummies in the box when she is out of her bedroom.

GET-DRESSED STENCIL

Getting dressed in the morning can be a bore for children! Try laying your child down on a large piece of lining paper and drawing around her with a thick felt-tip pen. This is a stencil of her body that will stay in her bedroom. It is to be called 'Flat Florrie' (or whatever your child's name is). At bedtime your child lays tomorrow's clothes on top of the stencil. The rule is that she doesn't come out of her bedroom until she is dressed. On seeing her dressed give her a lot of praise by thanking her for starting the day in such an organised way.

INCENTIVE SYSTEM

Creating an Incentive System means you have a way of focusing your child and guiding her to make changes. She will feel more involved in changing and more positive about it. The best Incentive System is one that your child shows an interest in from the start. For example, if your child loves trains then think of creating a chart involving adding carriages to an engine. For a child who likes fairies, the Incentive System can involve 'fairy dust'.

Explain the Incentive System to your child and then watch her face light up. Children generally want to please and they thrive on praise, so by using an Incentive System you can turn a negative behaviour into a positive one in just three days. There are certain rules that you need to follow when using an Incentive System and these apply to both you and your child, so you need to write up a list of them. When your child has completed the incentive, she can have a prize or a reward (see page 61). Here are some examples of Incentive System ground rules.

Your child does not ask for an incentive (a carriage/a brick/fairy dust). If this happens, the answer will be 'no'.
You NEVER take away an incentive (a carriage/brick/fairy dust).
The incentive always stays in a prominent place, where everyone can see it (unless it is a system for bedtime, in which case it stays in your child's room).
You do not bribe with the incentive ('If you put your shoes on I will give you an incentive').
You must notice every time the good behaviour is carried out. The more you reward, the faster the behaviour will be modified.
The child should not say, 'I put my shoes on so you have to give me an incentive.' You should say, 'I watch and see the good things and then I give the incentive. You cannot ask for one.'

Here are some Incentive System examples:

Train and carriages
Stage one: A picture of a train. Good behaviour means that another carriage is added. Twenty carriages means your child gets a reward. Stage two: Good behaviour leads to something being put into one of the carriages. A second reward is due when the carriages are all full.

Ribbon and hairclips
The ribbon hangs from a door handle. Good behaviour means that a hairclip is added to the ribbon. When the ribbon has 30 clips on it your child gets a reward.

Tree ribbons

Every time you notice the good behaviour you are looking for you give your child a ribbon, which she then ties to a tree. When the tree has 30 ribbons on it, your child receives a prize.

Faces (dinosaurs or people)

Cut out paper dinosaur faces using thick, coloured paper or card, but with ears, eyes and noses missing. The incentive is to add the missing features until the face is complete. Then your child can have a reward. You can also make human faces, but without features. If your child succeeds in being 'good' she adds eyes to one of the faces. When she has completed seven faces she gets a reward. Perhaps make the eyes out of buttons, which you can stick on, lips out of red sticky-backed plastic, hair and moustaches out of wool, and cut the other features out of coloured card. Be as crazy as you like!

Fill-it-up jar

Find a large jam jar and keep it in a prominent place where everyone can see it. If the jar is a mealtime incentive, then place it on the kitchen table. The idea is to fill it with pasta/marbles/coloured water/shells/stones – whatever is likely to inspire your child. When the jar is full give your child a prize/reward. If you decide to use pasta, get your child to paint it different bright colours first, that way it's more fun. You can give your incentives different names such as Mealtime Marbles.

Brick tower

Use Lego bricks, any other stacking bricks or magnetic stones for this incentive. You will need a base to secure the tower on. The aim is for the tower to reach a certain height, after which you give your child a prize or a reward.

Wee routine chart

If your child is shy about going to the loo at school (especially during classes), even to the point of not going to the loo all day and risking an accident on the way home, set up a sticker chart for her to fill in. Get her to think about convenient times to go (such as break times) and then reward her with stickers later.

String and pegs

Rig up a string in a prominent spot in your home. The location depends on the nature of what you are trying to achieve. If the three-day process involves food, then it is a good idea to have the string up in the kitchen or dining area. Fill a tub with ordinary clothes pegs and give your child a peg to put on the string every time she achieves the objective you are looking for. When the string is full she gets a prize or reward.

Mealtime chart

This incentive chart (see example below) is used to encourage good behaviour at mealtimes. Fill in the issues that you want to address with your child and reward her with stickers when things go well. Decorate it with your child so that she 'owns' it. Display it in a prominent place.

Day	Sitting nicely	Touches food	Cuts up food	Licks it	Chews it	Swallows it
Monday						
Tuesday						
add other days of the week						

Cutlery plate

Take a paper plate and draw lots of miniature forks and spoons on a coloured piece of paper. Cut them out. The aim is that every time your child uses a piece of cutlery at a meal, she can glue a cutlery miniature onto the plate. For example, if she uses her spoon at breakfast, she glues a mini spoon on to the plate. She has to use her cutlery for most, if not all, of the meal to collect the miniatures.

Fairy fun

If your child loves fairies, then create a fairy incentive chart with fairies on it (either drawn or cut out), where she has to give each fairy a magic wand and then a crown. The aim is that she has to give the fairies 30 things before she gets a prize.

Paper flower

Use this incentive if your child doesn't like having her nails cut. Cut out a paper flower with a centre and 20 petals – you can use brightly coloured tissue paper. Each nail you trim, your child cuts off a petal. When all the petals are gone, she wins a prize.

Incentive System Prizes and Rewards

An Incentive System should be carried out over five to seven days and you can give a prize or reward at the weekend. After repeating the system three times and having three family rewards you should then find that the behaviour has been corrected and become instinctive.

You continue without an incentive until the next challenge arrives. 'Prizes' or 'rewards' at the end of the Incentive Systems should focus on family time rather than on receiving material things. Note that little children love 'prizes' while older children prefer 'rewards', so you can decide what you call them according to the age of your child.

Here are some prize/reward ideas

- Go for a family bike ride and stop for a picnic/ice-cream.
- Build a den in the garden and all eat your dinner in it.
- Hold a games afternoon with board games and party games, finishing with a TV dinner.
- Hold a family face-painting event. Everyone paints one another's faces with face paint and then puts on a show.
- Have an afternoon cake-baking session and then take what you make into school to share.
- Arrange a sleepover for all the children (everyone has a friend to stay).
- Go on a family visit to the zoo.
- Go for lunch out in a restaurant and take board games to play while you wait for the meal.
- Build a den in the woods and take a flask of hot chocolate and muffins to eat.
- Make a family trip to the cinema.
- Stay up late and watch a family movie at home with popcorn and ice-cream.
- Book a special trip to the theatre.
- Have one-to-one time with one parent/child. Visit a café and buy a comic on the way to talk about over hot chocolate/babyccino.
- Each child has two friends over after school for party games and food.
- Organise a treasure hunt with chocolate coins.
- If your child is desperate for a particular toy, give it to her. Hide it in the house and give her a clue as to its location.

> **TAKE NOTE!**
> Take a camera on all 'reward events' and print out a picture and stick it on the fridge as a reminder for next time. You can create a collection of 'reward activities'.

JINGLE BELLS

Some children can walk silently from their bedroom to yours in the middle of the night and climb into your bed without you being aware of it. To alert you of your child's movements, put a string of jingle bells on the outside handles of your child's and your bedroom door. You will hear her coming and be able to return her quickly to her bedroom (using the Ragdoll Mode). The bells will also remind your child about what she is doing.

JUICE RULE

Once your child gets used to drinking juice frequently, it is very hard to break her of the habit and switch her to drinking plain water or milk, neither of which will spoil her appetite and are better for her nutritionally. Set up a Juice Rule that everyone knows about. At the start of a meal, before the food arrives, show your child the Juice Rule, which tells everyone what drink goes with what meal. Read it out and explain what she will be having. If she makes a fuss, move on to using the Shout Spot.

Breakfast	Milk or juice
Lunch	Juice – very weak, eventually changing to water with ice
Dinner	Water with ice cubes and a slice of lemon

JOURNEY BOX

Car journeys can be very dull for children. Have a box that you keep in between the car seats with things to do in it. Place a variety of interesting things in the box, such as: a slinky, a little notebook and felt-tip pens, mini puzzles, an old mobile phone, a disused set of keys. Ring the changes whenever you can so that your child can always expect to find something new in it. It's good to have this to hand if your child doesn't like getting into her car seat. She can climb in to the car to see what is in the box. Once her attention is taken by what is in it, this is when you can strap her in. Here are some ideas for the box.

Sticker books	Maze books
Small glow torches	Geomags
Baby puzzles	Blu-Tack to fiddle with
Pens and paper	Mirror and chapstick
Story books	An old set of keys

LANDMARK SPOTS

When you are outside and you feel confident enough for your child to scoot ahead and then wait for you at certain prearranged spots, give her landmarks to aim for. Stand on the street with her, bend down to her level and say, 'See the parked red car. Scoot to it and stop. I will meet you there.' Or, 'See the lamppost with the poster on it? I will meet you there.' Make sure you thank her for doing as you ask and having brilliant listening ears. When she waits at the prearranged landmarks, put a small coloured sticker on her scooter so that she can see how many she can collect. When she has collected a certain number she gets a prize.

LITTLE GLASS, BIG GLASS

Use this skill if you don't want your child to fill up on calorie-rich juice before and during her meal. Find two glasses: a sherry-sized glass and an ordinary tumbler. The little glass is to have 'before the meal' and the big glass is 'after the meal'. Put a jug of water on the table for your child to pour out water into the little glass and drink throughout dinner time if she wants. She needs to eat at least half of her dinner in order to have her 'after-dinner' juice in the big glass.

MENU PLAN

Children all have favourite meals that they would eat every single day of the week. In fact, if you ask a child what she wants for dinner she will often say the same thing several days in a row. Your child likes what is familiar and this is why it is important to offer her a broad range of foods. A menu plan can help with this (see example below).

Day	Dinner
Monday	Spaghetti with light tomato sauce (no lumps!)
Tuesday	Fish and chips with peas
Wednesday	Gnocchi with olive oil and parmesan
Thursday	Shepherd's pie with carrots
Friday	Sweet-and-sour chicken with rice
Saturday	Pizza – tomato and cheese topping
Sunday	Roast lunch (beef, potatoes, greens)

It is attached to the fridge and you can announce every morning what the evening meal is going to be. This prepares your child and makes her aware that there is a plan that isn't going to change and it's non-negotiable. Mealtimes are the one time when you do not give your child a choice. She can eat it or leave it, but she doesn't dictate what food she is going to have.

MONEY PURSE

When you are out shopping, let your child know what shops you are visiting before you go. Make it clear which shops you are *not* going into so that she doesn't assume you are buying things for her. Give her some money in a purse and tell her that you need to buy some birthday presents but that she is going to be in charge of paying! This is to give your child a role during the shopping trip rather than her thinking that she can just go into any shop and choose whatever she wants.

OCEAN SINK

If you need to give your child an incentive to wash her hands after going to the loo, fill the basin with warm, bubbly water. Drop some small plastic fish into it. Say, 'You must tickle the fish after you have been to the loo. They help get rid of the germs on your hands.' You can then get her to drop the 'washed' fish into a separate bucket or large plastic container.

OUT-OF-THE-WAY SHELF

Find a high shelf in an out-of-the-way place (or a high cupboard is just as good). This is in case your child does not want to share all her toys when a friend comes to play – particularly if there has been lack of sharing and fights on previous occasions. It's not an option to put all her toys up there. Before the friend arrives, sit down with your child and say, 'Now, James is coming to play after lunch today but you do not need to share all of your toys. Are there any special toys you would like us to put on the high shelf because they are precious to you? We can get them out again when James goes home.' You can then move on to telling her that she can share all her other toys nicely and if sharing doesn't take place she will have to sit on the Shout Spot. Once you have said this you must follow it through – even in company.

PICK A PORTION

Look at your child's hand. This is an indicator of how much food she needs to eat. Her fist represents the size of the carbohydrates she should eat (potato, rice, pasta). Her palm indicates the amount of protein (chicken, fish, burger). Her grasp indicates the vegetable portion size – she needs two of these on her plate. When served up on her plate this might seem like a small amount of food altogether, but it represents all the nutrients and goodness her body can consume and needs. It is fine if she eats more (though not too much), but she can survive on this seemingly small amount. This is her correct portion size.

PING-PONG FACE

If your son has a poor aim when he stands up to go to the loo, draw a face on a ping-pong ball and put it in the loo to float. Ask your son to aim at it. You will find that it gives him the incentive to try to aim accurately and avoid making a mess. The ping-pong ball can cope with being pooed on too and it won't flush away.

PYJAMA BEAR

If your child doesn't want to put her pyjamas on, leave her in the bathroom to put her pyjamas on and go into her bedroom saying that you are going to put some pyjamas on her teddy. Pull out some of your child's own clothes and tell her to get her pyjamas on and then come and see what teddy is wearing. Confidently walk away and shut the bathroom door. Your child will quickly pull her pyjamas on in order to see what you have dressed teddy in.

PLAN A DAY

Children like to know the order of what's happening in their day. A structure is particularly important for Negotiator and Fighter children (see pages 16–17). At breakfast, run through what's on the agenda today and write everything down in a list. This activity can be reassuring for your child and it also shows you are in control of what happens. It doesn't matter if your child is below reading age, just read everything out to her. You can use coloured paper, felt-tip pens and ask your child to decorate the plan with stickers – whatever you have to hand. Pin the plan up where everyone can see it. If your child suggests something that she wants to do but it's inconvenient, you can always say, 'That is something we will do this week but not today.' Here is an example:

After breakfast	Take the dog for a walk
Mid-morning	Play with playdough
Late morning	Post a letter
Early afternoon	Have a rest
Mid-afternoon	Go to the park
Late afternoon	Get out the train set
After dinner	Do some colouring
Before bed	Watch TV

PLAN AHEAD

Most children feel more secure if they know what the plan is and what to expect. They feel that someone is in charge. To help your child, create a chart whereby you write down what you are going to do on a piece of paper – this could be for part of the day, the whole day, the week or the summer holidays, for example. For an afternoon plan you might include such activities as: post letter, buy a birthday present for Christopher, buy milk and bread and collect dry cleaning. Here is an example of a week's outings.

Monday	Go to Steven's house
Tuesday	Go to the park
Wednesday	Playgroup party
Thursday	Go to Baby Bounce
Friday	Granny comes to stay
Saturday	To the zoo with Granny
Sunday	Out with Daddy

PLAY STATIONS

It may be too much to expect your child to just 'go and play'. So many children, particularly between two and four years of age, need a bit of guidance on this. When they are at nursery school, activities and toys will be set up in various places around the room, so that the activity is isolated and appealing-looking. This is something you can easily emulate at home.

- Place an activity at each end of the kitchen table.
- Put a puzzle on the rug in the living room.
- Have a pile of books in the corner of the kitchen.
- Set up the dolls' house or the train track on the floor.

Establishing play stations allows your child to graze one activity after another. As you see her exhaust one activity, you can then tidy it away together. Once all the activities have been explored you can stop and read a story together and then set out some fresh ones. Your child then starts to realise that there are things available for her to gravitate towards around the house while Mummy/Daddy continue with their jobs. Having all the toys mixed together creates confusion and even panic in the child's mind and on top of this they don't look very tempting.

SCREEN RULES

It's best for your child to know when she can/cannot have the screen (whether phone, ipad or the TV). If you don't have a framework of rules to work from she will continually ask to watch it. Here is an example:

We never watch TV/ipad before school.
We watch TV on a school night while Mummy is cooking dinner/ after dinner.
Ipad is after lunch on Saturday and Sunday for 30 minutes.
On Saturday or Sunday we watch a family film after lunch. Mummy and Daddy choose the film.
Sometimes, as a surprise, we get TV/ipad for being good. Mummy and Daddy choose when this is.

SHARE LADDER

Many siblings go through a phase of wanting what the other one has. This is a natural developmental stage. First, it's important not to jump in and sort out the dispute yourself, but remove yourself from the action and see whether they can resolve things themselves. If there is no hope of this, make a 'sharing ladder' for each child out of cardboard (cut up old cereal packets) and put a photo of the child at the bottom of each one. Each time they say, 'You can have it' or they back down from the argument move them up a rung on the ladder. When they get to the top they get a prize (something small that needs to be shared). Sometimes both children will go up the ladder for playing well together, while at other times they will go up it independently. When they are playing alongside one another amicably give them a prize.

SHOUT SPOT

This is a place in your home or outside (if necessary) where your child can be guided to sit (or stand) to let off steam – usually by shouting (or screaming or crying). Most children of toddler age will 'shout' if things don't go their way and this might escalate into a full-blown tantrum. It's best not to suppress your child's emotions, so she needs to vent her frustration in a safe environment and calm herself down in her own way – without anyone watching her. It's good for your child to realise that she can remove herself from a social situation to let off steam. You can identify a step at the bottom of the stairs, a little stool in the corner or a bean bag – or she can just stand. But she is not allowed to 'shout' in other parts of the home. The best place to establish a Shout Spot is usually the hallway, with a gate across the bottom of the stairs and all doors leading off it shut – and the front door locked. The area must be completely safe, so it's a good idea to move breakable objects. Your child needs to be isolated temporarily from other people and to feel deprived of their company. The area must be as 'boring' as possible.

If you are out and about – whether in a park, a shop or a relative's house – you can set up a temporary Shout Spot so that you can persevere with this part of the process. No one will mind – in fact they will applaud you for being a good, effective parent.

A note about 'shouting'

The word 'shouting' is used in this book instead of 'crying' or 'screaming'. This is because the activity needs to be seen as 'letting off steam' or 'venting frustration' rather than your child being emotionally upset (which can be much harder for a parent to be objective about and deal with effectively).

Shouting often happens when your child wants to express frustration but doesn't have the words. From about one year old a child can understand what is said to her, but cannot respond in words. So, in order to get what she needs or wants, she 'shouts'. It's a good idea to discourage this habit, which can continue for years otherwise (adults who shout to get their own way are not well thought of and may even require help with 'anger management') and that is why we make every effort to set up a Shout Spot and guide the child towards venting on her own – until she feels better.

SNACK CLOCKS

Make two 'snack clocks' out of paper plates. Mark the times when you plan to serve snacks on them. Explain to your child that two clocks mean there are two snack times a day – one in the middle of the morning and one in the middle of the afternoon. Find absorbing things to do until snack time arrives.

SNACK MENU

Before you pack the snack for going out, place all the available options on the kitchen table and ask your child to choose what she wants. She might choose what isn't on the table, so you need to then say, 'Take something from the table or nothing. You choose.' She then takes ownership of the snack, so that when she sees friends with their snacks she might make a bit of a fuss but fundamentally she knows that she chose her own snack.

| Mid-morning | Milk and rice cakes |
| Mid-afternoon | Juice and pieces of apple and banana |

TIMER

A timer is a handy household device and you probably already own one – you'll find that your child will respond readily to it if is used in the right way. Most ovens have timers inbuilt, but if you are out of earshot of the kitchen a portable one might be more convenient. It's as though your child takes the buzzing timer more seriously than your verbal instructions. You can create different 'kinds' of timer to use for different purposes (see the list below).

Come-back timer

When your child wants you to stay with her at bedtime, let her know what you are doing and that you will come back. Say, 'I am just going downstairs and I will set the timer for 15 minutes. I am doing the ironing and when the timer goes off I will come and see you. You will be fast asleep and I will plant a big kiss on your head.'

Sharing timer

If two children are arguing over a toy and you can see that the dispute won't be resolved by them, you can step in and introduce the timer. Say, 'Now I am going to set the timer for three minutes. Lily, you will play with the toy for three minutes. When the buzzer goes it is then Nancy's turn. Now, let's find something for you to do, Nancy, while you are waiting.'

Story timer

Using a timer to limit seemingly endless story times can be very successful. Perhaps your child likes 'reading' to you, but the story just seems to be going on and on – she may be playing for time by making up long story lines and subplots. Just set the timer for five minutes and ask her to wind up her story after the buzzer has gone. Then it can be your turn to read a story and her turn to listen.

Talking timer

Use a timer to limit your child's chatty interruptions, when you want her to be quiet so that you can talk and/or listen. This is especially useful if the phone rings and you need her to be quiet. You set the timer for four minutes (or whatever time you feel is reasonable) and ask her to be quiet and play until it buzzes, when you will talk to her. If it is someone on the phone your child knows you can let her say 'Hello' to them. But otherwise be quite firm over timing.

TIN-FOIL TACTIC

Light is a stimulant and children will wake early in the morning if there is daylight coming into the room. They can also find it harder to go to sleep at night in the summer months. Therefore try to keep the room fully blacked out. If you don't have fitted blackout blinds try this simple tip. Sprinkle the windows with water and line the glass with tin foil cut to fit the panes of glass exactly. This blocks out all light. Your child will find it far easier to sleep because she cannot see everything around her.

WAITING BEADS

Waiting is a hard life lesson, but one worth learning sooner rather than later. If you are making a phone call, sending an email or you are busy folding laundry, ask your child to wait. Have a shoelace with a knot in one end and a glass jar of buttons and beads. Each time she manages to wait (work on one to two minutes initially) hand over a bead and ask her to thread it onto the lace. When the lace is full give her a small prize. The way to work with this tool is to isolate three days in which your child has to wait for several short periods (for example, waiting for a bus, the doctor, dinner in a café, or to talk to someone). This will build up her understanding of waiting quickly.

WEE A RAINBOW

If your son's aim is a little shaky, try sprinkling 'hundreds and thousands' cake decorations around the loo pan and ask him to 'wee a rainbow'. He will love flushing and seeing all the colours merge into one and will try to improve his aim.

WRITE-IT-DOWN BEDTIME ROUTINE

This is a useful tool when you are both too tired to make decisions – it can prevent boundaries being pushed. Many children like to know 'what's happening next' in their lives. They feel comforted by a routine and like to know that others are going to do things the same way. The most important time for a routine to be in place is at bedtime. It can be helpful for your child to have it written down. She might not be able to read it yet, but she knows that it is something that everyone is following and she takes comfort in this. Here is an example of a bedtime routine:

Dinner time
TV time
Bathtime, pyjamas and brush teeth
Last wee of the day
Two stories while Jenny sits in her bed and Mummy/Daddy sit on the carpet next to her
Last big hug of the day
'I love you very much – see you at breakfast time'
Mummy/Daddy leave the room and closes the door
Knock on Jenny's door in the morning. That's when the day begins!

2 | Your skills

You know more than you think you know! You already have vast resources of knowledge, intuition and commonsense, not to mention parenting experience – and you know your child better than anyone else does. All you need to do is use the talents you already have for the three-day process. Here, a list of Skills used throughout the book explains how you can target your parenting problems in a really organised way. The Skills are arranged in alphabetical order.

ASK, TELL, WARN, ACT

This is an important skill – probably the most important. It's a handy way of remembering the sequence of events when you give your child an instruction that then needs further action and possibly sanctions.

- ASK your child to do something (nicely).
- TELL him, using a firm instruction (perhaps using your Teacher Tone).
- WARN your child about what you will be doing next (perhaps counting one, two, three).
- ACT by following through with whatever action is necessary. You might say, 'I have asked you nicely not to do that. Now we need to (name whatever needs doing instead).' You have to remove your child from what he is doing and if he shouts perhaps guide him to the Shout Spot.

BODY TALK

When your child says he has had enough to eat and asks to get down from the table, you might want to say, 'Now, you know your own body best. Are you sure it has had enough food to grow and be strong? The next food isn't coming until breakfast time.' If he says 'yes' you have to trust him and remain true to your word – don't give him any more food until breakfast. Babies need food in the night due to their rapid growth rate, but children aged two and up do not wake in the night hungry because of this.

EAR SWITCH

When your child continues to moan and whine rather than speak properly, tell him that you are going to turn off your ears. Bend down and make eye contact and say, 'When you whine like that I am going to choose not to listen until you use your wonderful voice instead. I am going to turn my ears off. They will only come back on when you speak nicely.' 'Turn' your ears, indicating that you cannot hear him. Say, 'This is what I will do when I hear you whining.' You will find that he whines far more when you turn off your ears, but you have to carry on as if you cannot hear him. It is only when he says something nicely that you quickly turn on your ears and say, 'What a lovely voice. What do you want to say?'

FAMILY LOO STOP BELL

This skill is to use with children who have accidents when they are out. Say, 'We have a family rule that everyone needs to visit the loo before we leave the house. I will go first and then open the door and ring the doorbell. Once everyone has rung the bell we can go.'

FOLLOW MY LEADER

Try this with the child who wants to be carried everywhere around the house. Bend down and say, 'I am not going to carry you around the house any more. I have to carry your baby sister because she can't walk.' PAUSE. 'You are going to be our leader. So wherever we go around the house you can always get there first.'

FREEZE RULE

This skill is to use with the child who takes off coats, hat and gloves when you are out, when it is too cold to do so. Have everyone put on their coat, hat and gloves on the doorstep before going out. The rule is, 'If you take off any clothing, we stop and we won't move until you have put them on again. So the more you take these things off, the later we are going to be. Now we don't want to be late, do we?' Once you have said this you must be consistent, so wrap up warm because you need to be prepared to follow through and stand still until your child puts his warm clothes back on.

MAGIC COAT FLIP

Try this if your child finds it hard to put on his own coat without your help. Lay the coat on the floor in front of him. The coat is upside down as he looks at it. He bends down and puts his arms in the coat sleeves. He then stands up and throws the coat over his back. Hey presto! He has put his coat on. This is a great achievement. Now part-zip up his coat and let him do the rest (it's a good idea to have a coat with zips rather than buttons at this age).

RAGDOLL MODE

Whenever you need your child to go somewhere without being stimulated, for example when you are returning him to his bed during the night, act like a ragdoll. Don't think of yourself as Mummy/Daddy but as a relaxed, slow and silent figure. Guide your child back to bed, or wherever you need him to be – act as if you are not there. It helps if you have your child facing away from you so he can't make eye contact.

SELF SERVE

Your child is likely to be more willing to come to the table and stay there if he is serving his own meal and you are sitting eating with him (even if your portion is very small). You can work on teaching him that he needs to take a little of everything, even the vegetables. This skill is not initially about eating the food, but to make a start by your child placing it on his own plate.

SIT IT OUT

If your child walks a short distance and them asks to be carried, he must choose whether he walks or sits in the buggy. Say, 'Buggy or walk?' If he starts to shout, sit him on the pavement and say, 'When you are ready, choose books or walking.' Take an empty plastic bag he can sit on if pavements are wet. Have a pile of books on his buggy seat waiting. Remain relaxed and calm, but be strong in believing that he is going to get into the buggy. Be prepared to follow through what you have said and wait it out until he does what he has been asked to do.

SLAP SLIP, DO YOUR BIT

Many children hate having suncream put on them. When putting on your child's suncream ask him to hold out his hands before you do anything. He then has to rub the cream into his own body. Sit him on the ground/floor and he is likely to rub it into his legs himself. While he is doing his part of the job you can do yours by rubbing the areas he can't reach. It is best not to talk during this task. Just remain quiet, to show your child that no matter what, the cream goes on!

SNIFF SOAP TEST

Some children don't like washing their hands after they've been to the loo. You need to impress on your child that this is really important for hygiene reasons. If he claims he has washed his hands but you strongly suspect he hasn't, simply say, 'Bring me your hands' and smell them for soap! If he hasn't, say, 'Nice try – back you go and get rid of those germs by washing your hands.'

TEACHER TONE

While your child was still a baby you probably mostly spoke to him in a soft, light voice. But now he is older you might need to employ a deeper, firmer tone that he will respond to better. The aim is for you to be heard and taken notice of. This might seem a bit strange at first if your voice is naturally light and high, but you will soon find that he responds much better to it when it is deeper. It's well known that children respond to men's voices better and you may have noticed this. Using your Teacher Tone will give

you confidence too. Try practising in front of a mirror using phrases such as, 'Right! Stop that. Let's find something else to do.' This doesn't mean raising your voice and shouting – it just means projecting your thoughts to him in a firm, confident way. Only use the Tone when you need to, so that your child notices it.

THE BACK

Showing your child your back is a highly effective way of closing the conversation and demonstrating your firm resolve. Just state what you have decided, turn your back to him and leave. That way he knows you are serious.

THE HAND

When your child is trying to interrupt you having a conversation with another adult, hold your hand up towards his face. Don't look at him. Keep focused on the adult. Say, 'Wait. I am talking' to your child. Quickly continue your conversation and wrap it up in a minute initially. Then bend down and say to your child, 'Thank you for waiting, what did you want to say?' The more you practise this the easier it will become. Start with short waiting times and then build up the time.

TUMMY PUSH

When some little boys first stand up to pee their aim is terrible. Try asking your child to push on his tummy just above tummy button. This causes his penis to 'stand up' slightly, giving a better aim.

WINDOW OF TIREDNESS

Most children are awake for 12 hours a day and asleep for 12 hours at night. By the time they reach three years of age they start to need nearer to 11 hours at night. It is important to notice your child's Window of Tiredness (the time when he is most likely to fall asleep easily) as this will help you learn when is the best time to settle him. As a guide, this tends to be around eleven and a half hours after he first woke in the morning. Therefore if your child woke at 06.30 he is likely to be showing signs of tiredness at 18.00. This is when you need to be getting him out of his bath and thinking about reading stories. If you say 'goodnight' to him during his Window of Tiredness he is going to find it much easier to fall asleep.

If you miss this window your child will get there at his 'second wind', but in the meantime may start to seem livelier than he was before,

running around and appearing to be fully awake. Once you have missed the Window you have to wait 45 to 90 minutes before the next one appears. If your child is taking a long time to fall asleep, you might be putting him to bed past his Window, so you can try to bring his bedtime forward.

WIPE TILL WHITE

Some children are unsure whether they have wiped their bottom properly and are therefore reluctant to do it themselves. They want you to 'check'. Show your child how to keep on using the paper until it comes away white. That is when you know that the job is done. Say, 'Wipe and wipe until all you see is white!'

YOU CHOOSE

It's good to let your child make his own decisions, though sometimes you just have to stand back and let him make the wrong choice. After all, this is how we all learn – through making mistakes.

So try saying 'you choose' and then turn your back and walk away, leaving him to make his own decision.

He makes either the right or wrong decision and knows what the reward and the consequence is. Once your child knows you are going to stay true to your word and remain consistent he will find it far easier to conform to what you want him to do generally. When you are asking your child to choose, keep the tone of your voice very positive. Don't stare at him after you have asked him to choose. Do the opposite, look away. Act in a way that says you trust he is going to make the right choice in a minute and do as you said.

Hand or Sit (an example of You Choose)

When your child needs to hold your hand when you are walking down the street but keeps pulling away, you need to simply sit him on the pavement. Say, 'You choose. Sit on the cold pavement or hold hands.'

Now start looking at your phone or talking to another child. Completely ignore him. As he starts to stand up, take hold of his hand and start to walk, talking about something you can see in front of you. If he pulls away, sit him down and start the process again. If he keeps pulling away after that it is because you haven't given him long enough sitting on the ground.

ZERO TOLERANCE

There are some behaviours that are completely unacceptable under any circumstance and need to be stamped on straight away. First, you need to agree with your partner and other people who look after your child exactly what these should be (for example, biting, bullying, pulling other children's hair, spitting, breaking things on purpose). Everyone needs to be completely consistent about reacting in the same way to the behaviour every time it happens and it needs to be dealt with immediately. Use the Ask, Tell, Warn, Act skill.

3 The five key areas that present problems

Sleeping, eating, behaviour, potty training and being out and about are the five key areas that present problems, identified as being triggers for causing difficulties in families. One area may feed into another and sometimes they are hard to separate and deal with effectively. For example, you might find that your child not sleeping deeply enough and for long enough affects his appetite and his general behaviour the next day – he becomes out of sorts and cranky. However, you have to start somewhere, so try to isolate a particularly obvious problem and deal with that first, using the three-day process. You may find that just solving this one thing has a knock-on effect and all the other issues seem to solve themselves. This chapter offers over 100 real-life scenarios that cover the five key situation areas. Search for your specific family problem, or one like it, and adapt it to suit your needs.

Sleep scenarios

This section explores a range of typical sleep problems. Have a quick look through and see whether any of them ring any bells for you. If you cannot find a problem that exactly applies to your situation, look for something similar and adapt it.

Importance of bedtime routine

Establish a good bedtime routine, which you stick to as much as you can. Assess when your child's Window of Tiredness (see page 76) is and plan when to have her bath, story and goodnight kiss. It's good to keep the order of events the same every night so that the routine becomes established in your child's mind. She will feel more secure.

Your child must be awake when you leave the room

Don't be tempted to rock your child to sleep or walk her around the room until she drops off. She needs to still be awake when you leave her to go to sleep by herself, otherwise you run the risk of her not being able to go to sleep without you. Go through the bedtime routine in the same order every night, say goodnight and leave the room. That way she can eventually learn to settle herself to sleep.

You must be in charge, not your child

Always be in control of the bedtime routine, so that you tell your child what is happening next. She will feel more relaxed and safe and know deep down that she is cared for. One way to do this is to talk about what you did today and then tell her what you plan for tomorrow.

My child gets up in the night and ends up in our bed

'Freya, aged two and a half, wakes in the night and quietly comes into our bedroom. We don't hear her but find her in our bed in the morning. We have no idea what time she comes in.'

LET'S DO IT!

YOUR TOOLS

Tin-Foil Tactic

Jingle Bells

Incentive System
(ribbon and hairclips)

See pages 54–71

YOUR SKILLS

Ragdoll Mode

See pages 72–77

WHAT TO DO

- **Make sure that your child's bedroom is nice and dark.** Remove any nightlights or lamps. Cover the windows in tin foil using Tin-Foil Tactic (tool). The landing has to be dark, too, so do the same there.

- **Hang Jingle Bells** (tool) from both yours and your child's bedroom doors – perhaps tape them to the handle to prevent then falling off.

- **Create an Incentive System** ribbon and hairclips (tool) .

WHAT TO SAY

- **The ideal time to talk to your child** is when she is in the bath and you are sitting, at her level, on the floor. You can get her full attention before the toys are put in the water. Say, 'Now Mummy and Daddy have decided that you are not going to sleep in our bed any more. You have your own wonderful bedroom and your own bed.' PAUSE.

- **Then say, 'Now I have put a special ribbon for holding hairclips** in your bedroom and every time you stay in your bed all night and don't sleep in Mummy and Daddy's bed you will get one to add to the ribbon.' Show her the hairclips. 'After bathtime we will look at the ribbon. When it is filled with clips you will get a prize.' PAUSE.

- **Go on to say, 'If you wake in the night** and your feet go walking, I am going to take you back to your bed. I will not talk to you. You will jump back into bed and stay there until breakfast time.' PAUSE.

- **Finally say, 'In the morning you get a hairclip** to put on the ribbon!' PAUSE. 'Now let's get out of the bath and find your ribbon.'

- **When you get to her bedroom** she may ask about the bells. Say, 'These make a nice noise when the door opens. You will hear me when I tell you breakfast is ready.' Show her by opening the door. 'If I hear the bells in the night, I know you need to go back to your bed.'

- **Now move on to her bedtime stories.** She is likely to continue with bedtime and not fully comprehend what your plan is. She will need to see you carry it out for real for her to understand fully.

ACTION IT!

- **Continue the normal bedtime routine.**

- **Pull her door to,** ideally close it. She will hear the bells jingle.

- **Hover on the landing** – she might 'test the system'. If she emerges, turn her around and guide her back, using Ragdoll Mode (skill). She might ask about the bells, say she is hungry or something similar. Don't speak to her or get engaged in a conversation.

- **Continue returning her to bed every time** – until she remains there.

- **Get ready to listen for the bells** and to follow the same regime throughout the night, if necessary. Carry on using Ragdoll Mode.

- **In the morning she gets a hairclip** because she didn't sleep in your bed. You achieved what you needed to do and after three consecutive nights you should see dramatic change. After she has had seven mornings of getting hairclips, give her a reward.

CARRY ON!

If the process does not work after three nights, or there has been a lapse, carry on. Adopt Ragdoll Mode every time you return her to bed and do not talk to her. She always gets a hairclip for learning something new and not engaging with you during the night. If you are consistently in Ragdoll Mode, you should see improvement – eventually she should sleep through. By the time the Incentive System is complete, your problem will be solved!

Why should my child not sleep in my bed?

There are families who co-sleep and this is absolutely fine, but there is a right way of doing it. The fact that your child is waking up and walking from one room to another indicates that she is not getting enough solid sleep.

Children grow both physically and mentally when they are sleeping, so it is important that their sleep is not disturbed on a regular basis. You would also like your child to be independent and know that she can sleep on her own without her parents.

You'll blink and time will flash by. Your child will be invited to go to sleepovers or a weekend at Grandma's house. You want to know that she is confident at bedtime and capable of solid sleep in her own bed, without you.

My child screams when I put him to bed

'George always used to be good at going to bed. But since starting nursery he screams when I say goodnight. I now stand outside his door until he falls asleep. He wakes at least once in the night and I stand by the door again. He insists that I stand there.'

YOUR TOOLS

Tin-Foil Tactic

Timer (come-back)

Incentive System
(trains and carriages)

See pages 54–71

YOUR SKILLS

Ragdoll Mode

See pages 72–77

LET'S DO IT!

WHAT TO DO

- **Ensure that the bedroom and landing are both dark.** Use Tin-Foil Tactic (tool) if you need to and remove any light sources that you were keeping switched on at night.
- **Use the come-back Timer** (tool) – one you can carry around the house.
- **Create an Incentive System** trains and carriages (tool) .

WHAT TO SAY

- **Wait until your child is in the bath** and sit on the floor so you are at his eye level. Say, 'Mummy and Daddy have decided that we are not going to stand at your bedroom door any more.' PAUSE.
- **Then say, 'We are going to say "goodnight" and use the Timer.'** Hold it up to show him. 'I am going to set it for ten minutes when I leave your bedroom and I will go downstairs to make our dinner.' PAUSE.
- **Now say, 'When it makes this sound.'** Demonstrate. 'I will come upstairs and see you are asleep. I will give you an extra kiss on your head and then see you at breakfast time.' PAUSE
- **Finally say, 'If you shout in the night,** you need to turn your body over and rest until sleep comes.'
- **When you go into his room with him after bathtime** explain the train and show him the carriages. Say, every morning you have managed to fall asleep and Mummy or Daddy haven't stood by the door you will get to choose a carriage. When all seven carriages are on the train you will get a prize!'
- **If he comes out of his room during the night** (though don't put the idea into his head by mentioning it) use Ragdoll Mode (skill).

ACTION IT!

- **Continue the bedtime routine** as usual.

- **At the end of stories have confidence in your voice** and say, 'Right! I am going to go downstairs. I will set the timer and after ten minutes I will come and see you fast asleep.'

- **Leave the room promptly.** He will try to keep you there, asking questions. Simply say, 'Today is finished, now. No more talking. You rest and I will be back in ten minutes.' Pull the door to, ideally closing it. Hover on the landing, but do not go into him.

- **He will moan, groan and shout,** but this is because he has been asked to do something he doesn't know how to do. Give him time. Don't go into the room – you will disrupt the process.

- **If he comes out of the room,** turn his body around (Ragdoll Mode) and walk him back again. Do not speak to him. This may continue until he accepts that you are not going to stand there.

- **If the initial departure ends up with you returning him to his room** the come-back Timer is not working. Stick with Ragdoll Mode and if he mentions the Timer say, 'We're not going to use it. It doesn't work.'

- **The more you engage with him,** the longer the process will take. Remain in Ragdoll Mode – you should see change in three days.

CARRY ON!

If, after three days of trying the process, your child still comes out of his room, keep repeating the routine and reinforcing the tools. Eventually they will take effect. Perhaps try using a new Incentive System – try dinosaurs instead of train/carriages. The most important thing is to remain consistent and remember not to engage with him at night.

Why shouldn't I stand by my child's door?

Children come into a light sleep six times during the night. Your child believes he cannot fall asleep without you standing by his bedroom door, so if he cannot see you he gets up. It is as though you have become a pillow and he cannot sleep without you.

This routine is exhausting for both of you. Broken sleep is damaging your performance as a parent the next day and your child needs to concentrate and be at his best – difficult if he has been awake in the night.

Your child needs to believe that he is capable of falling asleep on his own, knowing that all he has to do is be in his dark, warm, cosy bedroom.

My child won't let me leave the room after storytime

'Henry holds me around the neck after storytime and won't let me leave the room. He claims there are monsters in there.'

YOUR TOOLS

Tin-Foil Tactic

Dissolving Dust

See pages 54–71

YOUR SKILLS

Ragdoll Mode

See pages 72–77

LET'S DO IT!

WHAT TO DO

- **Make sure that the bedroom is dark** using Tin-Foil Tactic (tool) and that any other lights have been removed.
- **Check that the landing is dark,** but leave a small glow of light coming from downstairs.
- **Make your Dissolving Dust** (tool). This is just a jar with harmless powders in it – all mixed up.

WHAT TO SAY

- **When your child is in the bath,** bend down and make eye contact. Say, 'Now, I need to tell you something exciting about bedtime.' PAUSE.
- **'Look! I have found some Dissolving Dust** and the man in the shop said it definitely works!' Your child is now likely to ask what it is. Say, 'This is a dissolving dust for sprinkling around the windowsill and doorway in your bedroom. If a monster came past our house, this dust would make it sneeze and it would disappear without a sound. This stops any monsters finding their way inside.'
- **Your child might say, 'Monsters are not real!'** Now you know that his fear is not genuine. You can start to relax and realise he is saying it to keep you in his room. Say, 'Now, we are going to sprinkle this dust in your room after bathtime, then have our stories and I will say goodnight and go downstairs to do some ironing/emailing/cooking.'

ACTION IT!

- **Once your child is in his pyjamas and his teeth have been brushed,** take him into his bedroom and give him a spoon to sprinkle the dust over the carpet and window sill (sorry about the mess!).
- **Now he gets into bed** for storytime.

Why shouldn't I stay with my child?

Many children go through a stage where they claim they are scared. It tends to be a word that alarms us and we then react – your child looks for a reaction. He sees your worried reaction and this heightens his concern even more. It is always best to reassure your child that what he is thinking of doesn't exist or isn't possible, but this may not always settle him. Often fears are not rational or logical thoughts. Thoughts are not facts, but this is a hard concept for your child to grasp.

If you were to stay with him you would be reinforcing his fear by showing him that you are 'protecting him' from the visions in his head.

- **Before you start reading the stories** say, 'Now, we won't have any problem with monsters. We know that there are no monsters, but just in case, we now have the Dissolving Dust.'
- **Read his two stories** (avoiding the subject of monsters!).
- **Kiss him goodnight** and tell him you love him very much.
- **Confidently walk out of the room,** pulling the door to or closing it.
- **If he comes out of his room,** you need to simply walk him back in a slow Ragdoll Mode (skill). Say, 'We are not talking any more. No talking. Into bed and rest.'
- **When you have said this once, don't speak to him any more.** Return him to his room as many times as necessary, but do not stay with him.
- **Continue this through the night,** if necessary, and after three consecutive nights of being consistent you should notice a dramatic change taking place.

> **TAKE NOTE!**
> Dissolving Dust lasts one week, so it doesn't need to be sprinkled every night! After a week your child should be sleeping solidly and settling to sleep on his own.

CARRY ON!

If, for some reason, the process doesn't work after three nights (perhaps your child has been ill or disturbed by something else) you need to persevere. Remember that the Dissolving Dust lasts for a week, so continue with your routine of kissing goodnight, confidently walking out and then if he comes out again adopt Ragdoll Mode. Do not talk to him. After a few nights of your consistency he should be able to stay in his own room all night. Perhaps after a few nights you could replenish the Dissolving Dust, just to make sure the monsters have really been frightened off.

My child won't stay in his bedroom at night

'Johnny, aged three, keeps waking up and coming out of his bedroom after being said goodnight to and this sometimes goes on all night. He has numerous excuses as to why he "cannot sleep". I end up sitting with him until he falls asleep each time. He loves dinosaurs.'

YOUR TOOLS

Tin-Foil Tactic

Incentive System
(dinosaurs)

See pages 54–71

YOUR SKILLS

Ragdoll Mode

See pages 72–77

LET'S DO IT!

WHAT TO DO

- Make sure your child's bedroom is nice and dark. Cover the windows with foil using Tin-Foil Tactic (tool).
- Make sure the landing is also dark. Cover any windows with tin foil.
- Draw and cut out seven dinosaur faces and facial features (such as eyes) to glue/tack on to a chart using Incentive System dinosaurs (tool) each morning. The aim is that your child should complete one of the faces every day.

WHAT TO SAY

- **Explain to your child what is going to happen.** A good time to do this is when he is in the bath, before the toys go into the water. Make eye contact and believe fully in what you say. You need to be confident and sound convincing. Say, 'Now, we have decided that bedtime is going to be different tonight. We have found a way to help you to stay in your bed and not keep coming out of your room.' PAUSE.

- Now say, **'When you get out of the bath** and come into your bedroom, I have something to show you. Let's wash you quickly.' When he's in his room he will see the dinosaur Incentive System chart on his wall.

- **Sit down with him and talk** about how one dinosaur is missing his nose, the other an eye and so on. Say, 'Now every night you stay in your bed right through until breakfast you get to fix one of the dinosaurs on the Incentive System chart. When you have fixed all seven, after seven good nights, you get a prize.' PAUSE. 'Now, listen, it's important. If you come out of your room tonight, nobody will talk to you. We will take you back to your room and you will get into bed.'

ACTION IT!

- **Continue with the bedtime routine as usual** (bathtime followed by one/two stories while he sits in bed) and then say goodnight and tell him that the next time you will be talking to him is at breakfast time.

- **Pull the door to almost shut,** but ideally close it.

- **Hover on the landing,** but out of sight if and when he comes to the door.

- **If he steps onto the landing** turn his body around in Ragdoll Mode (skill), without speaking, and walk him back to his bed.

- **When he gets into bed.** Cover him up and walk away. Don't speak.

- **You are being calm,** floppy and slow in your Ragdoll Mode.

- **Do this every time he gets out of bed,** until he eventually 'gives in' and settles to sleep on his own.

- **No talking is very important.** Don't engage with him.

CARRY ON!

The same process might need to take place throughout the night. Adopt Ragdoll Mode every time and do not talk. He always gets to do a dinosaur face on the Incentive System in the morning as a reward for learning something new and not engaging with you during the night.

Over three nights, if you are consistently in Ragdoll Mode, you should see improvement and eventually he should sleep through. By the time the dinosaur face chart is complete, you should be home and dry!

Why should my child stay in his bedroom at night?

If your child can't settle himself and keeps waking up and coming to find you all night, his sleep pattern will be severely distrupted. Children aged two to three need 12 hours' sleep a night, while those aged three to five can manage on 11 hours. A child only grows, physically and mentally, when he is asleep and disturbed sleep affects his concentration during the day, which then affects his behaviour.

A child wakes six times a night. He comes into light sleep and then should return to sleep on his own. He sleeps solidly for the first four hours (19.30 to 23.30) and then every 90 minutes after he comes into a light sleep (at 23.30, 01.00, 02.30, 04.00, 05.30 and 07.00). If you settle your child at 19.00 by staying with him, he will expect you to return whenever he comes into light sleep. So he might call you between one and six times during the night!

Disturbed sleep affects him, but it also affects you and your ability to be a good parent, so your child learning to fall asleep on his own is one of the best life skills you can give him and your family.

My child doesn't fall asleep until 21.00

'Thea, aged five, goes to bed at 20.00. She lies awake and then turns on her light and plays until she falls asleep at 21.00. I have to wake her for school in the morning. She is very tired.'

LET'S DO IT!

YOUR TOOLS

Tin-Foil Tactic

Book of Thoughts

See pages 54–71

YOUR SKILLS

Window of Tiredness

Ragdoll Mode

See pages 72–77

WHAT TO DO

- **Firstly ensure her bedroom is dark,** using Tin-Foil Tactic (tool) if necessary. Light is a stimulant, so the more your child can see around her room as she lies in bed, the harder it is for her to fall asleep.
- **Observe your child and find her Window of Tiredness** (skill). It is likely to be around 19.00–19.30. This means she needs to have had her bath and her stories read to her by 19.00. This is when you need to leave her bedroom.
- **Create a Book of Thoughts** (tool).
- **Remove lamps or bulbs** if you think your child is likely to just turn lights on after you have said goodnight.

WHAT TO SAY

- **During dinnertime or bathtime** talk to your child about how bedtime is going to change. Say, 'Now, I need to talk to you about something.' PAUSE. 'I am a little worried that your body is not getting enough sleep. Children only grow when they are asleep. This also means your brain.' PAUSE. Say, 'I've decided that after I have read your stories at night you do not have a light on. You stay in bed and rest until sleep finds you. Do not get out of bed because that wakes up your legs, making it harder to fall asleep.' PAUSE. Say, 'After dinner/bathtime I will show you something in your room to help you to relax and sleep.'
- **In her bedroom show her/read her the Book of Thoughts.** 'Now, you can see your bedroom is darker. Let's turn the light off for a moment.'
- **Sit in the dark for a moment.** This will reassure you that she is fine about being in a dark room. If she says, 'I can't see' simply reply, 'When you are resting in bed you don't need to see. Your eyes will be closed.'
- **Sit her on her bed and explain the Book of Thoughts.** 'Now I am going to read you your bedtime story as usual and then we are

Can't I just leave my child to play after bedtime?

Your child is five years old and now at school. Every day she walks into her classroom and learns something new. Often everything she is taught is new to her. This involves a lot of concentration and it is hard to concentrate when you are tired.

Your child starts her day before her body naturally wants to – because she is falling asleep too late and not getting enough sleep. Children only grow physically/mentally when asleep and your child needs more sleep to help with her concentration.

going to choose two things for you to think about from your Book of Thoughts once the lights are off.' PAUSE. Say, 'You will lie in bed with teddy and tell him about the thing in the book you are thinking about. Your body will be relaxed and you will drift off to sleep.'

ACTION IT!

- **Ensure that your child has gone to bed at the right time** – during her Window of Tiredness. Aim to be reading stories at 18.45 and finding something to think about from the Book of Thoughts at 19.00.

- **Remove lightbulbs** if your child is likely to switch lights on again after you have gone. Be reassuring. Say, 'The light will come back in the morning. Now your body needs darkness for rest and sleep.' Tell her you love her and that you will see her at breakfast time.

- **You are asking your child to learn something new.** She might, initially, find settling difficult and keep coming out. Be ready on the landing to take her back to her bed using Ragdoll Mode (skill).

- **Talk to her only once,** say, 'We are not talking again until breakfast time. Get back into bed and rest. Don't try to sleep. Just lie and rest. Sleep will come to you.' After this you are in Ragdoll Mode. Keep returning her to her bedroom until she eventually tires and falls asleep.

- **Remain consistent for three consecutive nights** and you'll see change.

CARRY ON!

If your child starts to revert to former ways (perhaps she was ill and you left her light on), you will need to persevere for longer. Remember to be consistent with the tools, refrain from talking to her after you have settled her and stick to the bedtime timetable. You may need to talk to her again about what you require of her – to reinforce the process.

My child insists she reads the stories at night – and not me

'Katie, aged four, refuses to let me read to her. She reads two stories (in her own way!) and they go on and on – and on. She won't bring them to a close. Sometimes she is 'reading' to me for a whole hour!'

YOUR TOOLS

Write-it-Down Bedtime Routine

Timer (story)

See pages 54–71

LET'S DO IT!

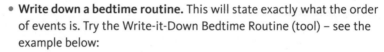

WHAT TO DO

- **Write down a bedtime routine.** This will state exactly what the order of events is. Try the Write-it-Down Bedtime Routine (tool) – see the example below:

Bathtime, pyjamas and brush teeth.
Into the bedroom and each choose one story. Katie chooses one and Mummy chooses one.
Katie gets into her bed and reads the first story to Mummy. The Timer is set – the story is to take no longer than five minutes.
Katie lies or sits on her bed and Mummy sits next to her on the carpet or a chair.
Mummy reads her story and Katie listens to it. Questions are asked at the end of the story. Katie and Mummy have a hug.
Mummy says, 'I love you very much. See you at breakfast time.' She confidently walks away and closes the bedroom door.

- **By posting this routine** on your child's bedroom wall it shows her that there is a clear routine that everyone is going to follow. You can read it to her and let her decorate it with stickers.
- **Use the story Timer (tool)** to show your child that her stories are to last for five minutes and the Timer will show her when the time is up.

WHAT TO SAY

- **At bathtime, when your child is in the water,** before the toys go in, you need to explain bedtime to her. Say, 'Now, I have decided that bedtime is going to be different from now on.' PAUSE. Say, 'After bathtime we are going to each choose a story book. You are going to read the first book to me and I am going to read the second book to you. When you read I am quiet and when I read you are quiet.'

- **Tell her about the story Timer.** Say, 'I have something that is going to tell us when it is the end of your reading time. It is a Timer in your bedroom. I will show you when you have your pyjamas on.'
- **In the bedroom show your child the Timer.** Say, 'Now, this is going to be set for five minutes because that's how long it takes you to read a story. It will buzz to tell you to finish your story and get ready for my story.' Demonstrate the buzzer. Say, 'Hop into bed and start your story. When you're ready to start, tell me and I'll start the Timer.'

ACTION IT!

- **Read through the Write-it-Down Bedtime Routine with her** the first night and let her put stickers on it. This will mean heading to bed slightly earlier.
- **Stick the Write-it-Down Bedtime Routine** on the wall/wardrobe door.
- **Choose one book each.** Ask your child to get into bed. Start the Timer as she begins reading. Once the Timer goes off, let your child's story come to a close. If she continues reading, stop her and say, 'My turn!' If she insists on carrying on reading say, 'You can finish this story in the morning, after we get dressed and before breakfast.'
- **When reading your story, make it clear** to your child at the beginning that she can ask questions at the end of the story.
- **Once both stories are read,** thank your child for 'story time' and tell her that you love her very much and you will see her at breakfast time.
- **Confidently leave the room** and pull the door to. Ideally shut it.

CARRY ON!

If your child reverts to old habits, keep the process going for a bit longer. Talk to her again about the Write-it-Down Bedtime Routine on her wall and read it out to her again. Stick closely to the routine yourself and use the Timer. She'll soon get it.

> **TAKE NOTE!**
> Your child may need reminding about what she has to do and why.

Why can't my child read to me for as long as she likes?

Your child is probably very strong-minded, liking to be in control, but she needs to know that you are in charge. At bedtime she has to wind down and relax before going to sleep and it's important for her to listen as well as 'read' to you.

By listening to your story she is learning. She has to concentrate and be patient in asking questions at the end. This is a skill that she needs to learn to prepare her for nursery and school.

My child refuses to put her pyjamas on after bathtime

'Daisy, aged two and a half, runs circles around me at bedtime, refusing to put her pyjamas on. I end up having to hold her on her bed and fight her to put them on. This has become a tricky pattern that I want to break.'

YOUR TOOLS

Pyjama Bear

See pages 54–71

LET'S DO IT!

WHAT TO DO

- **Find your child's favourite teddy bear** to make into a Pyjama Bear (tool). It should be a fairly large one, if possible.

- **Take a selection of clothes** from your child's drawers each night and dress her bear in them. You ideally want to be dressing him for bed, but putting the bear into day clothes at night is just as good – it could be turned into a joke.

WHAT TO SAY

- **When your child is in the bath** make eye contact and get her full attention. Say, 'Now, tonight is going to be a bit different at pyjama time.' PAUSE. Say, 'We are not going to have the shouting and I am not going to put your pyjamas on for you. You are going to do it all by yourself in the bathroom because I am going to be busy in your bedroom.' PAUSE.

- **Now show your child the teddy** you are going to dress. Say, 'This bear (state its name) is going to get ready for bed every night. I am going to get you out of the bath and lay your pyjamas on the floor in here. You will get dressed and I will go and dress bear. You will then come in and see what he is wearing. I am going to use different things from your bedroom.' PAUSE. Say, 'Then you will choose a story book and bear will choose one and you will sit together for storytime.' PAUSE.

Does my child have to wear pyjamas?

Some children do sleep in the nude, but you must ensure that the bedroom is warm enough. Children kick their covers off in the night and you do not want to be concerned about the bedroom getting cool in the early hours.

- **Let your child digest what has been said.** Avoid any unnecessary distractions. Her pyjamas need to be ones she can put on by herself.

ACTION IT!

- **Let your child pull out the bath plug.** Get her out of the bath and help her to get dry.

- **Lay out her pyjamas** and say, 'Tell me when you are ready. You say "go" and we will both get to it!'

- **If your child refuses to say 'go',** you can say it and confidently and promptly leave the bathroom and close the door. The chances are that when she is on her own she will get her pyjamas on.

- **If she comes out not wearing her pyjamas,** you need to promptly return her to the bathroom. You MUST remain consistent. You do not want her putting them on by your side in the bedroom as this is a slippery slope to her just running around while you dress a bear! The idea is that she comes out of the bathroom once she is dressed.

CARRY ON!

After three to five consecutive days of carrying out this process, your child should be getting her pyjamas on by herself in the bathroom, but the novelty might start to wear off. You can always say, 'Would you like me to stop dressing bear and you find another toy for me to dress?'

Eventually you will find that your child puts on her pyjamas without thinking and you no longer need to dress the bear.

> **TAKE NOTE!**
> Your child probably does want her pyjamas on – she is just testing your authority.

My child insists the bedroom light is left on

'Harry, aged three, always used to sleep in the dark but has recently insisted that the light is on. He claims he is scared of the dark. He wakes very early in the morning, as early as 05.00, and starts playing.'

LET'S DO IT!

YOUR TOOLS

Tin-Foil Tactic

See pages 54–71

YOUR SKILLS

Ragdoll Mode

See pages 72–77

WHAT TO DO

- **Return your child's room to darkness,** the way it originally was. Remove the bulb from your child's light if you think he will turn it on once you've left the room. Use Tin-Foil Tactic (tool) if necessary.

- **Play games in your child's bedroom in darkness.** You hide and he has to come and find you in darkness, for example. That way you can reassure him if he seems afraid of the dark.

- **Sit and chat in the darkness of his bedroom.** Play these games and chat. Do this in the afternoon, long before bedtime.

WHAT TO SAY

- **After you have played the games in his bedroom,** remind your child about how he isn't afraid of the dark. Say, 'Your body loves the dark. You are very happy when the lights are out.' PAUSE. Say, 'I have decided that we are not going to have your bedroom light on any more. It keeps you awake and wakes you up too early in the morning.' PAUSE. 'Tonight at bedtime I am going to turn out the light and it will not come on again until I knock on your door at breakfast time.' PAUSE. 'Do you understand? It is going to be how it used to be.' Don't expect him to answer you. Remain quiet for a moment, so that he can digest what you have said to him.

ACTION IT!

- **After bedtime stories, turn off the light** and then return to your child's bed. You might have taken the main lightbulb out and be reading by lamplight. You will need to remove the lamp or the bulb before you leave the room.

- **Sit on your child's bed** and tell him about three things that you are going to do the following day. Say, 'Tomorrow we have to go to the

Why should my child sleep in the dark?

Light is a stimulant. The darkness is a sign of closure: the end of the day. Just try it yourself. We tend to relax more when it is dark around us as opposed to when we are surrounded with brightness.

If your child is lying in bed and can see everything around him, he spends time looking, which can stimulate him awake.

He might then get out of bed and want to start playing again.

This scenario might not only happen when you put him to bed, but it might also occur very early in the morning when he comes into his final light sleep at around 05.00.

supermarket to buy some fruit. We are going to play with some playdough at home and then we are going to visit Grandma. Now settle down and rest and I will see you at breakfast time.' Talking about tomorrow will bring reassurance.

- **Confidently leave the room.** He might start to shout about the light, but you must tell yourself that he was fine this afternoon when you were playing in there together and he has slept in the dark before. Leave him to shout.

- **If he comes out of his room,** you need to go into Ragdoll Mode (skill) and return him to his bed. Do NOT speak to him. Remain calm and relaxed so that he senses your calm state.

CARRY ON!

The first night is always the hardest and the second might be just as challenging, but the key is to remain consistent. Carry on and don't give up. If you are not consistent and you stay with your child too long on his bed or agree to a 'little light' you are breaking the consistency and it will not be long before he has persuaded you to leave the main light on. You will be back to where you started.

Don't give up. Trust that the process will work and believe in yourself and your child. You can do it!

One of my boys wakes in the night and shouts until I go in

'We have two children sharing a bedroom (Jacob and Fred) and sometimes Fred wakes in the night and shouts for me. I immediately go to him because I am afraid he will wake Jacob. I sit with Fred for a few minutes and then he returns to sleep.'

YOUR TOOLS

Incentive System (dinosaurs)

Tin-Foil Tactic

See pages 54–71

YOUR SKILLS

Ragdoll Mode

See pages 72–77

LET'S DO IT!

WHAT TO DO

- **Create an Incentive System (tool) for both boys:** one for the fact that Fred shouts and the other for Jacob, for the fact that he is going to have to remain quiet and roll over and go to sleep when Fred makes the noise. They can have independent Incentive Systems, but they should both be of the same style (such as dinosaurs).

- **Ensure that the bedroom is dark.** Remove all light using Tin-Foil Tactic (tool), if necessary. Have the boys' beds as far apart as possible.

WHAT TO SAY

- **When the boys are in the bath together, sit and talk to them both.** Do this before the toys are put in the bath. Make eye contact with both children in turn. Say, 'Now, boys, I need to talk to you. You know that Mummy is getting very tired of getting up in the night because Fred is shouting.' PAUSE. Say, 'I have decided that I am not going to get up any more'.

- **Now focus on the child who is shouting at night.** Say, 'Fred, you are very good at settling to sleep when I say goodnight after stories. If you wake in the night, roll over and rest until you fall back to sleep.' PAUSE. Say, 'Everyone wakes in the night, but we roll over and go back to sleep'.

- **Now remain quiet and let the words sink in.** Then say, 'I have something in your bedroom that is going to help you sleep. We can look at it when you get out of the bath.'

- **Once the boys are in their pyjamas,** with teeth brushed, let them see the Incentive System dinosaurs in their bedroom. Say, 'Now you both have dinosaurs. But they all have their eyes missing. Poor things.' PAUSE. 'These dinosaurs are Fred's and these ones are Jacob's.

So, Fred, if there is shouting in the night you have to be very grown up and roll over, rest and go back to sleep. If you can do this you get to choose a dinosaur and put his eyes on in the morning.' PAUSE. 'So, Jacob, you must roll over and go back to sleep and you get your eyes for the dinosaur in the morning.' PAUSE. Say, 'The exciting thing is that after all the eyes are on you will both get a prize!'

ACTION IT!

- **After storytime, when the boys are in bed,** remind them of the dinosaurs. Say, 'So remember: I am not coming into your room. I am going to roll over and go back to sleep. You must do the same. I love you. See you at breakfast. I can't wait to do the dinosaur eyes!'

- **Confidently walk away and pull the door to** – or close it. Realise what you have said and that when the noise begins you must NOT go into the bedroom. You are asking Fred to break a long-held habit, so he will wake and there will be shouting. The only time you should be involved is if a child comes out of the bedroom and you have to walk him back in Ragdoll Mode (skill).

- **You might need to do this several times in the night** with both boys. It is going to be exhausting. Do it for three nights and you will see dramatic change – if you remain consistent.

CARRY ON!

You don't want to go back to your old ways after three nights. You will find that things will feel worse before they get better, so be prepared to ride through the initial difficult one/two nights. You can do it!

If after five nights things are better and you hear Fred (in the night) murmur and moan but return to sleep, this is a breakthrough. If all is going well but he suddenly shouts out one night, think before you go to him. If you do go to him, talk to him the following day to reiterate that you won't be going in again if he shouts.

> **TAKE NOTE!**
> You don't want the old behaviour to return before you even realise it.

Why can't I continue to go to my child when he shouts?

Broken sleep affects a child's potential. He may become tired and lose concentration. This is hard for him when he is at nursery or school. Solid sleep is when a child does his growing, both mentally and physically.

The fact that your child wakes in the night is not something he wants to do. He wakes and believes that he can only return to sleep if you go to him. You have both got yourself into a routine you don't want to be in.

My child screams during pre-bedtime hairwashing

'My daughter, Ruby, is two and a half and she starts screaming the moment she sees me reach for the shampoo. She refuses to tilt her head back and water goes in her face, but she still won't co-operate.'

LET'S DO IT!

WHAT TO DO

- **Find a big poster with a busy picture on it** that will appeal to your child and stick it on the ceiling above the bath. It needs to be a picture you can ask questions about. For example, 'How many apples are in the tree?' or 'What colour is the man's hat?'

WHAT TO SAY

- **When your child is sitting in the bath,** ask her to look up at the poster. PAUSE. Say, 'Now, that picture is to help us with hairwashing. When you look at it, it makes it very easy for me to put water on your head. It won't go in your face if you are looking up at the picture.'

- **Now explain that you are going to put water on her back.** Say, 'I am going to ask you to look up at the picture and I am going to wash your back, not your hair.'

- **Ask a question about the picture** as you pour water on her back and down to the ends of her hair (if it is long).

- **Slowly cover her back, not the top of her head, with water.** Continue asking questions about the picture all the time.

- **Now say, 'Guess what!** Your hair is all wet. You were so busy looking at the picture. Brilliant work!'

- **Now put a small amount of shampoo in her hair** without it being too obvious. Leave it there for a moment. Say, 'Okay, let's look up again and I will wash your back.' Do the same thing. Praise her enormously once all the questions have been asked and the task is done.

Can't I just avoid washing my child's hair?

The easy option is never the right one! Earmark certain days of the week to wash your child's hair and make her aware when these days are. Twice a week is fine.

If children's hair is not washed regularly their scalps can start itching, which can lead to an aggravated scalp. Therefore it is best to keep the hair clean.

ACTION IT!

- **Plan the two days in the week you intend to wash your child's hair** and remain consistent with those. Tell her at dinnertime whether tonight is a 'poster night'.

CARRY ON!

If your child refuses to look up at the poster, you are simply going to have to ask her to choose. Say, 'You can look up at the picture and ask Mummy questions and I ask you, or I can just pour water on you as you hold the flannel on your face.' You then have to do as you have said.

> **TAKE NOTE!**
> If you remain consistent, your child will eventually see the benefit of looking up at the poster.

The bedtime routine just goes on and on

'My child, Amelia, makes bedtime go on for too long, claiming she needs another hug, kiss or story. She is two and a half and always used to go to bed easily. This has now been going on for six weeks.'

YOUR TOOLS

Write-it-Down Bedtime Routine

Incentive System (tree ribbons)

See pages 54–71

YOUR SKILLS

Ragdoll Mode

See pages 72–77

LET'S DO IT!

WHAT TO DO

- **Write out the bedtime routine** with Write-it-Down Bedtime Routine (tool) and put it in your child's bedroom – see example below:

Bathtime followed by pyjamas and teeth-brushing.
Choose two stories and get into bed.
Mummy/Daddy sit on the floor and read as Amelia sits in her bed.
Mummy tells Amelia three things she will be doing tomorrow.
Mummy asks Amelia to tell her ONE piece of news from today.
ONE big hug and then a kiss
Mummy says, 'I love you very much. See you in the morning.'
The light is turned out and the door is closed.

- **Create an Incentive System** using tree ribbons (tool) to guide your child to not call out after you have left her room.
- **Ensure the room is dark:** no lights to stimulate her awake.

WHAT TO SAY

- **When your child is in the bath,** make eye contact with her and ensure she is focused on you. Say, 'Now, bedtime is going to be different tonight and from now on. We are not going to keep on talking and talking. I am not going to come back to your room if you call me. When I say goodnight, you need to rest. If you want to chat, talk to your teddy bear/rabbit.' PAUSE. 'When you have finished in the bath I have something in your bedroom to help you with this.'
- **Once you are in your child's bedroom** and she has pyjamas on, show her the Write-it-Down Bedtime Routine. Say, 'This is what is going to

happen every night. It will be the same whoever puts you to bed.'

- **Read out the Write-it-Down Bedtime Routine.** Point at each stage on the chart as you say it.
- **Now talk about the Incentive System.** Say, 'I have a jar of ribbons and each morning we are going to go downstairs and tie a ribbon to the tree in the garden. This is to show that you have gone to bed like a good girl and not called out.' PAUSE. Say, 'So each night when I say, "See you at breakfast time", this is the last time I am going to speak to you until ribbon time in the morning.' PAUSE 'There are seven ribbons and when they are all hanging in the tree you will get a prize!'

ACTION IT!

- **After storytime point to the routine** and say, 'Now we are going to get this just right.'
- **Carry out the stages** as they are written on the chart.
- **As you go to leave the room, say,** 'Remember! No talking until ribbon time. I can't wait to see what colour ribbon you choose. The tree is going to look so pretty!'
- **Confidently walk out of the room,** pulling the door to, ideally closing it. You now have to be true to your word. You must not return to her room or talk to her. If she comes out of the room, go into Ragdoll Mode (skill) and remain calm and silent as you return her to bed.

CARRY ON!

The first night is the hardest. Your child will shout, challenge you and insist you speak to her. Remain consistent and ensure you don't speak to her – you will see change. The moment you do speak to her she has taken the control back and you will have to start the process again the following night. Children are clever. They will try all manner of things and say all kinds of things. By the time the seven ribbons are in the tree, you will be home and dry. She must get a ribbon every morning.

Why limit the length of the bedtime routine?

Keep the bedtime routine to a limited time – you need your free time too. Aim for 20 minutes – from stories to leaving the room. If you stay for too long your child starts to get a 'second wind' and you miss the Window of Tiredness (see page 76). This means that she finds it hard to fall asleep when you leave the room. It could be 45–90 minutes before the next window arrives.

Eating scenarios

Eating is an area that seems to reveal a lot of parenting problems. Children can become picky eaters and it can be a challenge to get them to eat a balanced diet. But rest assured, if you try out the Tools and Skills recommended in this section, your child's eating problems will soon become a thing of the past. Please note that the three main meals are referred to throughout as: 'breakfast', 'lunch' and 'dinner'.

Importance of a mealtime routine
Try to stick to regular mealtimes. That way your child will know what is expected and will come to the table hungry and ready for food. Space out snacks so that he does not lose the edge from his appetite.

Mealtimes are family times
If possible, all sit down to eat as a family. Your child will start to understand that mealtimes are a social occasion and he will imitate those around him – eating the same food as them.

Mealtime rules
Decide on a 'code of conduct' for all the family. Write it up and post it where everyone can see it. For example:

- We sit nicely at the table.
- We serve ourselves nicely.
- We eat what we can and do not moan if we don't like the food.
- We ask nicely to leave the table and say 'thank you' for our meal.

My child drinks too much and then won't eat his dinner

'I know it is good for children to drink. My son, Ahmed, has two cups of juice before the meal arrives, but then will only have a couple of mouthfuls of food before saying he is full up and can't eat any more.'

LET'S DO IT!

WHAT TO DO
- **Take two glasses:** Little Glass, Big Glass (tool). The small glass is for before the meal and the big glass is for after the meal.

WHAT TO SAY
- **Explain what the glasses are for.** 'Now, look. Here are two grown-up glasses you can use. You are going to have to be very careful not to drop them. The little one is your juice glass to have before dinner.' PAUSE. 'The big glass can have juice in once you have finished your dinner.' PAUSE. 'I am going to put a jug of water on the table. You can pour water into your little cup and drink during dinnertime if you want.' PAUSE. 'You need to eat at least half of your dinner if you want your after-dinner juice.'

ACTION IT!
- **The little glass of juice** is on the table and the table is fully laid.
- **The big glass is out of sight.**
- **A small water jug is on the table.**

Continued ▶

YOUR TOOLS

Little Glass, Big Glass

Shout Spot

See pages 54–71

YOUR SKILLS

You Choose

See pages 72–77

Why shouldn't my child have drinks before a meal?

It is fine for your child to drink as much water as he wishes. He always will if he is truly thirsty. He can drink before and during the meal – this is fine as it won't affect his appetite. The difference with fruit juice or squash is that it is full of sugars and artificial alternatives and this causes your child to feel full immediately. If you let him drink lots before the meal, your child won't be able to eat enough. He won't feel full for long and may then claim he is hungry after the meal is over.

- **Once the little glass has been emptied,** you can suggest your child eats three mouthfuls.
- **Then let your child fill his glass with water** if he wants.
- **If he starts asking for more juice,** simply say, 'Your juice is waiting for you to eat this much lunch' (split off a small amount from the rest of the meal).
- **Continue eating your meal.**
- **If he refuses to eat,** just let him sit there until you have finished.
- **If he gets down,** you need to say using You Choose (skill), 'Now. Are you going to come back to the table and have a little something to eat or go to the Shout Spot (tool)?' PAUSE. 'You choose: chair or Shout Spot?'
- **If he comes back to the table,** this is wonderful. But if you are ignored, take him calmly to the Shout Spot. Say, 'Sit here until we have finished our food and then you can come back in.'
- **Leave him for the duration of the meal.** He might go up to his bedroom, but the main thing is that he is not in the kitchen disrupting the meal for everyone else.

CARRY ON!

All children put up resistance to change, but if you remain consistent your child will then accept it. He needs to know that he cannot make you change your mind before realising that this is the new way of doing things. Remain consistent and even if you don't feel firm at the beginning, it will be worth it in the end. Don't give up.

My child is a vegetarian, but he wants to eat meat

'We have raised our child, Ricky, aged five, as a vegetarian. Recently at school he has been saying that he wants to eat burger and chips. What do we do?'

LET'S DO IT!

WHAT TO DO AND SAY

- **Find a time to sit down** with your child and talk about how you feel about meat and the decision you have made with your partner about the 'burger school lunch' – that you don't want him to eat meat.

ACTION IT!

- **Plan for both of you to be with your child** when this discussion is happening – to show your child that you are united in the decision you have both made.

- **Be strong and confident in the decision** you have made and if you feel true to your word you must remain consistent.

CARRY ON!

If later down the line your child asks more and more about eating meat, you might have to change your approach. However, be aware that the more a child is told he cannot have something, the more he craves it and the last thing you want is a secret burger-eater.

Why must we make consistent joint decisions?

It is important that as parents you decide how you want to manage this situation and you agree and stay true to whatever decision you make. You then remain consistent with what you have agreed. Here are some options:

- If you are firm believers that your child should not eat meat, then you need to simply say, 'Meat is not something our family eats. You need to choose other foods at school.'
- You could allow your child to eat meat out of the house (at friends' homes and at school), but make it clear to him that meat never comes into his home.
- You could allow him to make his own choice and eat meat if he would like to.

My child refuses to sit up at the table

'Ellie, aged three, won't sit at the table and concentrate on eating. I am concerned about her weight. I follow her around the room feeding her as she plays.'

YOUR SKILLS

Self Serve

See pages 72–77

LET'S DO IT!

WHAT TO DO

- **Make sure your child has a chair** that is the correct height for her. She needs to be sitting with her tummy button, not her chin, close to the rim of the table. She needs to be able to look down on her food.

- **Place your child's chair at the back of the table** (against the wall, if possible)so it's harder for her to get down before the end of the meal.

- **Aim to sit and eat with your child** and don't get up during the meal. Place everything you need on the table before you start.

- **Put the serving dish of food in the centre of the table** and serve yourself a portion. It is important that your child sees you enjoying your food. She will follow your lead.

WHAT TO SAY

- **Sit down with your child** when she isn't distracted by any toys.

- **Make eye contact with her.** Say, 'Now, your special chair is at the table. This is so that you can sit with us at breakfast, lunch and dinnertime and we can all eat together.' PAUSE. 'The only food we are going to have is on the table.'

ACTION IT!

- **Show your child her special chair** and decorate it together with stickers or ribbons.

- **Carry out a morning activity** such as painting at the kitchen table with your child sitting in her special chair. Guide her to sit there as much as possible for table-top activities and play.

- **At mealtimes, have everything you need on the table** (including spare cutlery in case it gets dropped, paper towels for spillages, a water jug, food in serving dishes and dessert at the end of the table

Why is it so important for my child to eat at the table?

A mealtime is a social time for the family – it is not just when everyone eats, though that is important too. By sitting at the table and watching the family eat, this teaches a child manners, how to wait for food to come, social skills as well as, hopefully, good eating habits.

There are many situations in life when a child has to sit at a table, concentrate and 'wait'. The sooner you start to teach her this, the easier it is when she starts school, visits friends' houses and stays with relatives.

under a tea towel). This is so that you do not need to get up from the table once you are sitting down. If you get up – your child will want to get up too!

- **Once the table is laid,** guide your child to sit at the table.
- **Sit at the table and serve yourself.**
- **Give your child the serving spoons** so that she can serve herself using Self Serve (skill).
- **Relax and realise that if you sit with your child** she is likely to eat some food on her own because you are eating yours and she wants to imitate you.
- **Aim to chat about other topics,** not the food. Don't focus too much on your child eating. Understand that she will eat what her body needs (see page 65 for portion sizes) and after this she can move on to some dessert.
- **When your child indicates she wants to get down,** ask her to thank you for her meal and prompt her to say, 'Please may I leave the table?'
- **Ask her if she is sure she has had enough to eat.** Say, 'There isn't anything else now until dinnertime. Are you sure you have had enough?' You must trust her. The next meal is never far away.

CARRY ON!
It is important that if you try this three-day process at mealtimes you need to see this as a lifestyle change – something that you are going to continue to do in the long term. With consistency and your child realising that food is only eaten at the table, that she always has company there, she will adapt to this regime becoming the norm.

My child refuses to have vegetables on her plate

'Harvey sees vegetables on everyone else's plate, but screams and refuses to eat them if they are on his. I am now in the habit of not giving them to him.'

YOUR TOOLS

Incentive System
(fill-it-up marble jar)

Shout Spot

See pages 54–71

YOUR SKILLS

Self Serve

The Back

See pages 72–77

LET'S DO IT!

WHAT TO DO

- **Ensure that everyone comes** to the table to eat together.
- **Serve the food from the middle of the table.** Everyone helps themselves using Self Serve (skill).
- **Establish the rule that everyone has to put a little of everything** onto their plate (even if it is just one pea or one carrot stick).
- **Put a glass jar in the centre of the table** and a collection of marbles in a box on your lap using the Incentive System fill-it-up jar (tool).

WHAT TO SAY

- **Sit with your child** when he is not distracted by toys and explain mealtimes. Say, 'Now I have decided that we are all going to eat together at the table, but from now on you are going to serve your own food.' PAUSE. 'I am going to put the food in the middle of the table and everyone serves themselves.' PAUSE. 'Now the rule is that you have to put a little of everything on your plate.' PAUSE. 'So, you have to put the vegetables on your plate, but only a small amount if you want.' PAUSE. 'You don't have to eat them until the day comes when your body is ready for them.' PAUSE.

- **Now explain the fill-it-up marble jar.** Say, 'Now, I have a box of marbles and an empty jar. The jar is going to sit in the middle of the table. At mealtimes, when I see good behaviour and nice eating, I will give you a marble to put in the jar.'

- **Now give a few examples,** handing your child marbles. Say, 'You came to the table straight away. That means you have a marble. You have served yourself very well. That is a marble. You have served yourself vegetables. Brilliant! That is a marble.' PAUSE. 'Once the jar is full we are going to have a reward and do something fun as a family (the zoo, the cinema, a restaurant). Any ideas?'

ACTION IT!

- **Lay the table with everything you need on it** so that you do not have to get up once you are seated.

- **Place the food in the middle of the table.** Everyone serves themselves and you start to give praise using the marbles. If your child refuses to put vegetables on his plate, you can put the smallest amount on for him and quickly give him a marble. Continue talking about something different and what to look forward to after dinner (TV show, train set). Don't mention eating the vegetables. The fact that he has put them on his plate is a breakthrough. In time, putting vegetables on his plate will be the norm and eventually he will try them. There is no hurry. He will get there eventually.

CARRY ON!

If your child refuses to put vegetables on his plate you need to calmly remove him from the table and take him into the hallway using the Shout Spot (tool). Sit him on the Shout Spot. Remain calm. Say, 'This is a new rule. You have to put vegetables on your plate. You do not have to eat them. Now sit here and you can come back when you are ready to eat your dinner and leave your vegetables on your plate.'

Confidently walk away and leave him using The Back (skill). He will decide whether he is coming to the table or not. Don't be alarmed if you have two or three mealtimes where he would rather sit on the Shout Spot in the hallway. He is testing you. Remain consistent with this rule. He will conform, especially if you have served one of his favourite meals.

Do not worry if dinner is not eaten at all, a cup of milk or a yoghurt will line his stomach through the night and prevent hunger. He will learn in time and may even taste, and eat, his vegetables.

> **TAKE NOTE!**
> You are not 'forcing' him to eat the vegetables. They simply have to be on his plate.

Why give a child food when we know he won't eat it?

Your child's taste buds are maturing all the time. He might not like a food one week, only to start trying it the following week. It is important that there is always a variety of foods on offer for your child, including the ones he thinks he doesn't like. If veggies aren't on his plate, he never has the option of trying them because it has become 'accepted' by everyone that he never eats them.

When you get to this stage, your child starts to believe the same thing. By putting veggies on his plate you are showing your child that you are not giving up on him. Say, 'I know your body will want broccoli one day. That might be today! That is why it is on your plate.' If he is going to try it he will do it quietly when he feels least noticed. It will not happen if you are pressuring him.

I have to feed my child while he watches the TV/ipad

'I have got into the bad habit of feeding Alex, aged two and a half, while he watches a TV show at the table. Otherwise he refuses to eat. He goes to nursery two days a week and refuses to eat there, too.'

YOUR TOOLS

Incentive System
(fill-it-up marble jar)

Pick a Portion

See pages 54–71

YOUR SKILLS

Self Serve

See pages 72–77

LET'S DO IT!

WHAT TO DO

- **Ensure that the TV/ipad is completely out of sight.**
- **When you lay the table,** place everything you need on it for the whole meal, so that you do not have to keep getting up.
- **Place the food in the middle of the table** so that everyone can serve themselves using Self Serve (skill). You should eat the same food as your child.
- **Let your child know that after lunch** he can watch theTV/ipad while you tidy the kitchen and make a cup of tea!

WHAT TO SAY

- **Ensure your child is not distracted.** You want his full attention.
- **Talk to him** an hour before the meal. Bend down and make eye contact. Say, 'Now. I have decided that we are not going to have the TV/ipad on at the table any more when we are eating.' PAUSE. 'We are going to sit together and have our meal and then when we have finished you can watch the TV/ipad on the sofa'. PAUSE. 'Now I have this box of marbles. They are called 'mealtime marbles' (Incentive System fill-it-up jar tool). Every time you put some food in your mouth I will give you a marble to put in this jar (show him the jar).' PAUSE. 'When the jar is full you get a prize!'
- **Let him look at the marbles,** if he wishes, but then take them away and put the empty jar in the middle of the table. He now goes to play until the mealtime.

ACTION IT!

- **Lay the table with everything you need,** including spare cultery, paper towels and the second course concealed under a tea towel.

Why entertainment at the table isn't a good idea

If you introduce entertainment at the meal table your child becomes dependent on it and starts to believe that he can't eat any other way. He sees eating and entertainment as going hand in hand.

A child who is fed while he is being entertained (for example, watching a screen) becomes oblivious to being fed. Often he is not even sure what he is eating. It is not so much that the screen is on, it is the fact that he has no concept of 'mealtime' while it is on. However, as your child becomes older it is fine to have the occasional TV dinner with the family.

- **Have the food in the centre of the table** so your child serves himself, as do you. Use the Pick a Portion (tool) as a guide to portion size.
- **Say 'Now remember! Every time you put some food in your mouth,** I give you a marble and you put it in the jar!'
- **Now start to eat your meal** and let him follow your lead.
- **Do not be concerned about him using his fingers** at this stage. He is still learning, as he has been fed by you for so long.
- **The marbles should be a good enticement to eat.** He is likely to eat less than he usually does when he was being entertained (in front of the TV/ipad). This is because he was oblivious to feeling full before. Now he is reading his body better.
- **Accept it when he says he has had enough.** You can try and ask him to have two more mouthfuls, but don't push it.
- **Remember to take little steps.** Slowly he will eat more and start using cutlery and speeding up.
- **Be proud of both of you.** He might only eat a small amount to begin with, but he is doing it himself!

CARRY ON!

It is important that once you have made the decision to stop using entertainment (the TV/ipad) at mealtimes you must remain consistent and not reintroduce it. If you do, you will be back to where you started.

Most children forget to eat when the screen is on, so you would be back to feeding him yourself. Only try the three-day process when you are completely ready yourself because it is a lifestyle change not just a three-day wonder!

My child will only sit at the meal table for two minutes

'Clara will come to the table, stand and take between three and five mouthfuls, then say "I'm finished" and run off and play. This is making mealtimes very difficult with my other two children.'

YOUR TOOLS

Incentive System
(fill-it-up marble jar)

Shout Spot

See pages 54–71

YOUR SKILLS

Self Serve

See pages 72–77

LET'S DO IT!

WHAT TO DO

- **Have set places at the table.** Clara sits at the back, ideally between the wall and the table, if this is physically possible. This makes getting down more difficult. You sit next to her.
- **The table is laid with everything on it,** so that once you are sitting down with the children you do not need to get up again.
- **The food is in the centre of the table** and everyone serves themselves using Self Serve (skill).
- **Clara serves herself** and should eat what is on her plate and then sit at the table and wait for dessert.
- **Explain the Incentive System fill-it up jar** (tool). All the children need to be involved.
- **When Clara wants to get down she asks,** 'May I leave the table?' Make it clear: once she's got down, her food's gone, she can't return.

WHAT TO SAY

- **Sit all the children at the table** an hour before you eat.
- **Place the fill-it-up marble jar** in the middle. Say, 'I've decided we are all going to sit at the table together at meals and serve our own food.' PAUSE. 'Listen, Clara. You must sit at the table and eat everything you put on your plate. We are not getting down from the table early any more. If you do, you have to leave the kitchen and you can't come back. There will be no more food.' PAUSE. 'Do you understand, everyone? If you get down you have to leave the room. You cannot come back. I have a jar that we are going to fill up at mealtimes.' PAUSE. 'I have some marbles. Every time I see someone behaving nicely and eating well they can put a marble in the jar. When the jar is full we get a family prize!' Ask the children for their ideas on this.

ACTION IT!

- **Sit Clara** where it is least easy to get down from the table.

- **Bring her to the table last.**

- **Ask everyone to serve themselves.**

- **Ensure Clara is sitting on her chair.**

- **As the children serve themselves,** give them each a marble. As they start to eat well – a marble. Address each child individually. For example, 'Well done, Noah. You are eating nicely. You get a marble. Well done, Josh. Eating all your carrots. A marble. Well done, Clara, you are sitting so nicely. A marble.'

- **When Clara does try to leave the table,** ask her if she has had enough.

- **Give her the marble jar** and a bowl and ask her to count out the marbles while everyone finishes eating.

- **Now serve dessert.**

- **At the end of the meal,** everyone says, 'Thank you and may I leave the table?' This is how they earn their final mealtime marble.

CARRY ON!

If Clara does get down she gets her first warning. Say, 'Clara come back to the table quickly, we haven't had dessert yet. Let's count these marbles.' Guide her back to her chair. If she gets down again, say, 'You have got down twice. Do it again and you will have to leave the room and there will be no dessert for you.'

On getting down for the third time she needs to be taken to the hallway and put on the Shout Spot (tool). Say, 'Stay here until we have finished our meal and then you can come back in.' Nobody is allowed in the kitchen at mealtimes unless they are sitting at the table.

Be consistent. Clara will not like to feel that she is missing out, especially on dessert. By following this through a couple of times and her visiting the Shout Spot, she will learn and start to spend longer at the table.

> **TAKE NOTE!**
> Rules and boundaries in the home apply to everyone. Adults included!

Why is it important that my child sits down to eat?

Sitting down is important for your child's digestion, if nothing else. The body needs to remain still when we are eating.

In addition, mealtimes are social events and when the whole family is conforming there is no reason why one member can do what she likes!

My child won't sit at the table if it isn't his favourite meal

'Max is very stubborn. If the meal isn't sausages or fish fingers he refuses to come to the table. He just goes off and plays, saying, "I'm not hungry".'

YOUR TOOLS

Incentive System
(string and pegs)

Menu Plan

Shout Spot

See pages 54–71

LET'S DO IT!

WHAT TO DO

- **Lay the table with everything on it** so you don't have to get up again.
- **Tie a string across the kitchen** using the Incentive System string and pegs (tool) and when the children behave well at the table they are given a peg. They then attach it to the string at the end of the meal.
- **Announce in the morning** what dinner is going to be that day. Create a Menu Plan (tool), which will go up on the fridge/kitchen wall.
- **Explain the Shout Spot** (tool) to the children. This is, ideally, in the hallway. No toys are allowed there.

WHAT TO SAY

- **Sit the children down** an hour before the mealtime. You are all around the table and the string is hanging across the kitchen. The pegs are in your lap. The menu plan is on the table. Say, 'Now look. I have made a menu plan of what we are eating this week.' Go through the list Monday to Sunday. Dinners are the main focus. Say, 'Now, Max, we all know that dinner isn't always your favourite meal, but you must still sit at the table.' PAUSE. 'Do you understand? We sit at the table whether we eat or not.' PAUSE. 'No one is allowed to always have their favourite food.'
- **Explain the string and pegs Incentive System.** Say, 'Now, you can all see the string. Look, I have a box of pegs. I am going to give you a peg every time you are sitting nicely, eating well, making conversation, using your manners. After the meal, when you ask to get down, I will lift you up and you can put your pegs on the line. When the line is full up we will get a family prize.' PAUSE.
- **Explain the follow-up.** Say, 'Now, if you get down from the table and don't come back when I ask, you have to go and sit on the Shout Spot in the hallway on your own. No toys. You sit there until everyone has

Why must my child sit at the table if he's not eating?

It is important for everyone in the family to realise that mealtimes are social events, a time where you talk about your day, discuss holidays, weekend plans and other things. It is not about who eats what and how much is consumed. It is wonderful if your child eats well, but if he doesn't eat an entire meal every dinnertime he is still going to be fine.

For a child to feel relaxed to just sit and not feel pressured to eat is very important. Once he relaxes he is likely to eat, even if the food being served isn't his favourite.

finished their meal. Then you can go and play.' PAUSE. 'Do you understand?' If nobody answers, just say, 'Sit nicely, otherwise you will go on the Shout Spot in the hallway. Sit nicely and you get pegs!'

ACTION IT!
- **Now you have said it,** you must do it.
- **Everyone comes to the table** and it is laid with everything you are likely to need for the whole meal (to avoid you getting up).
- **Bring Max to the table last.**
- **If he refuses to sit down,** then you need to take him to the Shout Spot in the hallway. Say, 'Stay here until you are ready to sit at the table. Come back when you want to sit down with us.' Don't mention the food.
- **Everyone serves their own food.** Don't focus overly on Max to eat. Be proud that he is sitting there. Give him a peg for sitting still.

CARRY ON!
By remaining consistent, whereby Max is to sit at the table even if it isn't his favourite food, you will start to see him slowly trying different foods. Don't pressure him. Your main aim at this point is to have him sitting with the family.

Continue to take him to the hallway Shout Spot if he refuses to sit at the table. He must understand the clear message – if he is not going to conform to family meals he has to be on his own.

My child will only eat pasta

'I have three children. Two eat a good diet but my son, Tyler, aged four, will only eat pasta, which he has every night. Otherwise he won't eat.'

LET'S DO IT!

YOUR TOOLS

Menu Plan

Incentive System
(mealtime chart)

Shout Spot

See pages 54–71

WHAT TO DO

- **Create a weekly Menu Plan** (tool) around pasta- and carb-heavy meals. Aim to serve pasta two to three times in the week but introduce a small amount of sauce or some cheese to the dish. See below for an example of an appropriate carb-heavy Menu Plan.

Day	Dinner
Monday	Spaghetti with light tomato sauce (no lumps!)
Tuesday	Fish and chips (hoping he will focus on a few chips)
Wednesday	Gnocchi with olive oil and parmesan
Thursday	Your child's usual favourite pasta
Friday	Sweet-and-sour chicken with rice (aim for him to try some rice)
Saturday	Pizza – very plain topping (start with garlic butter and progress to margarita)
Sunday	Roast lunch (aiming for him to try the potato) – his usual favourite pasta for dinner

- **All the dishes are served with vegetables** and all three children serve themselves the same meal and eat together.

- **You then devise an Incentive System mealtime chart** (tool – see example below) to help Tyler slowly introduce himself to these new foods. Use brightly coloured stickers when things go well.

Day	Sitting nicely	Touches food	Cuts up food	Licks it	Chews it	Swallows it
Monday						
Tuesday						
add other days of the week						

Is it okay that my child only eats one food type?

Your child will not waste away! He is clearly managing to function on pasta alone, but life will be so much easier for him later on if he is confident with different types of food and is happy to eat a variety of foods – quite apart from getting a nutritionally balanced diet!

Travelling, visiting friends and going to restaurants all become a chore rather than a pleasure if he has a restricted diet.

WHAT TO SAY

- **Sit all the children together** at the table an hour before the meal and explain the new system. Say, 'Now, I have decided that in this house we are all going to have the same meal. I am not going to be giving you boring pasta every night.' PAUSE. 'Some nights will be pasta and other nights will be other foods.'

- **Now show them all the Menu Plan and read it out.** Ideally you want to start with the meal with pasta with the tomato sauce on it. This is the gentle change. Say, 'Now I know this is a challenge for you, Tyler, but I know you can do it! You only need to eat a little of what is on your plate, even one tiny mouthful. We will always have pudding.'

- **Now show Tyler the Incentive System mealtime chart.** Say, 'We are going to fill this in with stickers after every meal, for two weeks, and see how we improve as the days go by.'

- **Read the mealtime chart out** and explain it to him. Say, 'Now, remember, when we are sitting at the table we are not going to talk about food or watch one another eat. We are just going to talk about our days at nursery and school.'

> **TAKE NOTE!**
> It will help your child both now and later in life if he starts to vary his diet now.

ACTION IT!

- **Firstly talk to your other children** independently and make sure they understand that they are not to talk about food and Tyler. Say, 'Your brother might not eat, but just sit there. Don't tell him to eat or try and help. Just leave him to think. Understand?' You need them to acknowledge that they understand what you are asking of them.

- **Post the Menu Plan on the wall** and make the children aware of the evening meal before they head out of the door in the mornings.

- **Keep the Incentive System mealtime chart in a drawer.** You do this with Tyler quietly after each dinnertime.

- **When you ask everyone to come to the table** do not necessarily

Continued ▶

expect Tyler to eat. The aim is that he sits at the table and accepts what is in front of him. Say to him, 'Why don't you touch some of the food, pick it up, break it, lick it, nibble it. Think of your mealtime chart.' Once you have said this, don't talk to him about food.

TAKE NOTE!
If he has missed a whole meal, milk or yoghurt before bathtime will line his stomach and prevent him getting hungry in the night.

- **If he refuses to sit at the table,** he must take himself out to the Shout Spot (tool) in the hallway and sit there until the meal is finished.
- **When you take him to the Shout Spot say,** 'I don't expect you to eat the whole bowlful, but you can come and sit at the table. There is no pudding if you don't sit at the table with your brother and sister.'
- **Confidently walk away** and hope he will follow, otherwise you will have to follow through with the consequence (missing his meal).

CARRY ON!

This is not an easy challenge; it is one of the hardest, but the key to success is to be consistent. Your child must come to the table hungry, so don't fill him with snacks beforehand. If you go back to giving him pasta at every meal, you'll find it even harder to steer away from it next time. It may take six weeks before you see changes in what your child likes to eat. It is a slow process, but if he is not always given pasta and comes to the table hungry he will eventually eat what is in front of him.

EATING SCENARIO **9**

My child chews her food and spits it out

'My daughter, Harriet, has just turned two. She eats half of her meal and then the second half involves chewing and spitting it out onto the plate. The more I tell her to stop doing this the more she does it.'

YOUR TOOLS

Pick a Portion

See pages 54–71

LET'S DO IT!

WHAT TO DO

- **Think about your child's portion size.** Use Pick a Portion (tool). You might find that she does eat the portion size her body needs, but then plays by chewing the remainder but not being able to swallow it because she is already full.

WHAT TO SAY

- **Speak to your child** when she is not distracted. She needs to be fully focused on you. Say, 'Now. I have decided that when you feel full up you need to tell me. Give me your plate and I will get your pudding or you can get down and go and play.' This is all you are going to say to her. You are no longer going to focus on the chewing and spitting.

ACTION IT!

- **Sit down and, ideally, eat with your child.**
- **When the moment of chewing and spitting arrives,** just ignore it and continue to eat your own food. Be patient and just let her get on with it. It is a phase and she is doing it to get your attention. Call her bluff – ignore her!
- **When you have finished your food** say, 'Right! Let's get dessert.'
- **Take her plate and leave her sitting quietly.** This is a moment for her to register how you are behaving differently.
- **Eat dessert together** and then if the spitting occurs repeat what you did before. Ignore her and then remove her plate.

CARRY ON!

Remain consistent with the process. If you mention the fact that she is spitting to her, it will set you back and the activity will be likely to continue for longer. Let this phase take its natural course and, hopefully, burn out. Obviously if you are out or at a friend's home you need to stop your child before she starts chewing and spitting. Simply take her plate away saying, 'All finished'. Don't say anything else.

Why do children chew food and spit it out?

From as young as six months old children are experimenting with food. They are weaning. This process continues into the toddler years and even the school years. When we, as adults, try a new food it is really still a form of weaning!

When children wean they go through several stages. The first tends to be to just swallow the purée, but as thicker and more solid foods are introduced they need to chew. After the chewing process, children don't always swallow. They are still experimenting. If this experiment is focused on by an adult it becomes something a child enjoys doing to get attention. It is a phase and when ignored it will pass.

My child wants to be fed by me

'Natasha is now three and a half and since I had another baby six months ago she has been insisting I feed her. My baby is now weaning and I need to focus on his feeding.'

YOUR TOOLS

Beat the Balloon

Shout Spot

See pages 54–71

LET'S DO IT!

WHAT TO DO

- **Accept that this is a phase** your child is going through. The baby has now been in your home for six months and your older child needs to realise that she has to share her parents with her sibling.

- **Buy a packet of balloons** and make sure you can blow them up easily – some are harder than others. This tool provides a fun way to break the cycle you are both in. Use the Beat the Balloon (tool) for no longer than three days. You do not want it to become the norm that a balloon is needed at every mealtime.

WHAT TO SAY

- **Have both children at the table** five minutes before mealtime.

- **Look directly at your older child** and say, 'I have decided that I am not going to feed you any more. You are very grown up and I need your brother to watch you so that he can learn how to feed himself.' PAUSE.

- **Show her a balloon in her favourite colour.** Say, 'Now! We are going to do something fun with this balloon! Every time you put some food in your mouth I am going to blow the balloon up a little bit.' PAUSE and blow into the balloon a little bit. Say, 'The more you eat, the bigger the balloon will get.'

- **Blow and say 'mouthful',** then again – blow and say 'mouthful'. Repeat this several times until the balloon is fully blown up.

- **Then say,** 'When the balloon is this full it's because you have eaten lots of lunch. We can either tie a knot in it or we can let it go like this.' Let it go so that it buzzes around the kitchen.

Why should I guide my child towards feeding herself?

Try not to worry too much about you feeding your child. A natural point will come when she does want to feed herself. This will come accompanied with mess, but you just have to go with it. This is one of the moments when you see your child wanting to take control and gain her independence and you need to accept this. This phase can happen as early as eight or nine months of age. For other children it can be 12 to 18 months.

By the age of two your child will be able to use both a fork and spoon correctly but she will also still like to touch and feel her food, so she will still want to use her hands some of the time.

If your child goes from feeding herself to then wanting 'Mummy to do it' this is because she wants your attention. It is not because she is not able to feed herself.

ACTION IT!

- **Serve the meal** by putting everyone's food on the table, ideally including yours.

- **Put the balloon in front of you** and say, 'Let me know when you have your first mouthful and I will pick up the balloon.'

- **Now focus on the baby.** Feed him and feed yourself. Don't keep asking your child to put food into her mouth. Let her take the lead and tell you when she has eaten some food.

- **Don't praise her too much,** just say, 'Great job! Let's see how big this balloon is going to get today!'

CARRY ON!

Continue with the Beat the Balloon tool at mealtimes for two to three days and then progress to saying, 'We are going to have balloon time after dinner today. I am going to blow three balloons up and we are going to play a game.' From this you can progress to TV time after a meal as a reward.

If you find your child protests at the idea initially and starts to scream and shout, you need to take her to the Shout Spot (tool) in the hallway. Explain, 'You stay here until you are quiet and then you can come back and sit up at the table with us.' You need to be persistent with this process. Your child might even be prepared to go without her meal, but you must be ready to take this step because once you have started the process of change you cannot go back to feeding her again.

You must be ready to make the change. It is better to continue to feed her until you feel ready to move forward yourself.

My child always says he is hungry at bathtime

'Bertie, aged four, always says he is hungry at bathtime. I am concerned that he will wake in the night hungry, so I give him a snack before bed. He demands whatever he wants. It disturbs bedtime and we all end up going downstairs for snacks after bathtime.'

YOUR SKILLS

Body Talk

Teacher Tone

See pages 72–77

LET'S DO IT!

WHAT TO DO

- **After dinner, when the children are still sitting at the table,** talk to them about 'knowing their bodies' using Body Talk (skill). Here you are going to introduce the concept of 'supper'. This is the snack before bed brought forward a little timewise. The children eat this final snack downstairs and then everyone goes upstairs and stays there until breakfast time.

WHAT TO SAY

- **At the end of the meal,** when all the children are still at the table, sit with them and speak in a firm Teacher Tone (skill). Say, 'Now, I have decided that we are not coming back downstairs after bathtime. So if anybody wants a snack they need to have one now.' PAUSE. Now say, 'The choices are (list three things). So what would everyone like because after this the kitchen is closed until breakfast time?'

ACTION IT!

- **Give the children their three choices of snack.** Say, 'Now, you all know your bodies best. Who needs one last thing to eat before breakfast and who can wait until breakfast time?' PAUSE and wait for their choices.
- **After they have had their snacks,** say, 'Now. Everybody has had their supper. We are going to go for a bath and not come back downstairs. Everyone has a full tummy. Did you hear that, Bertie?' Wait for a response. Say, 'We are not coming back downstairs. The kitchen is now closed.'

Children don't need food whenever they feel like it

Many children say they're hungry because they fancy a snack and others say it to get a reaction from you. However, children are very rarely, if ever, really hungry. In fact, it is a good thing for a child to be hungry because then he gets to know his body's signals and enjoys the next meal when it arrives.

By giving your child too many snacks it can ruin his appetite for the next meal. If you think he is genuinely hungry, bring the next meal forward a little. This gives him more dietary goodness and nutrients than a snack will.

CARRY ON!

You might find that for the first two nights there is some moaning and groaning at bedtime, but relax! This is a habit, not genuine hunger. Stick firmly to what you have said and continue bedtime without giving your child any more food.

If you revert to having food after bathtime your child will then expect it every night. If, after two weeks of consistency, a weekend comes along and for some reason the children go downstairs after bathtime, this is fine. It is life. Make them aware that this is a treat and that you will go back to the normal routine of bath then straight to bed on Sunday, when it is a school/nursery the next day.

My child won't use cutlery

'My child, Abbie, is three and a half years old and uses her spoon and fork when she's at nursery. However, at home she only wants to use her hands, even with spaghetti and sauce! She makes a terrible mess.'

LET'S DO IT!

YOUR TOOLS

Incentive System (cutlery plate)

Shout Spot

See pages 54–71

YOUR SKILLS

Teacher Tone

You Choose

The Back

See pages 72–77

WHAT TO DO

- **Make an Incentive System cutlery plate** (tool). Take a paper plate and draw/cut out lots of miniature forks and spoons. The aim is that every time your child uses a piece of cutlery, after the meal she can glue a cutlery miniature onto the plate.

- **Make sure you serve food** that she can easily manage with cutlery over the next week.

WHAT TO SAY

- **Sit with your child at the table ten minutes before dinnertime.** Make sure you have her full attention. Make eye contact and use your firm Teacher Tone (skill). Say, 'Now. I have decided that there is a fun way to help you use your cutlery.' PAUSE.

- **Give her the paper plate.** Perhaps colour or paint it together.

- **Now show her the collection of little spoons and forks.** Say, 'Now, look at all these little spoons and forks. When you use your cutlery to eat nicely, at the end of the meal I am going to give you a glue stick to glue a spoon and fork on the plate.' PAUSE. 'When all of these are stuck onto the plate you will win a prize!' PAUSE. 'Now I know you find using cutlery easy because Mrs Brown tells me at school that you are one of the best eaters! When we have stuck the spoons and forks all over the plate we can take this to nursery to show her.'

ACTION IT!

- **Serve the food** and, ideally, sit with her and eat the same as her.

- **Use your own cutlery!**

- **Talk about your day.**

- **Now say,** 'Remember to use your cutlery so we can use the glue after dinner! You are being so good.' After three consecutive days of this your child should be instinctively using her cutlery.

When should my child start to use cutlery?

It is very important for children to experiment with their hands in their food in the early stages of weaning. However, some children are still learning to trust and enjoy food by the time they get to school age, so it's a good idea to let them touch their food.

If your child has already been using cutlery and knows how to manipulate it, she should be encouraged to do so.

- **Continue with the cutlery plate** for six to seven days. After this you know that the old habit has gone as her brain has been retrained!

CARRY ON!

If your child refuses to use her cutlery you need to ask her to make a choice using your Teacher Tone and You Choose (skill). Say, 'Now, listen. This is how it is going to be. You can either sit here and use your cutlery and then use the glue after dinner or you can go and sit on the Shout Spot (tool) in the hallway on your own until you are ready to use your cutlery.'

Now ignore her and continue eating your dinner. She may use her cutlery. If she does, don't say a word. Alternatively she will use her fingers. This is when you say calmly, 'Okay, you have made your choice. Come with me.' You hold her hand or support her under her arms if she refuses to walk and take her into the Shout Spot in the hallway. Say, 'You stay here and when you are ready to use your cutlery you can come back into the kitchen.'

Confidently walk away using The Back (skill) saying, 'Come back when you are ready.' If she returns and uses her fingers, you must persevere with the process. Remain consistent.

> **TAKE NOTE!**
> Don't be concerned if this process takes a while. This is a lesson your child will eventually learn. It is her choice as to whether she does it the easy way or the hard way.

My child is always saying she is hungry

'My child, Edie, aged three, is continually saying she is hungry. This prompts me to give her snacks. They are healthy snacks, but then she can't eat her meals – then she is hungry. It is a vicious cycle!'

YOUR TOOLS

Snack Clocks

Shout Spot

See pages 54–71

YOUR SKILLS

You Choose

The Back

See pages 72–77

LET'S DO IT!

WHAT TO DO

- **Draw two clocks using the Snack Clocks** (tool) on paper plates and put the snack times on them.
- **Serve the snack in a small bowl,** so it looks like a lot!
- **Don't make it carb-heavy** as this will fill your child up too much.
- **After a snack time** your child may ask for more. Be strong and say, 'No. Now it is time to wait for lunch/dinner.'

WHAT TO SAY

- **Make sure the Snack Clocks are clearly visible.**
- **Sit down with your child after breakfast** and explain that there are two snack times. Say, 'Now, these two clocks show when snack times are. Two clocks mean there are two snack times a day. One is in the middle of the morning and one is in the middle of the afternoon. Now, let's find some things to do this morning until snack time arrives and I find you something to eat and get myself a cup of tea!'

Does it matter if my child has lots of snacks?

You tend to know when your child is having too many snacks or the portion is too large – she will not be hungry for her main meals.

The best thing to do is to make your child aware of when the snack times are. Try one at mid-morning and the other mid-afternoon (10.30 and 15.30). These timings both leave a two-hour gap before the main meal.

ACTION IT!

- **Once you have put the clocks on the wall** and announced when snack times are you need to stay firm with the rule. Your child is naturally going to ask for snacks, but remind her when the next mealtime is and then distract her with an activity.

- **After three days of being consistent** with snack times you will see more enthusiasm at mealtimes. If not, you might want to reduce the snack portion sizes.

TAKE NOTE!
There isn't anything wrong with your child having snacks.

CARRY ON!

If asking for a snack turns into whining and moaning you need to ask your child to make a choice.

Bend down and make eye contact. Say, using You Choose (skill), 'Now, you choose. Stop that noise and come and do some playdough with me or go and sit on the Shout Spot (tool) and get all of this noise out of your system.' PAUSE.

Now stand up and walk away using The Back (skill) to put the playdough on the table. The moment she starts to whine and moan, calmly take her to the Shout Spot in the hallway. Say, 'Sit there and get all that silly noise out and when you are finished come and find me at the kitchen table with the playdough.'

Confidently walk away and leave her there to vent her frustration, if she needs to. Be consistent with this and you will have retrained your child's brain to accept snacks only twice a day (one portion only).

My three children insist I cook them different meals

'None of my children has allergies to foods. Each one is fussy in their own way. I dread mealtimes as I find myself cooking three different meals and then again for my husband and myself later.'

YOUR TOOLS

Menu Plan

Incentive System
(fill-it-up pasta jar)

See pages 54–71

LET'S DO IT!

WHAT TO DO

- **Sit down and give some thought** to how you could create meals using Menu Plan (tool) that would allow all the children to eat at least one thing on their plate.

- **If a meal contains carbohydrate, protein and vegetables** each child can find something they will nibble on if they are hungry enough.

- **Ensure they all see their favourite** on the menu one day per week. That meal can be accompanied with different things your other children would enjoy.

- **Reduce snacks to a minimum** to ensure that the children are really hungry before a meal. Ideally make sure there are at least two hours between the snack and the next meal.

- **Make the children aware** that there is only going to be one meal each night for all of you.

- **Create an Incentive System** fill-it-up pasta jar (tool), where the children are rewarded for all positive behaviour at the table. A piece of pasta goes into the jar every time you praise them. A full jar (after five to seven days) gets a prize! Here are some phrases to try:

'Well done, Becky, for sitting nicely, even though it isn't your favourite.'
'Thank you, Maddie, for eating all your vegetables.'
'Good boy, Nicky, for eating all the chicken.'
'Thank you, everyone, for not making a fuss!'

- **This is a very big step to make** and the children are going to resist initially. The challenge is to remain consistent because they will try every tactic in the book for you to give them what they want to eat.

- **Be consistent** for at least two weeks. Then you will see changes.

Why should my children all eat the same food?

Quite apart from the hard work that preparing different meals lands you with, children need to learn to experiment with new foods and accept different things that are put on their plates. A wide variety of foods will give them the balanced diet they need to grow strong and healthy.

WHAT TO SAY

- **Sit the children around the kitchen table.** Have the Menu Plan and Incentive System ready to show them. Say, 'Now. I have been thinking and I have made a big decision that I am going to stick to and not change my mind about.' PAUSE. 'From today I am only going to cook one meal at dinnertime. We are all going to have the same. I am going to sit with you as well and have the same.' PAUSE. 'If you don't want it, you need to just sit nicely at the table and wait for fruit and yoghurt. I am not going to get cross if you don't eat the main course, but I will be extremely pleased with anyone who tries a new food.' PAUSE.

- **Now explain the Incentive System fill-it-up pasta jar.** Say, 'For all good behaviour, no whining and fussing, and eating something from your plate, you will be rewarded by putting a piece of pasta in the jar.'

- **Give examples** that the children will relate to (see the chart of phrases opposite). After the phrase, PAUSE. Then say, 'When this jar is full there will be a prize! I think it'll take a week to fill the jar.'

TAKE NOTE!

It takes up to six weeks for a child to try and accept a new food item that has been presented week after week for six weeks. This exercise really does involve patience.

ACTION IT!

- **Now that you have said it,** you need to follow things through.

- **Sit with the children** at the table.

- **Have dessert prepared in advance,** so you only have to leave the table briefly. Allow the children to still have dessert, but let portion sizes relate to how much they ate of the first course. If only a little was eaten they only get a small dessert.

- **Continue to reward with pasta,** but talk about other topics at the table, not just food. The main aim is to keep everyone sitting at the table, whether they are eating or not.

Continued ▶

CARRY ON!

You will need to accept that there is going to be a lot of wasted food, but it takes time for children to trust food and put it into their mouths. They need to see it on their plate over and over again.

You need to remain dedicated to this process for two to three weeks and make notes of the slight positive changes you see.

Don't set yourself overly high expectations. You will not get to the stage of a 'perfect mealtime', but you should look back and think, 'Never again will I cook three separate meals!'

EATING SCENARIO 15

I don't want my child eating 'junk' food

'My child, Mandy, doesn't eat crisps and cake at home and we don't have "junk" food in the house. However, it can be difficult when she goes to parties because I don't want her to eat such foods. How do I make a compromise we are both happy with?'

YOUR TOOLS

Book of Junk Food

See pages 54–71

LET'S DO IT!

WHAT TO DO

- **Make a Book of Junk Food** (tool) that contains all the 'junk' food that is likely to be offered at parties or on playdates. Cut pictures out of magazines and stick them in.

- **Tell your child that she can choose** two items to have at the party and one item from the party bag. You could say that on a playdate she can have what her friend is having if she wants it, but to remember to stop and think about her body.

- **You can make your own 'junk' food rules,** but they need to be realistic and shouldn't leave your child feeling left out at a party, which is meant to be a happy occasion, after all.

WHAT TO SAY

- **Explain your decision about the 'junk' food.** Say, 'I have sat down with Daddy and we have decided that if you want to have some "junk"

Why it's important to allow some 'junk' food

It has been proven that if we are deprived of something, we crave it (we all know that in winter we crave the warmth of summer because we know we cannot have it).

There is a time for 'junk' food consumption, so maybe this could be reframed as 'party' food or 'playdate' food. This way you don't have the food in your home, but it is still allowed sometimes.

It is important to make your child aware of the damages of too much sugar/salt/artificial preservatives and by doing this and setting a good example you are likely to find that your child follows you.

food at a party or at a friend's house you can.' PAUSE. 'We think that two "junk" food items can be on your plate at a party. One of these might be the cake.' PAUSE. 'You can choose one "junk" food from your party bag.'

ACTION IT!

- **Once you have said this,** you need to accept it and action it accordingly. You can continue to add to the book and inform your child of the 'good' foods and the 'bad' foods.

- **You can educate your child** to make her own choices. It is up to her as to what she chooses.

CARRY ON!

Remember that by depriving her of some foods, she will crave them more. You don't want her to eat in secret as she gets older or hide things from you, thinking you wouldn't approve.

TAKE NOTE!
Be realistic. Children need to grow up knowing there are right and wrong choices, but we have to step aside and let them make the decision for themselves

My child won't drink water – only juice

'If I give my daughter, Julia, aged two, a cup of water she will pour it over the table and scream "juice" until I give it to her.'

YOUR TOOLS

Juice Rule

Shout Spot

See pages 54–71

LET'S DO IT!

WHAT TO DO

• **Set a Juice Rule** (tool) as to what drink your child can have and when. Here is an example:

Breakfast	Milk or juice
Lunch	Juice – very weak, eventually moving on to water with ice
Dinner	Water with ice cubes and a slice of lemon

• **Post the Juice Rule** on the fridge. Show this to everyone in the family. These rules are for everyone.

WHAT TO SAY

• **At the start of a meal, before the food arrives,** show your child the Juice Rule. She won't be able to read it, but she will see this as something you are taking seriously. Say, 'Now! This tells us what drinks we have with what meals.' Read it out to her. Say, 'So at dinner time it is water with ice. If you don't want to drink it, save it for me.' PAUSE. 'There is no shouting "juice". If you shout, I will ask you to stop or you can go to the Shout Spot (tool). You will sit there until you are quiet and then you can come in for your meal.'

ACTION IT!

• **Before the meal** make your child aware of what the drink option is this time. If she comes to the table shouting you can ask her to stop and then if she doesn't take her to the Shout Spot. It is important to leave her there until she is quiet and calm. Then she can come back to the table. Shouting is her way of protesting and hoping she can get you to change your mind. If you break, just once, you are right back at the beginning of the process.

Why should my child drink more water than juice?

Juice is often given to children during the weaning process as it is sweet and they like it. However, many juices are synthetically manufactured and are overly sweet, adding extra calories to the child's drink.

This can have a bad effect on sprouting teeth and your child's weight. If your child is thirsty, the most thirst-quenching drink is plain water. She can drink as much as she likes and it won't spoil her appetite.

CARRY ON!
It is important that you are consistent with this process. Eventually you can get to a stage where you don't even have juice in the house, if this is what you are aiming for.

Ensure you sit her on the Shout Spot if the volume increases or the whining is continual. After three consecutive days of staying true to the Juice Rule your child will have accepted the change.

TAKE NOTE!
If you want to introduce an Incentive System alongside the Juice Rule you can, but it's good to work without one initially.

My child throws food

'Megan has just turned two. When she has finished her food she throws the plate on the floor. This sometimes happens at the start of the meal.'

LET'S DO IT!

YOUR TOOLS

Pick a Portion

See pages 54–71

YOUR SKILLS

Self Serve

See pages 72–77

WHAT TO DO

- **Put the food for everyone into a dish or onto a platter** and let your child Self Serve (skill). Let her put her own dish/platter on a mat on the table/highchair tray in front of her.
- **If she throws the food on the floor** this is to show you that she doesn't want any more.
- **Don't give her any more of the food** she has thrown on the floor.
- **Sit your child in her highchair** without a plate. Don't put any other food in front of her.

WHAT TO SAY

- **Sit next to, or opposite, her and make eye contact.** Say, 'Now, we are going to have a nice meal today.' We are going to have our lunch together.' PAUSE. 'You are going to put your dish/platter of food onto your mat.' PAUSE. 'If you throw it on the floor the food will go into the bin. You won't have any more. You will get down!' Once you have said this you have to mean it. So only do this when you are truly ready.

ACTION IT!

- **Serve all the food into a dish** and place it in the centre of the table.
- **Serve yourself a small portion** of this food.
- **Always serve everyone at the table** before your child.
- **Give your child a spoon** and let her serve herself. The aim is that she serves herself a small amount using Pick a Portion (tool).
- **Let her eat what she wants to eat** while you focus on your meal.
- **DO NOT mention throwing** and don't use negative language.
- **Once she has finished her food,** and you can see the course ending, suggest pudding. Say, 'Now, let's put food you don't want in this bowl'.
- **Give her a bowl** and wait for her to give it back to you with her leftovers in it. Thank her for this. Say, 'Now let me get us a yoghurt.'

CARRY ON!

The key is that you sit with your child and let her take ownership of serving her own meal. She is more likely to throw her food if she is sitting on her own while you are the other side of the kitchen washing up.

Remain consistent in sitting with her and having a bite to eat with her. A child's meal should take between 20 to 30 minutes. This is not a long time to sit and have quality time with your child while eating lunch as well! After three consecutive days of being in the new rhythm the throwing should cease.

DO NOT be concerned that she is hungry. She can have her afternoon sleep/rest and then have a piece of fruit for her afternoon snack. This will carry her through until dinner.

TAKE NOTE!

If she does carry on throwing her food you need to take her down from the table and say, 'All finished.' You then ignore her while you tidy up. Do not focus on her. She is likely to be upset by the fact that you reacted and she now doesn't have pudding.

Why do children throw their food?

Children like to see a reaction. By throwing food on the floor your child receives two reactions: the noise/mess as the plate hits the floor and then your reaction! This makes the event very interesting for your child – plus she can do it three times a day!

Children are fascinated by the way a parent might react differently each time.

Sometimes we shout, other times we ignore, sometimes we give her more food and at other times we do not. Because our reaction is always different she will continue to throw out of curiosity – to see what we will do next.

This behaviour will only stop when we find a consistent way of managing it.

My child helps herself to food from the kitchen

'Our daughter, Tess, is nearly three years old. We have always encouraged her to be independent so she is very aware of where everything is kept in our kitchen and she is often found helping herself to biscuits or getting a yoghurt. This means she eats less at meals and survives on snacks rather than three square meals a day.'

YOUR TOOLS

Snack Clocks

See pages 54–71

LET'S DO IT!

WHAT TO DO

- **Firstly rearrange your cupboards** so that the snacks are not easy for your child to get at. In the fridge keep the things she likes (yoghurts) on the top shelf at the back. Tell your child about this new arrangement. It isn't a secret.

- **Decide on two snack times** per day. The ideal times are mid-morning and mid-afternoon (say around 10.30 and 15.30).

- **Draw two Snack Clocks** with the snack times marked on both. Your child can then compare these with the real clock to tell when it's time to have a snack.

- **At snack time place three types of snack** on the table and let her choose one. This way she has some control over her decision.

- **Stay firm over snacking.** Ideally you don't want your child to eat anything two to three hours before a main meal. This way she will be hungry for her lunch/dinner and be able to eat meals properly.

WHAT TO SAY

- **Sit down with your child** and show her the Snack Clocks (tool) you have created.

- **Say,** 'Now. We have decided that there are going to be two times in the day when we have a snack. When it is snack time I am going to put three snacks on the table and you have to choose one. Then I will choose one for me.' PAUSE. 'Now, I want to show you that the snacks have been moved to different places in the kitchen so that only Mummy and Daddy can reach them.' PAUSE. 'I will always make sure we don't forget snack times. One snack time is between breakfast and lunch and the other is between lunch and dinner.'

Why my child should not help herself to food

Many of us are tempted by 'treats' when we are bored or need a distraction. However, this is not a good habit to instil in a child. Food is for eating when we are hungry and it is for keeping the body strong and letting it grow – eating is not an activity for when we cannot find anything else to do. So instilling good eating habits is a wonderful life skill to give to your child.

ACTION IT!

- **Once you have explained the Snack Clocks** you need to follow the process through.

- **You have told your child** that there will be two snack times a day, so you must remain true to your word.

- **Your child will find it a challenge** for the initial three days because she is used to raiding the snack cupboard whenever she gets bored.

- **Ensure you have plenty of activities** and distractions for your child, to prevent the fallback cry of 'I'm hungry' being heard.

- **If she does say she is hungry** offer her her least-favourite fruit or vegetable to snack on. If she is genuinely hungry she will want it!

CARRY ON!

When you are making the decision that there are set meals and snack times it is important not to revert to letting your child have control over what she eats and when.

It is important to give your child independence, but not for her to think that she is in control of both you and the kitchen cupboards. She will soon get the message. Remember to always have some play ideas and activities at the ready for when she's run out of things to do. That way she won't even think about food.

Behaviour scenarios

You may find that your child adopts all kinds of bad behaviour habits, but don't worry, most of them can be sorted out using the three-day process. Try the Tools and Skills suggested in the following scenario examples and you'll be surprised how well they can work for you.

Importance of good daily routine
If you have established a good routine that you stick to most of the time, you will find that this will provide a good grounding for getting your child to improve her behaviour.

Be consistent!
Remember! Consistency is the watchword. Stick to what you intend to do consistently for three days at least and you will soon start to see your child's behaviour improving.

Take a positive view
Always assume that your child's behaviour can, and will, improve and that the three-day process will work for you. Talk to your child in a positive way and guide her towards the result you want. It will work!

My child follows me around the house

'My child, Holly, aged two, will play happily, but whenever I leave the room to put away the laundry, visit the loo or make a cup of tea she follows me, asking me to "come back".'

LET'S DO IT!

WHAT TO DO

- **Sit your child down and explain** what you are going to be doing.
- **Ensure you have your own tasks** for the three days of the process.
- **Make sure your child can count to ten.**

WHAT TO SAY

- **Sit down with your child** when there are no distractions for either of you. Say, 'Now, listen. I have got some jobs to do around the house today and you have lots of wonderful toys to play with.' PAUSE. Say, 'I am going to go and do my jobs while you are playing. I am only in the house and I always come back to the kitchen.' PAUSE. 'When I go out of the kitchen I am going to count to ten and then I will come back again. Come if you want or stay with your nice (name of toy).'

ACTION IT!

- **When you have given your child 'the talk'** you need to implement what you have said.
- **Have your list of jobs and let her know what you are doing.** Don't just slip away. Say, 'I am just taking the washing upstairs. I will be back when I get to ten. One, two, three...'

Continued ▶

Why shouldn't my child follow me around?

It is fine for your child to follow you around the house, as long as it is okay with you and doesn't disrupt what you have to do.

When a child follows a parent around it is because she doesn't want to miss out. So it's is a good idea to teach your child that she can't be involved in everything. Sometimes you need to just get on with what you are doing.

- **It is fine if she follows you,** but act as if she isn't there. Don't engage with her. You want this to bore her, so that she thinks twice before following you next time.
- **Continue counting aloud** and ensure you are back on ten!
- **When you get to ten,** engage with your child. Say, 'Right, I got the washing job done, what's next?' State the task and go and do it.
- **Aim to do your tasks for 20–30 minutes** and then sit and play with your child for 20 minutes before you start on chores again.
- **You will find that after implementing this consistently** for three consecutive days, your child will slowly stop following you around.
- **The problem won't be defused immediately.** Just remember to make your chores as boring as possible. She will then cease following you.

CARRY ON!

Keep your child informed about what you are going to do, where and she will start to feel happier about you carrying out jobs in other parts of the home. The counting will make her feel actively involved. Be strict with yourself about timing your tasks and then playing with her afterwards. That way, you will be able to build up more trust between you. She won't feel 'abandoned'.

BEHAVIOUR SCENARIO 2

My child continually interrupts when I am talking to someone

YOUR SKILLS

Teacher Tone

The Hand

The Back

See pages 72–77

'Francesca is a good girl, but when I need to talk to someone else she continually interrupts. I end up trying to have two conversations.'

LET'S DO IT!

WHAT TO DO

- **Spend three days** speaking to as many different people as possible. Include your partner on the phone. You need to get a lot of practice in for this one.

Why is it important to make my child wait?

By making your child wait you are teaching her both patience and consideration. It is important for you that you feel you can have a conversation with someone without having to involve your child every single time.

- **Practise your Teacher Tone** (skill) saying, 'Wait. I am talking'.
- **Warn your friends/family about** what you are doing. It can be off-putting when they are speaking to you and you look straight at them and use your Teacher Tone! They might be taken aback and then lose their train of thought. The important thing is that the adult conversation continues to flow after the Teacher Tone moment.

TAKE NOTE!
The sooner your child learns that she doesn't always come first, the better!

WHAT TO SAY

- **You don't need to explain to your child** what you are going to do. The way for the child to learn is through consistency.

ACTION IT!

- **When you are talking to an adult and your child interrupts,** even if it is with a polite 'excuse me', keep your eye contact locked with the adult you are talking to.
- **Hold your hand up in front of your child's face** (don't look at her). Using The Hand (skill) say in a firm Teacher Tone, 'Wait. I am talking'. Now rapidly continue talking to the adult.
- **If your child continues to interrupt,** repeat the same thing again and then turn your back on her using The Back (skill).
- **Pause or conclude the adult conversation** after one or two minutes and then immediately bend down and say, 'Thank you so much for waiting. What did you want to say?'

CARRY ON!

The more you practise this technique the better you will become and the faster your child will learn. Remain consistent. You need to remember not to return to the old way of letting her interrupt because she will then think it is acceptable again and you will be back to where you started. This is a scenario you need to practise, practise, practise.

My child doesn't listen to anything I say

'Kyle is three and a half years old. He has never listened to me. I ask him to do something and I just get ignored. He just does what he wants. He loves Lego.'

YOUR TOOLS

Incentive System
(brick tower)

See pages 54–71

LET'S DO IT!

WHAT TO DO

- **Ensure that when you are asking your child to do something** you bend down to his level and look into his eyes. The chances are that if he is not looking into your eyes his ears aren't working!

- **Create an Incentive System** brick tower (tool). Take some small bricks with a platform to build on (Lego is ideal). You are going to call them 'listening bricks'. You will need 40–50 bricks (in a box).

WHAT TO SAY

- **Sit down with your child.** A good place to sit is at the kitchen table. Have the bricks and platform near by. Say, 'Now, I have something here that is going to help you with your listening.' PAUSE. Say, 'You have brilliant hearing, so this is going to be easy for you.' PAUSE.

- **Put the platform on the table.** Say, 'I have decided that every time I ask you to do something and you do it I am going to give you a listening brick from this box!' Show him the box, but don't open it. 'There are a lot of listening bricks in here. When you have built a tower with all the bricks you will get a prize (see page 61)!' PAUSE.

- **Open the box, show him the bricks.** He can play with them at the table on the platform. Say, 'So I ask you to do something. You do it. You can have a brick.'

- **Put the bricks back in the box,** saying, 'Now let me take the bricks back.' Put them all back in the box. 'So, when I say, "shoes on" and you do it – you get a brick. When I say come to the table at dinner time. You do it – brick. When I say, "upstairs for bathtime" and you do it – brick. Forty bricks means a prize.' PAUSE.

- **Now say, 'So we are going to start right now.'** State a task and watch him do it and then give him a brick.

Why is it so important that my child listens to me?

When a child listens to an adult it shows that he respects them. It is fundamentally important that your child learns as soon as possible how to respect you.

ACTION IT!

- **The important thing about building the tower** is that you remember to reward your child with a brick every time he does as he is asked.

- **Remember to have eye contact with him and be close to him** when you are asking him to do something.

- **Don't forget to award the brick.**

- **The aim is that a minimum of ten bricks** is put on the platform each day and by day five the tower is complete. This means you give a reward at the weekend and then immediately start the tower again.

- **After three towers over a two-and-a-half to three-week period** you should have trained your child's brain to listen and you should be asking him to do things in a direct and clear fashion. Be sure to use eye contact.

TAKE NOTE!
Respect starts at home and then flows out into your child's social world.

CARRY ON!

Consistency is the key to success with this one. When your child doesn't seem to want to listen to you, be sure to get down to his level and insist on establishing eye contact with him first, so that you are fully communicating and you know he is listening to you. Then tell him what it is you want him to do. Reinforce this with the Incentive System – in this case the brick tower. Perhaps change the type of incentive if he seems to be losing interest in it. Before too long, with your consistency, your child should be able to take in what you are saying and follow through with the action you are asking of him. You'll soon find that he will show you more respect than he did before.

My child won't play on her own – she needs me with her

'Ava is nearly three years old. She wants me to entertain her all the time. She cannot instigate play. I feel as though I'm her playmate and cannot get anything done around the house. My chores have to be done when she is in bed at night and I don't get my own evening.'

YOUR TOOLS

Timer

Play Stations

See pages 54–71

LET'S DO IT!

WHAT TO DO
- **Organise the toys** so that you can see each different activity in a separate box or place on a shelf.
- **Use your Timer** (tool) or make sure the oven timer works.
- **Assess the toys** and think whether you need to acquire more 'independent play' toys/activities. These might be worth investing in.
- **Take a look around your home** and visualise where you can lay out five different activities using Play Stations (tool). For example, on the sofa, in the corner of a room, on a beanbag, in the hallway or on the kitchen table.
- **Check that the Timer works!**

WHAT TO SAY
- **Have breakfast together** and while she is eating talk to her about the structure of the day. Say, 'Okay. We are going to do things a little differently this morning.' PAUSE. Say, 'After breakfast I am going to lay out toys and activities for you around the room and you are going to decide what you want to play with first.' PAUSE. 'While you are busy I have to do some of my own jobs. I am not going to be playing with you.' PAUSE. Say, 'I have to (state three tasks such as 'do the ironing', 'phone the dentist' and 'hoover the upstairs'). When I have finished we will play together.'
- **Show her the Timer.** Say, 'Now I am going to set the Timer for 20 minutes. This gives you time to play and time for me to do my jobs. When we hear the buzzer it is "together time".'

Why is it important for my child to play on her own?

It can be exhausting for you to feel that you are your child's chief entertainer and can't get any of your tasks done unless she is out of the house or in bed. This is not realistic in life, neither is it sustainable.

It is important that your child sees you doing things for yourself. This helps her to grasp the concept that the world doesn't just revolve around her. Playing on her own is allowing her creativity and independence to develop and her understanding that 'Mummy is busy doing something for herself at the moment.'

ACTION IT!

- **Set out the activities** and allow your child to choose some if she wants to. Once they are laid out DON'T start to play with her. Say, 'I am going to set the Timer and get my jobs done.'

- **Set the Timer** and then get on with your jobs.

- **Your child will come to you** and continue to ask, 'Is the time up yet' or 'Please come and play'. You need to continue with your tasks and not engage with her too much. Don't make eye contact and just say, 'I will see you at buzzer time.'

- **This is going to feel very foreign to your child,** but if you carry out this system two or three times in the day for three consecutive days she will soon learn the importance of 'me time', 'Mummy time' and 'together time'.

CARRY ON!

If you continue with this approach, you should soon find that your child will start to respect you and your time and learn to use the Timer to guide her in this. Be consistent in your approach and be sure to follow through with the process – don't make eye contact when you are going off to do your chores. She'll soon get the idea and start to be more independent in her play.

My children fight over their toys constantly

'Sam, aged three, and Will, aged four, always want to play with the toy the other one has. I am constantly refereeing and end up taking away whatever it is they are fighting over. There are sometimes more toys on top of the wardrobe than on the floor!'

YOUR TOOLS

Share Ladder

See pages 54–71

YOUR SKILLS

The Back

See pages 72–77

LET'S DO IT!

WHAT TO DO

- **Create two Share Ladders** (tool) and put the children's photos at the bottom of each one. You need to be able to move the photos up the ladders (but never down).

- **Create enough play space** so that the children have room to play without being on top of one another.

WHAT TO SAY

- **Sit the children down without any distraction** at a distance from one another – so that they cannot wind one another up. Have the ladders and photos to hand. Say, 'Right. You both know I am tired of having to take your toys away when you fight over them. I am going to stop doing this. I am going to let you decide on sharing and not taking toys from one another.' PAUSE. Say, 'I have something here to help us.' Give them both the photos. Make the 'mistake' of giving them each other's so that they have to swap, but without you intervening.

- **Now put the ladders on the table.** Say, 'Now you are both going to go up the ladder and win a prize. Listen to how you can go up the ladder.' PAUSE. 'This is for every time you share. Every time you, Sam, let Will have the toy, you go up the ladder. Every time you, Will, let Sam have the toy, you go up the ladder.' PAUSE. 'If you are fighting over a toy and one says, "Oh, you can have it" that gets you up the ladder again.'

- **Now show the children how they go up the ladder** on a piece of Blu-Tack. 'Give your brother the toy – up the ladder.' Do it. 'Play nicely together – up the ladder.' Do it. 'Let your brother have what you are playing with – up the ladder.' Do it.

ACTION IT!

- **Once you have explained the ladders,** action the system.

- **Set out toys** for the children and start by playing with them. Then prepare to leave. Say, 'Right! I have to go and peel the potatoes for dinner, so you can both play nicely. Sam look after Will and Will look after Sam. I am listening and watching to see who goes up the ladder.'

- **It is important that you keep an ear out** for what is going to occur.

- **When you hear the first disagreement,** approach so that you can see them but they cannot see you.

- **Wait and see if they can defuse the situation** by themselves.

- **If things start to get physical** and you need to step in, simply say, 'I wonder who is going to be kind and give that to his brother. Think of your ladders!' The chances are they will both let go of the toy and you can let them both go up the ladder. 'Now remember. If you hand the toy over, you go up the ladder.' Say, 'You are great boys. You know how to play nicely.'

- **Confidently walk away** using The Back (skill) saying, 'Remember ladders.'

- **When they have played nicely for 15–20 minutes** without any disagreements praise them both and let them both go 'up the ladder'. The aim is for it to take three days to get to the top of the ladder. 20–30 rungs are needed. One child will reach the top before the other, but try to keep them relatively close. If they are too far apart the one behind will lose faith and is likely to misbehave in frustration.

CARRY ON!

It may take a little longer than three days to sort this one out. Keep reinforcing the ladder tool and you will eventually realise that the children are not fighting so much over their toys – if at all. Peace at last!

Why is it important for children to share their toys?

Children learn so much from their siblings. They learn about waiting, sharing and consideration. Before they learn these skills there is a lot of disagreement. This is because both children think they are the most important and that they are right.

You want your children to be able to share with friends and to allow their friends to choose activities when they are together. This is why it is best to start teaching them the importance of respecting one another at home as soon as possible.

BEHAVIOUR SCENARIO **6**

My child refuses to let me brush his teeth

'Every morning and every night my son, Oscar, aged two and a half, refuses to let me brush his teeth. He will "do it", but not properly.'

YOUR TOOLS

Brush Song

Shout Spot

See pages 54–71

LET'S DO IT!

WHAT TO DO
- **Buy a new toothbrush and paste** (obviously a flavour he likes.)
- **Aim to keep duplicate brushes upstairs and downstairs.** This is so that you don't have to go upstairs after breakfast to brush teeth.
- **Arrange a mirror** suitable for your child to brush in front of.

WHAT TO SAY
- **Talk about teeth-brushing beforehand** – while he is eating his breakfast. Say, 'Now, I have decided that both of us are going to brush your teeth. I have telephoned the dentist and he said that all children, until they are nine years old, have their mummy brushing their teeth.' PAUSE. 'When you are nine you will be brushing yours on your own.'
- **'Now I have a new brush and paste** for you and a nice mirror in the cloakroom downstairs/by the sink in the kitchen. You are going to brush first and then I am going to brush. My brushing is going to be very quick. I will sing a song called the Brush Song (tool) and when I get to the end of the song I have finished!' (The song 'The Animal Fair' is the right length.)

ACTION IT!
- **After breakfast, go straight to teeth-brushing.** Don't allow any play to start first.
- **Show him the new toothbrush** and as he brushes, sing your song to show him how quick it is. Then say, 'Right, now it's my turn, get ready. One quick song.'
- **Start singing and get on with the job** with confidence. Don't hesitate or hover, giving him time to protest – just do it!

Why must I brush my child's teeth? Can't he do it?

It is not until a child is nine years of age that he is capable of brushing ALL of his teeth properly.

Unfortunately foods today contain preservatives and sugars, quickly causing holes to appear in milk teeth and destroying big teeth. Children need to know that they can brush their teeth first, but that Mummy/Daddy needs to 'finish off the job'.

- **Praise and thank him** once this is done and tell him that you will be ringing the dentist to tell him how good he is and that he won't be getting any holes in his teeth.

- **If your child is adamant** that you are not brushing his teeth sit him on the Shout Spot (tool) and tell him to stay there until he is ready. Say, 'We cannot play until your teeth are clean.'

- **Keep returning him to the Shout Spot until he is ready.** Do not back down as this is an important issue of health and hygiene.

- **Once you have done this consistently for three consecutive days** he should get used to the routine – and your singing!

CARRY ON!

This is a battle that it is worth fighting – for the sake of your child's teeth. Make use of the Shout Spot to press home the fact that you are serious. Bit by bit he will understand that you mean business. And when he's all grown up he'll thank you for a perfect set of gnashers!

My child won't get dressed in the morning

'It's always a rush before nursery in the morning as I chase my three-year-old, Jamie, around the kitchen to get dressed. He sees it as a game, but I find it a frantic and stressful way to start the day.'

YOUR TOOLS

Get-Dressed Stencil

Incentive System (optional)

See pages 54–71

YOUR SKILLS

The Back

See pages 72–77

LET'S DO IT!

WHAT TO DO

- **Use the Get-Dressed Stencil** (tool). Take a roll of lining paper and a thick black pen. Use poster paint to paint the stencil a flesh colour.
- **Ensure that your child's clothes are organised** in the wardrobe/drawers so that you can choose the clothes quickly before bedtime.

WHAT TO SAY

- **After lunchtime** sit down with your child and talk about the afternoon activity. Get his full attention. Say, 'Now, I have an idea that is going to make getting dressed in the morning a bit easier.'
- **Now produce the art materials.** Say, 'We are going to draw around your body and then draw in your face and lay this upstairs in your bedroom. It is called "Flat Jamie" and it's going to hide under your bed until storytime tonight.'
- **Place the stencil under the bed,** ready to talk about it at bedtime. Say, 'Before we have stories we are going to get out "Flat Jamie" and dress him in the clothes you are going to wear tomorrow.'
- **Get out the clothes** to dress the stencil. Or lay out two outfits for your child to choose from. Say, 'In the morning you are going to take Flat Jamie's clothes off, get dressed and put your pyjamas on him!'

ACTION IT!

- **Draw around your child** and draw his face on the stencil and place it under his bed/in his bedroom.
- **After bathtime, before stories,** dress the stencil in an outfit of your child's choice.
- **Read your child's bedtime stories.** Say, 'Now, remember, in the morning it would be a lovely surprise if you get dressed and put your

pyjamas on Flat Jamie. Then we'll go downstairs and see what we are going to have for breakfast. We might even have (state his favourite).'

- **Confidently leave the room.**

- **In the morning** your child might surprise you by getting dressed, but if he's still in his pyjamas simply say, 'Okay Flat Jamie. Time to put your pyjamas on.'

- **Start by helping your child remove his pyjamas,** especially if he is still sleepy. Say, 'Now, I am going to go and get dressed and when I come back, see if you can surprise me by getting yourself dressed.'

- **Confidently walk away** and trust him using The Back (skill).

- **If he follows you,** simply return him to his bedroom and say, 'Start getting dressed and I will come and help you once I am dressed.'

- **Walk away.**

- **This regime needs to continue** until he realises that you are not going downstairs for breakfast until he is dressed. You need to start this process early so that you are not feeling time-pressured.

CARRY ON!

If you have decided to use this process, you must carry it through. If you dress your child one morning he will assume you'll do the same the following morning and you will be back to chasing him around the room. Stand your ground and realise that this is for his benefit. Think of his developing independence. If you do not see improvement on day three or you find all goes well until day five and then he regresses, put an Incentive System (tool) in place alongside the stencil. The process needs to last for seven to ten days before a prize is given. Remember that he gets the reward every morning because you are determined you are not getting him 100 per cent dressed. A little assistance is fine, but don't slip back into old ways.

Why should my child dress himself? Why can't I do it?

It is always challenging when teaching your child something new because, the fact is, you could get the task done so much quicker! When you are working against the clock it is tempting to dress your child because you can do it at speed, but there needs to come a time when he dresses himself. A child gets a true sense of achievement and independence from doing this.

Start by 'part-dressing' your child and slowly but surely find yourself saying, 'You can do it!' Once your child is dressing himself, it is one less job for you to do!

My child cannot decide what to wear in the morning

'My daughter, Rosie, aged three, is very particular about her clothes. We lay out her clothing the night before at bedtime, but in the morning she refuses to put the chosen outfit on and proceeds to take everything out of her wardrobe.'

LET'S DO IT!

YOUR TOOLS

Incentive System

See pages 54–71

YOUR SKILLS

You Choose

See pages 72–77

WHAT TO DO

- **Have the clothes organised** so that it is easy to pull out two outfits at the end of the day.
- **Devise an Incentive System** (tool) that incorporates your child's interests (fairies, trains). Decide the right time to start this process because once you start, you need to continue.

WHAT TO SAY

- **After bathtime, lay two outfits out on the floor** of your child's bedroom. Say, 'Now, You Choose (skill): now or in the morning. What outfit is your (day of the week) outfit?'
- **Don't try to persuade her either way.** If she says, 'Neither' you need to remain calm and say, 'Well you need to choose one because if you stay in your pyjamas you will be in your bedroom all day!'
- **If she cannot choose at night** simply say, 'Let's have our stories now. You can choose in the morning. Both outfits are lovely. It is going to be a surprise for me to see which one you choose.'
- **In the morning** go into her bedroom and mention her favourite breakfast. Say, 'I've decided to make pancakes! Now, choose your outfit and take off your pyjamas. I'm going to brush my teeth and I'll be right back.' Leave her to think through what she's going to wear.

ACTION IT!

- **Lay the two outfits out the night before.** Your child might claim she wants to wear something different (her green jumper). Say, 'Well, that's in the wash. You're choosing from these for tomorrow.'
- **If she won't choose,** stay where you are, remain calm and say, 'Choose in the morning.'

- **In the morning** start by helping her to remove her pyjamas. Say, 'Now you choose and start by putting your knickers on. I am just going to brush my teeth. I will be straight back.'
- **Leave the room, closing her door.** She must be left alone to think this through for herself.
- **If she refuses point blank to get dressed,** you need to bend down and make eye contact. Say, 'Now. You are staying in your room until you are dressed. I am going to go to my bedroom to do my make-up. When I come back I want to see that you have chosen your clothes.'
- **Confidently walk away.**
- **This process needs to continue** – you leave her alone and then return. Chances are she is going to get very cross because you are showing control and things are different from the way they were yesterday. Eventually she will choose her clothes. You might want to help her put them on the first day if she has exhausted herself protesting and choosing. Praise her for eventually choosing and reward her using the Incentive System (tool).

CARRY ON!

It is important that you remain positive and calm because your child is not going to conform immediately – protest will come first. Ensure she doesn't have access to her wardrobe and can remove all the clothes. You need to feel confident that she is in a safe environment and cannot hurt herself if she gets cross. If she has been shouting, eventually it will exhaust her and you can calmly say, 'Now, let's go and make pancakes. What outfit? I will help. Let's go.'

You cannot force her, so you need to let her take as long as she wishes, but she must not go downstairs for breakfast until she is dressed. Consistency is the key. She will stop the fight when she realises she isn't going to win!

Why does my child find it hard to choose?

It can be very overwhelming for a child to choose something from a large selection. She would have the same problem if you went into a toy shop and said she could choose something. The choice is too great. She finds herself not only focusing on what she can have, but all the things she won't have once she has decided. It is no different when she is choosing clothes. She probably wants to wear more than one outfit and gets frustrated because she knows she can't.

My child never puts on his own shoes and coat

'Charlie is now at nursery school and the staff want me to teach him to put on his own coat and shoes. He sits on the stairs in the morning and just whines "I can't do it". I end up doing it as we have to dash out of the house so that I am not late for work.'

YOUR TOOLS

Shout Spot

Incentive System (optional)

See pages 54–71

YOUR SKILLS

Magic Coat Flip

Teacher Tone

See pages 72–77

LET'S DO IT!

WHAT TO DO
- **Ensure your child can easily find and reach** his own coat and shoes.
- **Arrange coat hooks low down** and a box that is easy for storing his shoes. This means that not only can he find them to put on, he can also put them away when he takes them off.
- **Buy your child's coats with zips, not buttons.** This makes life easier.

WHAT TO SAY
- **Say, 'Now. Mummy and Daddy have decided that it is time** for you to always put on your own shoes and coat. We will do it together, which means that we will be busy putting our shoes on while you are putting yours on.' This is important – when you are busy he is less likely to ask for help. If you are standing over him watching, he will just wait for you to do it for him.
- **Say, 'Now, we can all do our own shoes,** so I'm going to put them on the bottom step to put on. Then it is Magic Coat Flip (skill) time!'
- **'Whoever gets their coat and shoes on first** can ring the doorbell and wait on the front step. That might be Mummy or Daddy or you!'

ACTION IT!
- **Make sure you allow enough time** for this process so that you don't feel time-pressured. The last thing you want is the stress of running late and then having to give in and do the task for him.
- **Put the shoes on the stairs** and lay the coats out for the Magic Coat Flip. 'Okay. I will meet you at the door. Magic Coat Flip time! Let's go.'
- **You might have to approach your child** and make eye contact to tell him to come to the door.

- **At the door** guide your child to sit on the bottom stair and start putting your shoes on. Say, 'Great work. I can't wait to see the Magic Coat Flip and hear you ringing the doorbell.'

- **Now ignore your child for a moment and sort yourself out.** Make sure you are completely ready to go before you focus on him.

- **If he is sitting there refusing** to put his shoes on and you know he is perfectly capable of doing it, you need to close all the doors leading off the hallway and leave him sitting on the Shout Spot (tool). Say, 'We are going to wait out here. Come when you are ready.' Stand slightly out of sight and leave him to get on with it.

- **You might find that shouting starts,** but you need to let this happen. Your child is now seeing how far he has to go to get you to dress him. Once he is quiet, approach him and guide his feet into his shoes, but he must do them up and put on his coat himself. Say, 'Right! Do your shoes up and on with your coat. That doorbell is waiting to be rung!' Ensure his coat is in front of him. Say, 'I will go and wait on the doorstep. Once your coat is on, ring that bell and we can go.'

- **Stand outside as you did before.** Now think of what you might see on this trip that will entice him to come. For example, 'I hope you are coming soon. We want to see if Mrs Smith's cat is sitting on the wall.'

CARRY ON!

This process needs to continue until your child has put his coat on. You have started this process, so you don't want to back down. Once you have shown your child that shoes and coats are his responsibility it will become habit. If, finally, you have to go and put on his coat for him you need to make a point of saying in a firm Teacher Tone (skill), 'I am NOT doing that tomorrow. You are a clever boy who can put his shoes and coat on by himself.' Don't see this as a failure. Just start the process again the next day and, if necessary, create an Incentive System (tool).

> **TAKE NOTE!**
> This short-term pain has long-term gain.

Why should my child put on his own coat and shoes?

Families are often in a hurry when leaving the house, so life becomes a bit easier when everyone can put on their own shoes and coat. Children must have this skill when they are at nursery and go into their school years. No child wants to be the one who can't do it and is therefore the last to reach the playground because he needs the teacher's help. Independence breeds confidence. Children love to say 'I can do it on my own'.

My child cannot accept the word 'no'

'If my daughter, Emily, aged three, asks for something and I have to say "no" she will scream and shout. This can go on and on, so I tend to give in and she gets what she wants. I know this is wrong, but I don't know how to break the cycle.'

YOUR TOOLS

Shout Spot

See pages 54–71

YOUR SKILLS

Ragdoll Mode

The Back

See pages 72–77

LET'S DO IT!

WHAT TO DO

- **Identify the Shout Spot** (tool) and perhaps put a beanbag there.
- **Sit down with your child** and explain to her that when you have to say 'no' that doesn't mean she has to scream and shout.
- **Let her know that you have a Shout Spot in your home** and this is where anyone who wants to shout goes.

WHAT TO SAY

- **When all is calm,** sit down with your child and explain how you are now going to behave with her. Say, 'Now, you know when Mummy sometimes says "no" and you start to shout. Well, I want to help you with this. Mummy and Daddy have decided that it is okay to shout, but we now have a special place in our house to go and do it.' PAUSE. 'I can go there, Daddy can go there and we will take you there if you need to shout.' Show her the Shout Spot. 'You can sit and shout and when you are finished you can come and find me. I will probably be in the kitchen.' PAUSE. 'BUT I need you to know that once I have said "no" I am not changing my mind. Do you understand?'

ACTION IT!

- **Have the Shout Spot ready and waiting at all times.** Stay strong, stick to your word and don't be nervous about saying 'no'.
- **After three consecutive days** of being consistent, she should grasp the concept of 'Mummy says it and means it.'
- **When you first have to say 'no'** and her shouting begins you may have a gut feeling that it is not just going to stop.
- **Approach your child,** turn her body away from you and walk her to the Shout Spot in Ragdoll Mode (skill). When she is in front of it say,

Why is it important to stick to 'no' once you've said it?

Nobody likes the word 'no'. It is a disappointment, but it is part of life, so the sooner a child can comprehend it the better. The earlier you start saying it, the easier it is.

Hearing 'no' builds on a child's understanding that the world doesn't revolve around her. Try 'no but yes'. Keep the thought process of saying 'no', but tell her when she can have what she is asking for. For example, 'I know you want a biscuit, so do I. We are not having one now. We are going to choose out of the biscuit barrel after lunch.' Or, 'We are not watching TV now. Our TV time is after lunch. We will watch it then.' Practise these 'no but yes' sentences.

'It is okay to shout. Shout here. When you are quiet come back.'

- **Confidently walk away** and close the door behind you using The Back (skill). The aim is that she is in the hallway and nobody can see her. No child likes being watched when they are frustrated and cross.

- **If she comes back into the kitchen** still in a cross state, return her to the Shout Spot as before. You do not need to say anything to her.

- **Continue this process** until you can sense her calming down. Once the rage has gone, this shows you that she has accepted what you said. She has accepted 'no'.

- **Now distract her** and don't talk about the incident. Say, 'Let's go and get that playdough out and make some cakes and build a café!' She might want to stay on the Shout Spot. Say, 'I am in the kitchen setting up the playdough. Come and find me when you are ready.'

- **When you are eventually playing and all is calm** mention the incident briefly. Say, 'Next time Mummy says "no" try your best not to shout.'

- **Now stay positive** and remember that this was the first big step towards your child realising that 'no means no'.

CARRY ON!

It is so important to remain consistent. If you are going to make this change you need to understand that if you suddenly turn a 'no' into a 'yes' she will see this as returning to the old way.

Aim for three consecutive days of one or two visits per day to the Shout Spot and by the end of the week she will have a clear understanding that 'shouting gets you nowhere!'

TAKE NOTE!
The more often you implement the word 'no' the faster she will learn.

My child won't be quiet when I am on the phone

'Mark is three years old and if he hears me on the phone he will break off from playing to try and speak to me. He then demands that he speaks to whoever is on the other end. I often have to hang up and call back when he is in bed or at nursery.'

YOUR TOOLS

Timer
(talking)

Waiting Beads

See pages 54–71

LET'S DO IT!

WHAT TO DO

- **Gather together the items you need:** a Timer that makes a loud noise when time's up to use as the talking Timer (tool), a shoelace and some pasta/beads/buttons to thread onto the lace.
- **Line up several phone calls** over the three consecutive days of the process – to make and receive at home while your child is with you.

YOUR SKILLS

Teacher Tone

See pages 72–77

WHAT TO SAY

- **Sit down at the kitchen table with your child.** Put the phone on the table for him to see, but make sure it is out of his reach. Say, in a firm Teacher Tone (skill), 'Now, I need to talk to you about something.' PAUSE. Say, 'You know that Mummy gets very cross when you make a noise when I'm on the phone – I try to listen to what the other person is saying but you keep making a noise. That is going to stop now.'
- **Produce the Timer.** Say, 'When the phone rings I am going to set the Timer for four minutes. You have to be quiet and play until it buzzes, when I will talk to you.' PAUSE. 'If it is someone on the phone you know I will let you say "Hello" to them. Do you understand?' PAUSE. 'Now, I have something to help you to be quiet.'
- **Now produce the shoelace and beads/buttons** for the Waiting Beads (tool). Give your child the shoelace, but hold onto the threading items. Say, 'When you are quiet while I am on the phone, AFTER the call I am going to ask you to choose something out of the tub. You can put it onto the lace.' PAUSE. Say, 'When you have put 15 things on the lace you will get a prize!' PAUSE.
- **Now put the tub in front of him.** Say, 'So what must you do to get something out of the tub?' This is where you hope he says, 'Stay quiet when you are on the phone'. If he doesn't, then simply say it for him.

Why is it important for my child to be quiet?

Your child cannot always be involved in everything you are doing. The sooner he realises that sometimes Mummy does things for herself and Daddy does things for himself, the better.

A child starts life believing that he is the centre of the universe and as much as you love him, there is a fundamental lesson to be learnt that he is a small part of a much bigger picture.

By asking your child to remain quiet you are teaching him to respect you, to be patient and understanding.

ACTION IT!

- **Aim to have/make five phone calls** each day for three days.

- **Be realistic** and only set the Timer for two minutes initially and then up it to three, four and five minutes.

- **If you need to speak for 10–15 minutes,** ensure your child has an activity he is engaged in before you make that call. For example, get the water tray out, put playdough on the table, get out the painting things. Let him know that it is going to be quite a long call and he will get to choose two items from the tub to thread onto the lace.

- **After three consecutive days** you should both be in a rhythm with the Timer so that it becomes standard behaviour for your child to be quiet while you are on the phone.

CARRY ON!

It is common for children to say, 'Who are you speaking to – can I talk?' when you are on the phone. Remain consistent and realise that if you revert to giving him the phone straight away you will both slip back into old habits. You have to remain strong with this one.

It would be nice to ask your child if he would like to make a phone call every so often. You can set the Timer and when it buzzes he gives the phone back to you. This will reinforce the system to him and make him realise that it is used for everyone in the house, not just him.

Finally, if you need to make a call that is going to last for more than 15 or 20 minutes, there is nothing wrong with turning on the TV or giving him the ipad to watch. This is called 'life'!

My child screams and shouts when I turn off the TV/ipad

'No matter how long my son, Ollie, has been watching TV, when it is time to turn it off he screams and immediately tries to turn it back on again. How long should I let him watch? Does it matter if he has unlimited screen time?'

YOUR TOOLS

Screen Rules

Timer

Shout Spot

See pages 54–71

YOUR SKILLS

Teacher Tone

The Back

See pages 72–77

LET'S DO IT!

WHAT TO DO

- **Sit down and decide what the Screen Rules (tool) are.** Write them out clearly so that the whole family knows. See the example below:

We never watch television/ipad before school.
We watch television on a school night while Mummy is cooking dinner/after dinner.
Ipad is after lunch on Saturday and Sunday for 30 minutes.
Ipad is after dinner on Saturday and Sunday for 30 minutes.
On Saturday or Sunday we watch a family film after lunch. Mummy and Daddy choose the film.
Sometimes, as a surprise, we get TV/ipad for being good. Mummy and Daddy choose when this is.

- **Have a Timer (tool) that has a loud buzz** to indicate when TV/ipad time is up. You can use the oven timer if this can be heard clearly.

WHAT TO SAY

- **Sit down at the table with your child and have the Screen Rules** in front of you. Say, 'Now, we have decided that we are not going to have shouting any more when the TV/ipad is turned off.' PAUSE. Say, 'You are a grown-up child and I don't want to hear that awful noise.'

- **Now say, 'We have made some rules** so that everyone knows when we are allowed to watch the TV/ipad.' Now read them out and let your child decorate them. Say, 'We are going to stick these on the fridge so that whoever comes to visit knows the Screen Rules.' PAUSE.

Why is it important to limit screen time?

Children between the ages of two and three and a half have an attention span of 20 minutes (on average). This means that they will focus 100 per cent on what they are watching for this length of time. After this period they will 'glaze over' and just be looking at images and colours. This explains why certain children's TV shows last for between 6 and 20 minutes. A child can manage three episodes for six minutes or one 20-minute show.

Children aged between three and a half and five years of age tend to be able to concentrate for much longer, but it is unclear for how long. Some are able to sit through a film, but how much they comprehend varies from child to child.

So the ideal time to turn off the TV/ipad is before your child goes into his 'glazed-over' state. It is also best that he knows at what stage the TV/ipad is going off before it is put on. For example, you could limit your child's viewing to three Peppa Pig episodes and then he can head up for his bath.

Unlimited time watching TV/ipad might keep your child quiet, but from the ages of two to five years he cannot sustain long periods of comprehension. He is in a 'glazed-over state', almost daydreaming, rather than learning and benefiting from the show. So it would really be better for him if he was playing or doing something else.

- **Now get the Timer out** and put it on the table. Say, 'This is the Timer and at the beginning of your TV/ipad time we will set it together.' Now set it for 30 seconds. Say, 'At the end of your TV/ipad time the Timer will make a noise and this is when you, me or Daddy turns the screen off.' Make the Timer buzz. Allow your child to turn it off. Say, 'Once the TV/ipad and Timer are turned off, it will then be time for dinner or bath or play. There will be NO shouting.' This is said in a firm Teacher Tone (skill).

- **Now say, 'We have a Shout Spot** (tool) in our house. It is in the hallway on the bottom stair.' PAUSE. Say, 'If anyone wants to shout, they can. But on the Shout Spot. We will take you to the Shout Spot to have a shout and when you have finished and all is quiet you can come and find us.' PAUSE. Now say, 'But I don't think we will need to use the Shout Spot very much because I know you are going to turn the Timer and the TV/ipad off when you need to.'

ACTION IT!
- **Have a day where the TV/ipad is used two or three times.** The ideal time is at a weekend, when you don't have to factor in nursery/school. The more you practise this system the faster your child will learn.

Continued ▶

- **Remember to set the Timer before the TV/ipad is turned on** and that your child starts the Timer as the show begins.
- **When the Timer sounds,** take it to your child and place it in front of him. Say, 'Please turn this off and the TV/ipad too.' It is important not to get into a discussion along the lines of 'Two more minutes/five more minutes'.
- **If the programme has only a few minutes** (five) to run, sit and watch the final part with him and then ask him to turn it off. The key is not to be hesitant about turning it off and not to be nervous of hearing the shout. You know where the shout goes – to the Shout Spot. Alternatively walk away using The Back (skill) and let the shout fizzle out on its own. Once your child knows you will not change your mind and turn the TV/ipad back on he will stop shouting.

CARRY ON!

If there are times when you do let him watch TV/ipad for longer than usual it is important to make it clear that this is a 'special treat' and tomorrow he will be back to the Screen Rules. You do not want him to think that he is taking control. This is something you need to remain consistent with because it all too easy for the TV/ipad to be used far too much, with your child not interacting and socialising.

BEHAVIOUR SCENARIO **13**

My child always shouts from elsewhere, 'Come here, Mum!'

'My son, Zach, is four years old and he is continually calling me to go to him. He will want to ask me a question or show me something. Should I go to him every time he calls?'

YOUR SKILLS

Ear Switch

See pages 72–77

LET'S DO IT!

WHAT TO DO
- **Explain the Ear Switch** (skill) to your child.
- **Once you have done this** you need to action it.

Why my child needs to change his behaviour

It is far better to teach your child that by shouting he gets no response from you. He knows where you are and he needs to come to you – not the other way around. By continually shouting he will see this as the norm and expect you to drop everything and come to him every time. He is not learning to respect you with this behaviour.

- **Make sure you only set this rule when you are ready to take it forward.** Your child will protest and shout louder and louder before he finally accepts the change, so you need to be feeling strong.

WHAT TO SAY

- **Bend down and make eye contact** with your child and say, 'I have decided that if you shout my name from another room I am not going to come. If you want to speak to me you need to come and find me.'

- **Now say,** 'I am going to switch my ears off when I hear you shouting at me.' Show him what you mean by turning your ears (see Ear Switch tool). Say, 'I will only turn them back on when you come into the room and speak to me nicely.' PAUSE. 'Do you understand?'

- **He might not answer,** so just say, 'Great! No more shouting.'

ACTION IT!

- **When he shouts your name,** simply say, 'I am in the kitchen if you need me'.

- **From this point on you are to ignore his shouting** because you have 'switched your ears off'. So do not respond to anything he says.

- **He needs to really believe that you have turned off your ears** and that he cannot be heard.

- **Only turn your ears back on** when he addresses you face to face.

CARRY ON!

By remaining consistent, you are likely to find that after three days he has corrected his behaviour. You must remember to remain consistent and when he shouts say, 'I am in the kitchen if you need me.'

> **TAKE NOTE!**
> You have to make sure that you do not shout to him from another room! The rule applies to everyone!

My child wants me to carry her everywhere

'I have a two-and-a-half year-old, Isla, and a seven-month-old baby, Isabella. My toddler insists that I carry her, not the baby – the moment Isla sees me holding Isabella she demands to be picked up. So I have to carry both of them up and down the stairs both at once. I feel I am ignoring Isabella to deal with Isla's demands.'

YOUR SKILLS

Follow My Leader

You Choose

Sit it Out

See pages 72–77

LET'S DO IT!

WHAT TO DO

- **Explain to your child** that you are not carrying her any more. As you hear yourself say it, mean it and stay true to your word. This means that you are to do this when YOU are ready. There is no hurry. Choose your time carefully and then dedicate three consecutive days to making the change.

WHAT TO SAY

- **Say, 'Now, Mummy and Daddy have decided** that you do not need to be carried around all the time, especially in the house.' PAUSE. 'You can walk. You have very strong legs.' PAUSE.

- **Use the Follow My Leader** (skill). Say, 'You can be the leader and walk in front or you can wait and then come and find me.' PAUSE.

- Say, **'When we are out, you can choose** using You Choose (skill) to hold hands or look at your books in the buggy. Carrying you is not good for Mummy's back.'

ACTION IT!

- **Once you have said this,** action it as soon as possible. It is going to be tough and your child may scream and shout to try and get her own way.

- **Start the process at home** and tell yourself that you are going to do things around the house and that if your child wants to come with you she will have to follow. Say, 'Right, I am going upstairs to put away the washing. Stay here and play if you want to.' She is likely to want to come and will approach you to be carried. Say, 'I am carrying the washing. Your sister is staying down here in her play den. Come if you want to.'

- **Confidently walk up the stairs and let her follow** if she wishes. Don't say anything else.

- **You have started what you are going to do** and you have given her choices. Now leave her to make her decision. This might involve her shouting and you might find that you return downstairs and she is still there. Say, 'Remember. I don't carry big girls who have strong legs.' Give her time before you find another task to do. Continue this through the day. The more you do it, the faster she will learn.

- **Make a small trip out** where she has to decide to walk or sit in the buggy. Simply go to the local shop and back again. If she walks a short distance and then asks to be carried, she must choose. Say, 'Buggy or walk?' If she starts to shout, use the Sit it Out (skill). Sit her on the pavement and say, 'When you are ready, you choose "books or walk". Take an empty carrier bag she can sit on if pavements are wet. Have a pile of books on her buggy seat waiting. Remain relaxed and calm, but be strong in believing that she is going to get into the buggy.

- **If you start to feel nervous** and doubt her, she will sense this and continue to shout, trying to get back control and be picked up and carried. Once the shouting has stopped, give her a book to hold and just sit her in the buggy. Start talking about the book to distract her.

- **If she protests,** sit her on the pavement and repeat the process.

CARRY ON!

After three consecutive days you will see dramatic change. All children will test a new system and try to break it. By remaining consistent, your child will accept the change and adapt. On occasion you will have to carry her. Tell her that it is a treat and won't be happening tomorrow. If you occasionally 'slip', quickly return to independent walking.

> **TAKE NOTE!**
> You are strengthening her muscles as well as her independence.

When should I stop carrying my child and why?

Once your child is sturdy on her feet she is capable of walking. The more she walks the stronger her limbs become and the further she will be able to walk.

There is nothing wrong with picking up your child and cuddling her. The thing you do not want is that she starts to use you as a mode of transport. It is far more interesting for her to be carried around at a higher level, but this doesn't help your child build her strength and independence.

It's a good idea to encourage your first child to be as independent as possible before a second one arrives. However, with twins you will have to find a different solution. It is very dangerous to carry two children at once, especially when going up and down stairs.

My child can't play with her toys for long before she's bored

'Olivia has her own playroom. All the toys are tipped over the floor and then, within ten minutes, she doesn't know what to do. She comes to find me and wants to do whatever I am doing.'

YOUR TOOLS

Play Stations

See pages 54–71

LET'S DO IT!

WHAT TO DO

- **Sort and organise your child's toys** so that they are in certain boxes, depending on what they are.
- **Remove all toys that are too young** for her, no longer used or broken.
- **Aim to rotate the toys.** Put some away ready to bring out next month and keep others out that she may not have seen for a while.
- **Devise areas using Play Stations** (tool) in the playroom and at the kitchen table, where your child can play. Put toys at each station.

WHAT TO SAY

- Say, '**Now, each morning after breakfast** I am going to set out some toys for you to play with.' PAUSE. Say, 'Some will be here in your playroom and some will be downstairs on the kitchen table.' PAUSE.
- Say, '**I am going to watch as you play with the toys nicely** and I am also going to do my own jobs. When you have finished playing with the toys we will put them away together and get out some fresh ones.' The aim is that toys are rotated through the day and you guide your child to play and then step away. Always have an activity, such as painting, sticking and glueing, playdough or colouring, ready at the kitchen table.

ACTION IT!

- **After breakfast or in the afternoon,** when your child arrives home from nursery, set out four activities in each corner of the room. Ideally place one activity on a small table with a chair. Say, 'Right! You have some fun things to do here. I am going to start this puzzle with you and then I need to peel some vegetables.'
- **Once you have started her off and she is engaged** in what she is doing, go into the kitchen and set an activity out on the table.

Why it is important for my child to entertain herself?

Every child should know the feeling of being bored. Then when she reaches beyond this moment she finds something to do and can become creative.

It is important that your child is guided to think for herself. You can give suggestions and set up activities, but ultimately she needs to feel comfortable in her own company and happy to entertain herself.

Realistically, life is about spending periods of time alone, so this should be seen as an enjoyable time not one of uncertainty or boredom.

- **When your child comes in** she can choose to return to where she's just come from or look at what is on the kitchen table. Either way you need to continue with your chore – don't stop until you have finished. She needs to have periods of time where she has to find something to do and not depend on you to entertain her. It is important that she sees you busy, saying, 'When I have finished my job I will come and see you.' The longer you leave her and don't engage with her, the more quickly she is likely to find something to do.

- **If she says 'I will help you'** you need to respond with, 'This is something I want to do on my own. You have lots of things you could go and find to do.'

TAKE NOTE!
You may have found that your child is now at a stage where she needs toys with a purpose: puzzles, Lego, magnetic games, maze books, building a shop, playdough, making cakes and building a café, mosaic cards, threading beads and cards.

CARRY ON!

It is important to remain consistent and dedicate an initial three consecutive days to sorting out the issue. By setting out her toys you will start to reflect on whether she does have enough toys/the right toys to stimulate her. Many children are given things that are aimed slightly higher than their age, so this should be avoided.

Remain consistent and don't find yourself going back down the path of entertaining her. Remember to always have an activity on the kitchen table so that when she follows you into the kitchen you have somewhere to guide her to.

My child refuses to 'wait'

'No matter what I am doing, if my child, Jessica, wants me she will moan and whine until I stop what I am doing. She just won't wait.'

LET'S DO IT!

YOUR SKILLS

Teacher Tone

The Hand

The Back

See pages 72–77

WHAT TO DO

- **This scenario involves using a firm, clear Teacher Tone** (skill). Use a tone that makes your child stop and hear that you are being serious in what you are asking of her.

- **Stand in front of a mirror and practise your Teacher Tone.** Say the words, 'Wait. I am talking' in a strong, clear way. Initially you might feel as though you are shouting, but this is not the case. It is a voice that your child will take notice of.

- **Now drop your voice so that it is deeper.** Think of it as being 'like a man's voice'. Children respond far better to a deeper, stronger voice. Practise, practise, practise.

WHAT TO SAY

- **You do not need to explain anything** to your child. If you use your voice correctly, this will stop her in her tracks.

- **Your child will continue to try and interrupt,** but you must blank her and conclude your conversation within 30 seconds to one minute.

ACTION IT!

- **Plan three consecutive days** where you will be speaking to several friends in person and your child has to wait for you to finish. The more you practise the better – the faster your child will learn.

- **Start the conversation and make your friends aware** of what you are going to do. This will help relax you.

- **When you talk to your friend, you remain focused on her,** don't look at your child – hold your hand up in front of her using The Hand (skill).

- **When your child approaches and starts to talk,** hold your hand up towards her face so that she sees it clearly. Say (in your Teacher Tone), 'Wait, I am talking'.

- **Now quickly pick up the flow of the conversation** with your friend again and continue for 30 seconds to one minute. During this time

Why is it important for my child to wait? How long for?

Waiting isn't an easy lesson for a child to learn, but it is essential. Life sometimes consists of a lot of waiting and the sooner you learn how to remain calm and wait the more relaxed you will be.

Start by being consistent and having your child wait for very short periods of time: 30 seconds to one minute – and then build on that. Eventually you should be able to have your child wait for between three and five minutes while you complete a conversation before turning your attention to her.

you need to turn your back on your child using The Back (skill) and ignore her if she is trying to interrupt.

- **After 30 seconds to one minute,** bend down and say, 'I have finished talking now. What did you want to say?' Very often your child does not have anything to tell you – she just wanted to interrupt!

- **When you do this for the first time,** tell her what she has just done. Say, 'You must NOT talk to me when I am speaking to someone else. You just stand and wait there until I have finished.' Then say, 'If you see me holding my hand up, this is because I need to hear what my friend is telling me. You won't have to wait for long, but you must wait quietly. Do you understand?' She might not respond, but you can reinforce the message by saying, 'Wait quietly'.

TAKE NOTE!
Your child should be able to remain quiet for a long time if she has an activity to engage in.

CARRY ON!

Now that you have practised and carried out the process over three days, continue to use it. Don't lapse and go back to talking to your child the moment she interrupts. By doing this you will find yourself back where you started.

Stay strong with the Teacher Tone and The Hand. Build on the time you make your child wait and you will find that as she gets used to this system she will interrupt but realise that she is not going to get your immediate attention. She might just go off and play! This does eventually happen if you remain consistent.

My child won't give up her dummy

'My child, Elise, is now three and a half years old and still insists on carrying her dummy with her everywhere. It is constantly in her mouth.'

LET'S DO IT!

YOUR TOOLS

Dummy Box

See pages 54–71

YOUR SKILLS

Ragdoll Mode

See pages 72–77

WHAT TO DO

- **Find an old shoebox and decorate it** alongside your child. Use paint, glue and collage, stickers – anything you can find. This is your Dummy Box (tool).
- **Use plenty of colourful ribbons** to tie the dummies up in a tree in your garden or outside the front of your home.
- **Stage one is to put the dummies** into the Dummy Box in your child's bedroom. Only bring one out during rest time and at bedtime.
- **Stage two is that the dummy fairy** comes to visit the dummies that are hanging in the tree. She takes the dummies to babies who need them and leaves a present in the tree instead to say, 'Thank you'.

WHAT TO SAY

Stage one

- **Sit at the kitchen table** to decorate the shoebox. Before you start, make eye contact with your child. Be firm, confident and true to what you are saying. Say, 'Now, your dummies are not going to come downstairs any more. In fact, they are going to live in your bedroom. They are going to live in this Dummy Box.' PAUSE. 'The box will open when you are in bed. Your dummy is only for rest and sleep time.' PAUSE. 'If you need to rest in the day and you want a quiet dummy time you can do that in your bedroom.' PAUSE. 'Now let's decorate the box and then we will put your dummies in it and take it upstairs.'

Stage two

- **After a week of the dummies** being kept in the box in the bedroom, now comes the big step of parting with them completely. After dinnertime, before bath, tie a ribbon around the dummy handles and bring the Dummy Box downstairs. Ensure your child has your full attention. Say, 'Now, it is time to give these dummies to little babies

Why must my child say goodbye to the dummy?

When a child constantly has a dummy in her mouth it prevents her from speaking clearly. She is not using her tongue as she would normally because it is wrapped around the teat of the dummy. The words do not form correctly.

At the same time the dummy can force her teeth to grow at an angle, particularly the front two teeth.

Developmentally it is far better to lose the dummy as soon as possible.

who really need them. The dummy fairy is coming tonight with a present for you!' PAUSE.

- **Open the Dummy Box.** Say, 'We need to hang these in the tree outside and the dummy fairy will swoop down and put them in the bag on her back.'

ACTION IT!

- **Now that you have said it,** you must follow it through.
- **Decorate the Dummy Box,** put the dummies in it and keep your child busy during the day – as a distraction.
- **After three consecutive days,** she should have adapted to only having her dummy at bedtime.
- **Carry out stage two only when** you are 100 per cent ready. This is a big step as your child doesn't really know how to settle to sleep without sucking on the dummy.
- **Hang the dummies in the tree** with your child. You need to act positive and be confident that this is going to work. Your child needs your strong, confident guidance.
- **At bedtime she will ask** for her dummy. You must make sure that ALL the dummies are out of the house.
- **She may well start shouting at bedtime,** but you need to continue the routine as usual and avoid talking about the dummy. Say (once), 'We don't need a dummy any more and I can't wait to see what the fairy has left us in the morning.'
- **Leave the room** at night as you always do. Your child might shout in frustration, but leave her to do so.

Continued ▶

TAKE NOTE!
Don't stay with
her to fall asleep
as this will
introduce another
challenge that will
then need fixing!

- **If your child comes out of her** room go into Ragdoll Mode (skill) and keep returning her.
- **Remain hidden on the landing in the dark** so she doesn't fully wake herself by going downstairs.
- **Once she is asleep** on night one, go outside and take down all the dummies and throw them away. Don't keep any – you might be tempted to give one back to her.
- **Hang a present on the tree** instead of the dummies for your child to find in the morning.
- **After three consecutive nights** the dummy will be a distant memory.

CARRY ON!

This task is a challenge, but it can be done and you will feel so much better when your child isn't dependent on her dummy any more.

During stage one remain consistent with the dummy staying upstairs. Keep the Dummy Box in a high place so that you are in control of it and your child has to ask for it. She only gets to open the Dummy Box when she is on or in her bed and ready to sleep.

Stage two is a challenge, but if you remain calm and in Ragdoll Mode she will be settling to sleep independently by night three.

BEHAVIOUR SCENARIO 18

When I try to discipline my child he just covers his ears

'I am totally in support of disciplining my child, Robbie, but when I try to explain that his bad behaviour is not acceptable he shuts down and refuses to listen or look at me.'

LET'S DO IT!

YOUR TOOLS

Shout Spot

See pages 54–71

WHAT TO DO

- **When all is calm** and well sit your child down and talk to him about what is going to happen when he covers his ears when you are talking.
- **Ensure you have a Shout Spot** (tool) in your home.

Why is it important not to ignore this behaviour?

Your child is being extremely defiant and this shows lack of respect to you. It is important that he learns to understand that he has to listen to what people have to say – even if he doesn't like it. This is a hard life lesson, but an important one.

WHAT TO SAY

- **Sit down with your child** during a quiet moment and explain what is going to happen the next time he covers his ears.

- **Bend down** and ensure you have his eye contact. Say, 'Now, I have an idea about what to do when you cover your ears and don't listen to me'. PAUSE. 'When you are not ready to listen, I am going to take you into the hallway and ask you to sit on the Shout Spot until you are ready to listen to me.' PAUSE. 'You can sit there for a little while or a long while.' PAUSE. Say, 'I will come and see you there and talk to you. If you cover your ears again I will walk away until you are ready.' PAUSE. 'You are a very clever boy and I hope you aren't going to cover your ears any more, but if you do, you know where you will sit until you are ready to listen.'

ACTION IT!

- **You might find that as you start to talk** about this he covers his ears. He is doing this because he doesn't want to hear that he has done wrong or talk about doing something wrong.

- **If he does cover his ears** you can ask him to uncover them, but if he doesn't you can take him to the hallway to the Shout Spot. Say, 'Stay here and I will come back when I am ready.'

- **Leave him out there for a while.** He might go to his bedroom. Let him do this. Eventually he will want to come back into the living area, but he cannot do this until he has listened to what you have to say.

CARRY ON!

This is a task you must remain consistent with. Every time he covers his ears he is to sit on the Shout Spot. If you are consistent you will find that over time he will start to correct himself. He will start to cover his ears and then stop himself. When this happens, thank him for listening to you so well.

My child refuses to let me wash his cuddly

'Toby has a cuddly that he drags around the house and takes to bed. It really is disgusting, but he refuses to let me wash it.'

YOUR TOOLS

Cuddly Box

See pages 54–71

LET'S DO IT!

WHAT TO DO

- **Find a box that you can decorate with your child** and explain that this is the Cuddly Box (tool).
- **Earmark a high shelf** or top of a wardrobe where the Cuddly Box can be kept.
- **Find the 'quick wash'** button on your washing machine!

WHAT TO SAY

- **Sit down with your child** and make eye contact with him. Say, 'Now I know that your cuddly is very precious to you and I have decided that from now on he is going to stay in your bedroom and live in his own Cuddly Box.' PAUSE. 'When you are downstairs and playing, your cuddly will be sleeping in his Cuddly Box on the high shelf in your room.' PAUSE. 'At night you will lift the lid and have him in bed with you while you sleep.' PAUSE. 'Do you understand? We will decorate this box and this is where cuddly will stay. In your bedroom.'

ACTION IT!

- **Decorate the Cuddly Box** together with paints, glue and collage.
- **When the box is dry,** take it to your child's room together and put the cuddly in it.
- **Return downstairs** and get your child busy, to keep him distracted and occupied.
- **If he asks for his cuddly,** say that he can have him but that he has to lie on his bed. Say, 'Would you like to have a little quiet time on your bed with cuddly and then pop him back in the Cuddly Box when you are ready to come back here?'
- **Take him to his bedroom** and lift the Cuddly Box down from the high shelf/top of the wardrobe.

Why life is easier if the cuddly stays upstairs

Many children have a comforter (an old blanket or a soft toy, for example) and this is a nice thing that you would not want to remove from your child altogether. As he becomes a toddler, it is far easier to decide to make a rule whereby the comforter is just for when he sleeps and rests in his bedroom. It isn't something that goes downstairs or out of the house.

This means that your child is independent during the day and not feeling the 'need' to have some form of security in his hand.

It also means that there is less chance of losing the cuddly and when it needs a wash it can be done in a day and be back in his Cuddly Box ready for bedtime (or after-lunch rest, if necessary).

- **Let him open the Cuddly Box** and leave him for his quiet time.
- **He will come downstairs** when he is ready. If he has the cuddly with him you need to take it back to his room together, pop it in the Cuddly Box and put it on high shelf/top of the wardrobe.

CARRY ON!
Remain consistent. You must make sure that the cuddly stays in the Cuddly Box upstairs on the high shelf/wardrobe because if you 'give in', even just once, your child will assume that you have gone back to the old way of letting him carry it everywhere.

TAKE NOTE!
By doing this, after three consecutive days the cuddly will only be looked forward to at bedtime and the 'dragging around' phase will have passed. This frees up some time for you to get it into the washing machine!

My child ignores people when they say 'hello'

'When my parents or friends come to visit, my daughter, Eliza, aged five, refuses to say "hello". She hides behind my legs and will stay there until she flies back to her toys to play.'

YOUR TOOLS

Don't be Shy Prop

See pages 54–71

LET'S DO IT!

WHAT TO DO

- **Make your child aware** that you have visitors coming.
- **Find something (with her involvement) for her to show them.** This is the Don't be Shy Prop (tool) and it can be anything your child is proud of such as a toy, a swimming badge or a cake she has helped to bake.
- **When the guests arrive,** ask your child to open the door and, as she does, to say, 'Hello' before they do. This is a 'hello race'. Who can get there first?

WHAT TO SAY

- **Sit down with your child** and say, 'Now. After lunch Grandma is coming.' PAUSE.
- **Explain your plans.** 'I have decided that when we have visitors you are going to open the door for them.' PAUSE. 'We are then going to have our own little game and that is to see if we can say, "Hello" before they do!' Say, 'I am going to count up the "hellos" and when you have said ten you will get a prize.' PAUSE. 'Now. Let's find something that we would like to show Grandma. How about your new ballet certificate or your new book?'

ACTION IT!

TAKE NOTE!
Have the door keys in your pocket just in case someone gets locked out!

- **After explaining the door-opening exercise,** practise it, with you on the doorstep and your child opening the door. She has to try to say, 'Hello' before you do!
- **After this exercise,** place the Don't be Shy Prop near the door. Your child is going to show it to Grandma. It always helps a child if she has the prop in her hands – she then feels that the object is being focused on, not her.

Why it is important to help a shy child/not ignore them

Shy children often need a little 'push' to help them overcome initial moments of shyness when they are socialising. Your child needs to find a way to introduce herself and say, 'Hello' quickly before she feels the shyness creeping up on her.

The more you help your child with this, the sooner she will learn ways of managing her shyness.

CARRY ON!

It is important to remain consistent with this process, so each time the door is knocked on your child needs to open it and say, 'Hello' as quickly as she can. She might even say it from behind the door, but the point is that she is saying it!

This process is something that needs to be ongoing. You are really helping her with something that challenges her – shyness. It is great parenting because you are helping her to accept the way she is, but finding methods to help her.

My older child is continually bullying his younger brother

'The moment my back is turned my older son, Ethan, aged four and a half, is teasing his younger brother, Rufus, aged three. Poor Rufus is always moaning and crying. This is exhausting.'

LET'S DO IT!

YOUR TOOLS

Shout Spot

See pages 54–71

YOUR SKILLS

Teacher Tone

You Choose

See pages 72–77

WHAT TO DO

- **Initially, ignore** the behaviour.
- **Wait for your younger child to come and find you.** Engage with him in an activity you have set out on the table. Ignore your older child.
- **DON'T get caught up in the reasons behind the disagreement,** simply focus on something else with the younger one.
- **If the younger child has really been hurt** then send the older one immediately to the hallway to sit on the Shout Spot (tool).

WHAT TO SAY

- **Sit down with both children** when they are not distracted by toys or TV. A good time to talk to them is when they are eating. Say, 'Now. I have decided, Rupert, if Ethan upsets you, you are to walk away. No moaning and whining. Just walk away and come and find me.' PAUSE.
- **Find your firm Teacher Tone** (skill). Say, 'Ethan, if I have found that you have hurt Rufus badly you will be sitting on the Shout Spot in the hallway for a long time.' PAUSE. 'I am NOT having violence and hurting one another in our house.' PAUSE. Say, 'Do you understand?' using your strong, firm, confident voice.

ACTION IT!

- **Allow the children to go and play** and accept that it is only a matter of time before a disagreement occurs.
- **Leave the children and wait** for Rufus to come to you.
- **Start to set out an activity** on the kitchen table, or wherever you are. Playdough, moon sand and colouring are all good options.

Why it is important to ignore this behaviour initially

When siblings tease each other or argue with one another you need to see it as a moment where they are strengthening one another's characters. They are finding out who is 'king pin' and they are learning to stand up for themselves.

Of course, if you detect that the behaviour is actually bullying or simply that too much physical force is being used, you need to step in, but initially let the children see if they can resolve the disagreement between them.

- **When Rufus comes in moaning,** simply say, using You Choose (skill) 'You can come in here and get on with the playdough or go back into the playroom with your brother.'
- **Continue with what you are doing in that room** and the chances are he will climb up to the table to play with the playdough.
- **Your older child will wander through** and then start to play with the playdough as well. The 'incident' doesn't need to be discussed.
- **However, if you can hear** that your older child is being particularly unkind or has hurt your younger child, you are to take his hand and calmly walk him to the hallway. Say, using your strong Teacher Tone, 'Stay on the Shout Spot until I am ready. I am NOT having that behaviour in this house.'

CARRY ON!

Remain consistent with this process. Have a cupboard in the kitchen with activities you can set out on the table for when one child comes in moaning about the other. This is so that you are prepared and can act quickly.

Simply say, 'That was *your* argument with your brother. Not mine. I don't need to hear about it, thank you.'

Don't return to being a referee. Your children come to you and you distract them – or the behaviour is so severe that your older child finds himself on the Shout Spot.

My child won't stop aggravating our family dog

'The moment my back is turned Gregory, aged four, aggravates the family dog by pulling on his tail, holding his front paws and making him walk too fast, and showing him food he knows he cannot have. This is really upsetting me.'

YOUR TOOLS

Shout Spot

See pages 54–71

YOUR SKILLS

Zero Tolerance

See pages 72–77

LET'S DO IT!

WHAT TO DO

- **You have already spoken** to your child and told him how unkind this behaviour is, but he is not listening to you. He now needs to be told the consequence of cruelty to animals. Use Zero Tolerance (skill).

WHAT TO SAY

- **Sit your child** down in the hallway on the Shout Spot (tool) with the dog present. Ensure you have your child's full attention. Say, 'Gregory. I need to talk to you about something quite serious now.' PAUSE. 'I have told you lots of times about not aggravating the dog and you haven't listened to me.' PAUSE. 'I now have a new plan. When I see you upsetting the dog I am going to take your hand and bring you out here to sit in the hallway on your own on the Shout Spot.' PAUSE. 'You will stay here until I am ready to come and get you. You can go to your bedroom if you want, but you will not be coming into the kitchen, where I will be with (dog's name).' PAUSE. 'Now, I know you can stop this silly behaviour with the dog, which is making me sad, but if you forget, you will go to the Shout Spot. Do you understand?'

ACTION IT!

- **You need to follow through with what you have said,** so the moment you see your child progressing from playing with the dog to aggravating him he visits the Shout Spot.

- **Just take him calmly by the hand** and don't say anything at this stage.

- **When you get to the Shout Spot,** bend down and make eye contact. Say, 'Stay here until I come and get you'. The aim is that he starts to moan and shout, wanting to come back into the kitchen with you.

Why it is important to intervene in such situations

It is said that you should never trust a dog 100 per cent. It would be awful if your child caught the dog off-guard or in a bad mood and he snapped at him, or, worse still, bit him.

- **Allow your child to shout louder and louder** and then become quiet. It might take him a while before he starts to shout and it might then take him a while longer to calm down again, but you must allow him to feel the pain of being excluded from the family.

- **When you do let him back into the kitchen** you do not need to mention anything. He knows why he was out there. It is now his decision as to whether he bothers the dog again or not.

CARRY ON!

You must remain consistent with this process. After three days of making visits to the Shout Spot your child should learn about how there is no benefit to upsetting you and the dog.

After seven to ten days of leaving the dog alone, you could have the dog 'buy' your child a small gift to say, 'thank you for being nice to me!'

> **TAKE NOTE!**
> It is great when children are confident with animals, but they need to learn to respect them as well.

My child insists on whispering in public!

'My child, Isa, is always trying to whisper to me when we are with other people. She doesn't want others to hear what she has to say. I find this very embarrassing and if I refuse to let her do it, she starts to get upset, cry and shout.'

YOUR TOOLS

Shout Spot

See pages 54–71

YOUR SKILLS

You Choose

The Back

See pages 72–77

LET'S DO IT!

WHAT TO DO
- **Organise three consecutive days** where you will be socialising with friends.

WHAT TO SAY
- **Sit with your child** just before your guests arrive or you are due to go to a friend's house or meeting place. Say, 'Now listen. I have decided that I am not going to let you whisper in my ear any more. If you try to do it I am going to cover my ear.' PAUSE. 'You can talk to me in a quiet voice and it's a private chat that others don't need to hear. But NO whispering.' PAUSE. 'Do you understand?'

ACTION IT!
- **Now that you have said it,** you have to action it.
- **Make your friends aware** that you might be dealing with a few tantrums over the three days, but after this your child should have corrected her behaviour.
- **When she leans in to whisper,** move your body away or stand up and continue talking to your friends.
- **Finish talking to them** after a couple of minutes and say, 'What would you like to tell me? You can use your quiet voice.'
- **When she does this, praise her** and say, 'It would be great for everyone to hear you ask to have a drink. You don't always need to use a little voice.'
- **If she starts to shout** because you refuse to let her whisper you need to bend down and say, 'Stop this noise and talk nicely or we will find a Shout Spot (tool) like we have at home.'

Why my child should be taught not to whisper

Whispering is seen as rude and can make people feel very uncomfortable if they see others doing it in front of them.

Children need to know that this behaviour makes others feel uncomfortable. You can always try whispering to your partner in front of your child so that she grasps how it feels.

The reason why a child tends to whisper is because she wants your full attention. It is usually in a social environment because she just doesn't want to share Mummy/Daddy with anyone else.

Don't instantly assume your child is shy. This is not likely to be the case.

- **If she continues,** use You Choose (skill) to say, 'Stop or Shout Spot.'
- **If she continues after this,** walk her to a suitable Shout Spot corner near by and say, 'Sit there. When you are quiet come and find me.'
- **Confidently walk away** using The Back (skill) and leave her there.

CARRY ON!
Remain consistent and after three consecutive days of you showing your child that you are no longer allowing her to whisper in your ear she will stop even trying. She might talk to you in a quiet voice so that you have to go close to her face to hear her, but the important thing is that the whispering no longer happens.

TAKE NOTE!
In a public place you need to be able to see her, but you do not need to stand next to her all the time. This is the attention she craves.

My child refuses to get into the buggy after the park

'Sophie is happy to get into the buggy at home before we go out, but on the return journey she will refuse to get into it. I sometimes have to force her and often end up walking down the street with her screaming in the buggy.'

LET'S DO IT!

YOUR TOOLS

Bag of Tricks

Shout Spot

See pages 54–71

YOUR SKILLS

You Choose

See pages 72–77

WHAT TO DO

- **Create a Bag of Tricks** (tool) by collecting a bagful of small items that your child would not usually play with at home. These might be things that you would need to monitor – you can easily do this while she is sitting in her buggy. Examples include: a purse with coins in it, a small pot of playdough, a note book and biro, a slinky, a bunch of keys, a mirror and chapstick, an apple, a string of beads, an old watch or a mobile phone.

WHAT TO SAY

- **Wait until your child is playing** at the park and you want her to come to the buggy.
- **Bend down and make eye contact.** Using You Choose (skill) say, 'Now, choose one more thing to play on and then we are going to go to the buggy and see what is in the Bag of Tricks'. Let her play on one more apparatus and then take her hand before she can go anywhere else. Say, 'Quick! Come and see the bag of wonderful things'.

ACTION IT!

- **Once you have asked your child to choose** one last thing to play on, you then take her hand and guide her to the buggy. Say, 'Let's see what is in the Bag of Tricks today.'
- **Arrive at the buggy** and give her the Bag of Tricks to hold.
- **As she looks in the Bag of Tricks,** swoop her into the buggy and do up the clasp. Say, 'Now what's inside the Bag of Tricks?'
- **Engage with her for a moment** and then start pushing the buggy. The first time you do this will be a novelty. It is important that the Bag of Tricks is only played with in the buggy and that you rotate the items.

CARRY ON!

It is important to remain consistent and not return to forcing her into the buggy. If she refuses to get into it or even to hold the Bag of Tricks you need to identify a Shout Spot (tool).

- **Bend down, make eye contact** and say, 'We are not going back to the park. You Choose: sit on the ground with no Bag of Tricks or jump in the buggy and see if you can find the mirror for me.'

- **Give her a moment to see if she responds.** If she doesn't, simply sit her on the ground (on your designated Shout Spot) and say, 'Stay there until you are ready to look in the Bag of Tricks.'

- **Stand up and act busy with your phone.** You want to ignore her and show her that you are calm. If she senses your tension she will act up more, thinking she can 'break' you.

- **After she has become quiet** or has sat on the Shout Spot for three to five minutes quietly say, 'Right! I want a piece of that apple in the Bag of Tricks.' Say this in a confident, fun voice. Scoop her up, with the Bag of Tricks, sit her in the buggy. A protest means she goes back to sitting on the Shout Spot.

- **This time leave her a little longer.** You are waiting for boredom to set in so that she wants to look in the Bag of Tricks. How long it takes her is variable from child to child, but once this process is started you must not break it.

- **Eventually she will get into the buggy** and you can feel pleased that you have achieved your goal. Next time you will find that she will not sit it out for quite so long.

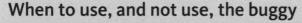

When to use, and not use, the buggy

There is a stage in your child's development where she still needs to use the buggy as she cannot walk the whole distance to the park/shop/Granny's house and back again – plus enjoy her time while she is there.

Perhaps a journey can start with your child walking and when she decides she is tired she sits in the buggy. By doing this on the outward journey as well as the journey home it makes life easier and it also builds your child's leg strength and her stamina for walking distances.

Eventually you reach a stage where she can walk the full distance, but you have to allow the time to do this at her own speed, not yours.

If you are in a hurry you might have to use the buggy, so take a Bag of Tricks hidden under the seat.

My child refuses to have his seat belt done up

'Every time I lift up Jack, aged two and a half, to put him in his car seat he starts shouting. I end up having to push him into the seat to strap him in. He then shouts at the start of the journey, but eventually quietens down.'

YOUR TOOLS

Journey Box

See pages 54–71

YOUR SKILLS

You Choose

See pages 72–77

LET'S DO IT!

WHAT TO DO

- **Make sure you have told your child** why he is getting into the car, where he is going and if it is a 'quick' or a 'long' journey. Tell him before you go to the car.

- **Have a Journey Box** (tool) with a collection of things to do in the car. This can sit between the back seats or in a foot well. The items need to be regularly rotated and just kept for the car, not taken out.

WHAT TO SAY

- **Bend down and make eye contact** with your child while he is eating breakfast. Give him your full attention.

- **Explain that you are going in the car** after breakfast to travel to (name destination). State whether it is a short or a long journey. Say, 'Now, things are going to be different when we are in the car.' PAUSE. 'Mummy and Daddy have bought a box of things to look at and play with in the car.' PAUSE. 'This box is going to always have something new in it to look at. It is our Journey Box.' PAUSE. 'We've also decided you are going to climb into your seat all by yourself. You can then get something from the Journey Box and look at it while I buckle you up!'

- **Perhaps reiterate,** 'Do you understand? Journey Box and climb in all on your own!'

ACTION IT!

- **Dedicate three consecutive days** to going on two or three journeys each day. You could make little trips to the library, shops, café and park – drive to all of them. The more practice your child has, the better it will be.

Why? It's a question of safety

Eventually your child realises that the battle isn't worth having because he is not going to win it. The seat belt has to be worn or we are not going anywhere!

- **Always state where you are going** before you get out to the car. Make eye contact when you tell your child.
- **Don't let time be a constraint.** This is not a pressure you need to put on yourself. Let your child climb into the car. It may take time.
- **Once he is in the chair,** buckled in with something to entertain him from the Journey Box, you need to thank him. Say, 'It's so nice to have a grown-up child who gets himself into his seat and can sit nicely looking at things out of the Journey Box. I am so pleased with you'.

CARRY ON!

If you have a child who, even with the incentive of climbing in and the Journey Box, still refuses, simply sit him on the ground close to his side of the car with the door open. You stand behind him so he cannot run off. Using You Choose (skill) say, 'Now, you choose. You can sit on the pavement and wait until you are ready or you can start to climb in!' Now guide him to climb, though he is likely to push you away. Sit him on the pavement and calmly say, 'Sit there and when you are ready, climb in.'

Now ignore him and either talk to someone else and discuss the Journey Box contents or simply start looking at your phone and acting busy. This body language shows him that you are not bothered and he can sit there all day if he wants. Some children quietly stand up and start to climb in the car. If he does this, let him do so without saying anything and then strap him in and simply kiss him on the head. This is where actions speak louder than words. Some children will sit on the ground for a long time. If this is the case, ensure he has nothing to do. You are waiting for him to get bored and start to climb in. Give him a positive push by saying, 'Oh, there's something you are going to love in the Journey Box.' Stand him up and guide him. If he resists, you need to sit him back down and calmly say, 'Okay, you are not ready yet.' Be patient because after a couple of challenging moments like this, with you remaining calm, he will soon learn that you are in control – not him!

TAKE NOTE!
There is no choice on certain things in life and safety is one of them.

My child tells me what to do

'My daughter, Mia, aged three and a half, insists on being in control of everything. She dictates who sits where, who walks upstairs first, what music we listen to in the car. We are now in a pattern of asking her what she wants rather than telling her what we are doing.'

YOUR TOOLS

Plan a Day

Shout Spot

See pages 54–71

YOUR SKILLS

Teacher Tone

See pages 72–77

LET'S DO IT!

WHAT TO DO

- **Plan the day ahead using Plan a Day** (tool) ready to sit down and explain it to your child.
- **Practise your Teacher Tone** (skill).
- **Find a location for your Shout Spot** (tool).

WHAT TO SAY

- **Sit with your child at the beginning of the day** and as you are eating breakfast explain the structure of the day to her. This is to show her that you are in charge of it: there is a plan and it isn't going to change. For example, say, 'After breakfast we will brush teeth and then we need to head out to the shops. We are going to (name the shops and what needs to be bought).'
- **State what she can choose at the shops.** 'When we go into the supermarket you can choose the green top or the blue one.'
- **State what will happen when you get home.** Say, 'After shopping we will come home and do some colouring and then have lunch. We will have TV time after lunch and then we will go to the park. Then we will collect dry-cleaning, come home and cook dinner. You can help me with chopping veggies. Tonight after dinner and bathtime Daddy will read your story while I do my work. That is our day!' PAUSE.

ACTION IT!

- **You now need to start the day as you stated** and remain true to your word that this is its structure and you are sticking to it.
- **When she 'tells' you to do something,** such as fetch her something or get her a drink or colour a picture in a certain way, this is when your Teacher Tone needs to come into play. Say, 'You can ask me to help you with something and I will, but if you are asking me to do something that you can do yourself, you have to do it – not me.'

- **Now continue with what you were doing** and ignore her. She needs to digest what you have just said to her.

- **The next time she instructs you to do something** you either say (using Teacher Tone), 'You can do that yourself. You don't need me. I am busy.' Or 'Ask me by saying, "Please Mummy, can you (state the request)?".' If she asks for it nicely and it is not something she can do herself, then simply say, 'You asked in such a kind and polite way, of course I can (for example, get a drink) for you.'

- **When she instructs you** to, 'Play with me' or 'Read me a story' simply say, 'I don't want to do that right now' and continue with what you are doing. Ignore her when she is being 'bossy' or when she can do the task herself. It is only when she asks for something nicely and with respect that you are prepared to assist her.

CARRY ON!

The change in your approach might cause her to shout in frustration, 'You are not listening to me. You are not doing what I say.' She is acknowledging the change but you must not respond. The basic message is that if you talk to people this way they don't listen.

If the shouting continues, you need to guide her to the Shout Spot in your hallway. Say, 'It is okay to shout. Do it here. When you are quiet you can come and find me and we will get the playdough out together.' Confidently walk away. It is normal behaviour for a child to 'shout out' when change she doesn't like is occurring. Remain consistent in saying 'no' to some of her demands. When she shouts, pop her on the Shout Spot. After three consecutive days your child should understand that 'Mummy doesn't like being spoken to like that. If I do she walks away.'

Why must I not do everything my child tells me to?

If you find yourself conforming to your child's every wish, she will grow up assuming that this is the way she can talk to everyone. She will be most shocked when she hears another child say she doesn't want to play 'that game' or whatever. On the day your child starts school she will have to do as she is asked and it will come as a huge surprise when she realises she not the one calling all the shots. It is best to get a balance and teach your child how to ask rather than tell and also to understand that things cannot always be done her way.

My child whines when she doesn't get her own way

'Lola is four years old and will often whine rather than talk. This drives me mad and I continually say, "Use your big girl voice" but it doesn't seem to work.'

YOUR SKILLS

Ear Switch

The Back

See pages 72–77

LET'S DO IT!

WHAT TO DO

- **Sit down with your child** and explain that you do not like her 'whine voice'. Let her know you will be turning your ears off using Ear Switch (skill). They will only be turned on when her 'nice voice' returns.

- **You need to be ready to remain consistent** for the initial three days and thereafter. Only start with the change process if you feel ready. If you are not completely dedicated to it, postpone it until you are.

WHAT TO SAY

- **Sit down with your child** and make sure that she is 100 per cent focused on what you are saying.

- **Make eye contact with her.** Say, 'Now, I have decided to make a change to something. You know that I really don't like it when you use your whining voice like this (demonstrate)?' PAUSE. 'You have such a lovely voice that you use so nicely at nursery/school.' PAUSE. 'Now, when you start to use your whine voice I have decided that I am going to turn my ears off. I will turn them back on when the nice voice talks to me again.' PAUSE.

- **Show her how you 'turn' the top of your ears** to stop listening to her whine. Say, 'Now, I want you to try your best to keep your nice voice on today. I don't want to turn my ears off because then I cannot hear what you are saying.'

- **Now continue to get on with something.** Say, 'Right! I need to load the washing machine (or whatever). You could get out your new sticker book and felt pens.' Leave her to think through what has been said to her. You know it won't be long before you need to turn off your ears!

Why the whining has to stop!

A lot of children whine incessantly and get their own way by doing it. It has become the norm for them – a habit that is quite a challenge to break.

Therefore, aim to stop the whining before your child views it as her normal way to communicate and get whatever she wants.

ACTION IT!

- **As soon as your child starts to whine,** give her a warning, 'Speak nicely because I don't want to turn off my ears. What do you want?'

- **If she whines, then show her how your ears are turned off** and then turn your back using The Back (skill) and 'get busy'. You are genuinely acting as though you cannot hear her. Her volume will get far worse before it gets better. She might scream and shout to try and get you to listen, but you are not going to make eye contact while she is speaking in her whining voice or shouting.

- **The moment she addresses you in a nice calm voice,** turn on your ears and say, 'How can I help?' Don't mention her shouting – because as far as she is concerned you didn't hear it!

CARRY ON!

You will find that the noise worsens before it improves, but if you remain consistent for three days you will find that she will start correcting herself far quicker and before you know it the whining habit will have passed.

Remember that if you start answering her when she whines again, rather than ignoring her, her whining will come back.

Get everyone on board. Every adult in the home should 'switch off their ears' when they hear the whine or the threat of one. If older siblings are turning off their ears too tell them not to do this because this should just come from your child's parents and main carers. Say, 'If you don't like the way your sister is talking you simply go to your bedroom for some peace and quiet.'

My child refuses to share when his friends come to play

'No matter what the other child wants to play with my son, Alfie, aged three, will snatch things away from them and say "mine". This causes tension and embarrassment with my friends.'

YOUR TOOLS

Out-of-the-Way Shelf

Shout Spot

See pages 54–71

YOUR SKILLS

Teacher Tone

The Back

See pages 72–77

LET'S DO IT!

WHAT TO DO

- **Create an Out-of-the-Way Shelf** (tool) using an empty shelf or cupboard where certain special toys can go that your child doesn't want to share with friends.

- **Find your Teacher Tone** (skill) to talk about sharing.

- **Ensure you have a Shout Spot** (tool) and make your friends aware that when their children come to play it is likely to be used. They might want to warn their children if they are particularly timid.

WHAT TO SAY

- **Ensure you have your child's complete attention.** Talk to him, making eye contact, when he is not distracted by toys or screens. Say, 'Now. I need to talk to you about something very serious. We are going to work harder with our sharing.' PAUSE. Say, 'Your friend (Adam) is coming to play after lunch and we are not going to snatch toys from him. We are going to let him play with our toys.' PAUSE. 'Adam is not going to break your toys. He is not going to hide your toys and he knows he must not take them home.' PAUSE. Now say, 'I want us to go and look at your toys before Adam arrives. I have a special cupboard and we can put the toys in it that you don't have to share: the things that are precious to you.' PAUSE.

- **Take him to his toys** and say, 'Are there particular toys you would like to put away until Adam has gone home?' Your child has to give you a certain number, but he cannot hide his entire collection of toys away in the cupboard.

- **Guide him with certain toys** that have caused conflict in the past. Say, 'Now, all your favourite toys are put away, so you can let Adam play with everything else.' PAUSE. Say, 'Is he going to break your toys? No. Is he going to take them home? No.' PAUSE.

Why is it so important to guide my child to share?

There is an argument in favour of letting children try to resolve disagreements for themselves and this is often how they learn about sharing. However, if you find that your child is continually taking toys from other children, just for the sake of it, then you need to address the problem.

Too much 'taking from others' and pushing and shoving can cause other children to steer away from your child and this is very hurtful to watch.

The sooner you teach your child that sharing is a good thing to do and that his own toys won't be taken away for ever, the easier he will find it to make friendships and bond with other children.

- **Suggest some other activities.** Say, 'I think we should make playdough together/make some cakes you can decorate when Adam arrives.'

- **Now make or bake together.**

- **Finally you need to walk him to the Shout Spot** in the hallway and sit him on it. Say, 'Now. If there is any pushing or snatching when Adam is here I am going to bring you straight to this Shout Spot. You will sit here until I am ready to let you come and play again. Do you understand?' He is not likely to answer. So you say, 'Right! Now we are going to have a lovely afternoon. I don't want to have to send anyone to the Shout Spot for snatching or pushing.'

ACTION IT!

You need to accept that once you have said this to your child, you need to action it. Aim to have three days of at least four social occasions. These need to be with good friends who will support you going through this process.

- **Give the children space** and don't hover over your child, as if you are expecting him to misbehave. Trust him. It is different now because you have a process in place.

- **Set out toys** for the children to engage in and step away and chat to your own friend.

- **If the children start to disagree,** let them have a moment to see if they can resolve the issue. If you can see and are quite certain your child is to blame, take him straight to the Shout Spot. Say, 'Now. That was snatching. I don't like it. Stay here until I come and get you.'

- **Confidently walk away** and leave him in the hallway using The Back (skill). All doors need to be shut (lock the front door). He will shout and might even come back into the room where you are. If he is still

Continued ▶

cross and shouting, take him back to the Shout Spot. Say, 'I am not ready yet. Stay here until you are quiet. I will come and get you.'

- **After this you need to keep returning him to the Shout Spot in silence** until he is quiet for a moment. Go to him and say, 'All finished. Now let's go and have a nice time. We could get the playdough out.'
- **As you walk to the room where everyone is** stop, bend down and say, 'Let's play nicely. I don't want to put you back on the Shout Spot.'
- **When the playdough is out on the table,** let the guest unwrap it and divide it in half. This guides your child on how to share.
- **At every opportunity** ask your child to 'Give that to Adam, please' (a dinner plate, cutlery, cup). The guest should be given food first.

CARRY ON!

Sharing is something all children have to learn. It is up to parents to teach and guide as well as let the children resolve things for themselves.

Once you have implemented the Shout Spot and sharing, be consistent. Have several occasions where friends come to your home and your child is asked to be kind and share. Use the Shout Spot when needed and after three or four times of being put on it your child should start to understand that he will be excluded if he snatches and pushes.

My child refuses to let me play with the baby

YOUR TOOLS

Incentive System
(fairy chart)

Shout Spot

See pages 54–71

'Poppy is three and a half and my son, Leo, is six months. Poppy will climb on me if I am holding Leo and she refuses to let me play or sing to him. She tells me to play with her. She loves Leo very much.'

LET'S DO IT!

WHAT TO DO

- **Create an Incentive System chart** (tool) that you know your child will engage with. If she loves fairies, then create a chart where she has to give each fairy a magic wand and then a crown. The aim is that she has to give the fairies 30 things before she gets a prize.

WHAT TO SAY

- **Bend down and make clear eye contact.**

- **Have this conversation when the baby is sleeping.** Say, 'Now. I have something that is going to help you with sharing Mummy with Leo.' PAUSE. Say, 'There are times when I want to read Leo a story or sing him a song and you just have to wait a minute until I have finished and then it is your turn!' PAUSE.

- **Now show the Incentive System chart with fairies on it.** Have a box with the cut-out wands and crowns that she has to stick on. Say, 'Now, every time you let me have a moment with Leo, when I have finished we are going to come straight to the fairy chart and give one of them a wand or a crown. When they all have their crowns and wands you are going to get a prize from a fairy!' PAUSE. 'The prize will be hidden in the garden! It is not there yet because you don't have all the wands and crowns on the fairies.'

ACTION IT!

- **Now that you have heard yourself say this,** you have to action it.

- **Aim to have three consecutive days** where you spend time putting your baby first.

- **The aim is that your child earns** between six and eight wands/crowns a day. After five days you should have broken the habit of her shouting when you spend time with the baby. She will get her prize and you can start the Incentive System again, if necessary.

CARRY ON!

If you find that your child is still being very demanding and is refusing to let you spend time with the baby, you are going to have to talk to her about the Shout Spot (tool). This is where she will have to go if she refuses to listen when she has to wait her turn.

Why should my child learn to share me with the baby?

It is important that your toddler has one-to-one time with you when the baby is sleeping, but that she also starts to learn how to share you. This can be done by involving her as much as possible with small tasks such as collecting nappies and giving the baby toys, but ultimately she has to sometimes learn to wait and realise that the baby must come first.

This is never easy for a first child, but it's a good life skill. Life doesn't revolve around only her!

My child refuses to go upstairs on her own

'Alice, aged four, refuses to go upstairs on her own. If she wants something from her bedroom I have to go with her. She is fine downstairs if I have to go upstairs and leave her for a few minutes.'

LET'S DO IT!

YOUR TOOLS

Bottom-Stair Song

See pages 54–71

WHAT TO DO

• **This is something you should only instigate** when you feel truly ready. You have to believe that you are capable of being strong for your child. She needs a little push in the right direction.

WHAT TO SAY

• **Sit with your child** on the bottom stair in the hallway.

• **Ensure you have her full attention.**

• **Make eye contact with her.** Say, 'I want to talk to you about something. I have an idea to help you with going up the stairs to collect things from your bedroom.' PAUSE. Say, 'When you need something, I am going to come to the bottom stair and sit here while you go up. I will not move. You will know I am here because I am going to sing the Bottom-Stair Song (tool).' PAUSE. 'I am sure you will be up there in a flash and be back before I have finished the song!' PAUSE.

ACTION IT!

• **Now say, 'Let's try it!** You run up the stairs to your bedroom, pick up what I left on your bed and come straight back.' Say this in a happy, confident voice and then say, 'Ready, steady, go.'

• **Start to sing** and remain looking in front of you. She should just run upstairs and back again, or at least get part of the way.

• **Praise her** when she returns, but don't overdo it. She has achieved something quite normal, so don't make too much of a fuss.

CARRY ON!

If she still refuses to go upstairs, then you can simply say, 'Okay, maybe next time.' She might want to know what is on her bed, but you can

Why should I guide her to do this alone if she is scared?

It is very common for children to go through this stage and part of the reason is to control you (getting you to do it instead!) and the other part is that they are a little anxious about going up there on their own.

The easy option would be to fetch and carry for your child, but this is not the solution. It is important that she overcomes this challenge so that she feels comfortable about walking around her home without you.

simply say, 'The lights are all on up there. You will be able to see what it is. Tell me if you need me to sit on the bottom stair.'

Confidently walk away and leave her to think about what you have said. You have given her an incentive to go up and you have given her a system to help her, but she just isn't ready.

Leave it at that and wait until another occasion when she wants something from upstairs. It is important that you tell her you are not going to collect things for her from upstairs and you are not going up again until bathtime. She needs to know that this is something she has to fix herself. You can be reassured that she isn't overly scared, otherwise she wouldn't remain downstairs playing when you go upstairs to the bathroom or to do chores. She will get there when she is ready. It is important not to pander to her or make an issue of it.

TAKE NOTE!
This is all about being an independent child, which leads to confidence: two qualities that make life far easier for her.

My child bites

'My son, Finlay, is two years old (just) and he is not yet speaking very much. When we are out socially and also at his nursery he bites the other children when they come close to him.'

LET'S DO IT!

YOUR TOOLS

Shout Spot

See pages 54–71

WHAT TO DO

- **Make sure that for the next three days you are socialising** with friends you feel comfortable with and trust.
- **Arrange playdates** knowing your child is going to bite at least once.
- **Have arnica cream at the ready for the victim.** This, if put on immediately, can reduce or prevent bruising.
- **Find an area in your home** away from the living area that will be your Shout Spot (tool). The area needs to be as 'boring' as possible.

YOUR SKILLS

Teacher Tone

Zero Tolerance

The Back

Ragdoll Mode

See pages 72–77

WHAT TO SAY

- **Before the playdate,** bend down and make eye contact with your child. Use your firm Teacher Tone (skill) and say, 'Now we are going to have a lovely time playing when Jenny and Sam come today. If there is any hurting or biting, I will be taking you into the hallway and you will sit on the Shout Spot on your own for a long time. Now, let's make sure we are nice and kind. Let's find some toys to set out to play with. Your friends are going to be knocking on the door very soon.'

ACTION IT!

- **When your friends arrive leave the children** to play on their own (to a degree). Trust your child and don't act too concerned. You have a plan for what to do. The sooner you implement the process, the faster he will learn that biting is not something he does any more.
- **When your child lunges towards someone** with the intention of biting, do your best to leave it until (almost) the last minute.
- **Ask a friend to focus on the hurt child.** Remember the arnica cream.
- **Hold your child's hand** and as calmly as possible walk him to the Shout Spot. Don't say anything to him as you are walking there.
- **If he refuses to walk,** stand behind him, hands under his arms and walk him to the hallway (in Ragdoll Mode).

> **TAKE NOTE!**
> Make your friends aware of what you will be doing. Tell them when the children are not listening.

Why is it so important to stop a phase like biting?

When a child bites, initially there is a dramatic reaction to him – from the victim, the parent of that child and the parent. This reaction can fascinate the child and therefore he will tend to repeat the act. For as long as there is a reaction to the activity it may continue. This is why there are certain behaviours that are termed Zero Tolerance (skill) – and this is one of them.

- **Bend down and make eye contact.**
- **Using your firm (very firm) Teacher Tone** say, 'We DO NOT bite.'
- **Stand up and say,** 'Sit here until I come and get you.'
- **Confidently walk away** using The Back (skill), ensuring all hallway doors are shut, including the front door and the gate to upstairs.
- **Check the victim and make your apology.** Let everyone know that you intend your child to stay out on the Shout Spot in the hallway for at least 15 minutes.
- **If your child comes back into the living area,** even if he is saying 'sorry', turn him around and walk him back into the hallway. Say, 'I am not ready yet'. Say this only once and then leave the hallway.
- **From now on,** if your child comes into the living area, turn him around and walk him back to the Shout Spot. DO NOT look at or talk to him. Being ignored and excluded is one of the hardest forms of discipline for a child. As a biter he has gone from creating a lot of drama and attention on him to being excluded and ignored.
- **He needs to remain in the hallway** until he starts to feel the pain of being away from everyone. He will start to shout and cry. Leave him. Your aim is that he feels pain, like the poor bitten child does.
- **Only when he starts to calm down** and goes quiet is he allowed back into the living area.
- **Go to your child and bend down and look him in the eye.** Use your Teacher Tone and say, 'You can come back in the living room now to play. Remember – no biting.'
- **Do not carry him or hug him.** Walk with him and guide him to play again with the other children.
- **At this stage you need to feel** that 'the system worked'. He felt the pain of isolation. By feeling this pain he will think twice before he bites again.

Continued ▶

CARRY ON!

It is extremely important to remain consistent. Your child needs to stay on the Shout Spot until he is really upset about being on his own and the message that he is being excluded for biting sinks in. This is a situation where your discipline needs to be very firm. Any form of violence is Zero Tolerance. If the biting continues, you need to think about how long you isolated him for because it might not be long enough. Don't think, 'How long has he spent in the hallway?' Think, 'Can I hear him feeling as if he is as hurt as the bitten child was?' Be strong and remain consistent. Aim to arrange as many social occasions as possible over the initial three days of the process, but continue after this period to ensure that you are disciplining him in a really effective way. Firm guidance can cause the biter to stop biting in three days. However this doesn't mean that the behaviour won't come back, so remain consistent.

BEHAVIOUR SCENARIO **32**

My child empties her drawers and wardrobe every day!

'My child, Phoebe, empties the clothes out of her chest of drawers every morning before we go in. She is just two years old. She sleeps well. It is infuriating to start the day by tidying her clothes away.'

LET'S DO IT!

YOUR TOOLS

Get-Dressed Stencil

See pages 54–71

WHAT TO DO

- **Draw around your child** and together paint the picture of her without any clothes on using the Get-Dressed Stencil (tool). This picture is to remain in her bedroom.

- **Remove some of her clothes** from the drawers to eliminate some of the mess.

Is my child just going through an annoying phase?

The answer is 'yes'. Choose to ignore it by not saying anything and simply throwing her clothes back in her drawers – until the habit stops. Or tell her not to do this and give her an incentive (Get-Dressed Stencil) to stop.

WHAT TO SAY

- **After bathtime show her the stencil** you made with her earlier and dress it together by placing clothes on it to be worn the following day. Say, 'Now. In the morning I can come in and help you get dressed.' PAUSE. 'I do not want to find lots of clothes on the floor.' PAUSE.
- **Now say,** 'If the only clothes that are out of the drawers are these ones, I will stick a sticker on "Flat Phoebe". Then when we get dressed before breakfast there will be another sticker. When you have 12 stickers you will get a prize.'

TAKE NOTE!
You will have to judge whether your child can comprehend this at two years of age. Some children can; others cannot.

ACTION IT!

- **Make 'Flat Phoebe'** and lay it out in the centre of the floor.
- **When it is time to say goodnight** and turn out the light say, 'Remember! Tidy room In the morning and get dressed together. Two stickers!' In the morning your child will always get a sticker for getting dressed, but if the clothes are all over the floor you do not need to mention the second sticker.

CARRY ON!

If your child's behaviour continues, you might want to consider turning the chest of drawers around to face the wall so that she can't access it. Alternatively you can simply accept that what she is doing is a phase and put the clothes in the drawers rather than folding them each morning.

This behaviour isn't permanent. Don't focus on it and it will soon become boring to your child.

My child refuses to come home after a playdate

'When I collect my four-year-old daughter, Anna, from a playdate at someone else's home she always runs and hides and I can't seem to get her to come home without it ending in shouting and tears.'

YOUR TOOLS

Incentive System
(ribbon and hairclips)

Plan Ahead

Timer

See pages 54–71

LET'S DO IT!

WHAT TO DO

- **Sit down with your child** and show her your diary and explain that you would like to arrange some playdates.

- **Ask her who she would like to come and play** and whose home she hopes to go to in return.

- **Talk to her about what happens** when you pick her up.

- **Explain the Incentive System** ribbon and hairclips (tool).

- **Make her aware that you are prepared to cancel** the playdate, though this is the last resort.

WHAT TO SAY

- **After discussing your diary and arranging playdates** using Plan Ahead (tool), now sit down and say, 'Now last time you went to play at Maisie's house can you remember what happened when I came to collect you?' She might talk about what happened or just become quiet and thoughtful.

- **Go over what happened.** Then say, 'This is not going to happen again.' PAUSE. 'Now we have decided to have lots of playdates and I am going to telephone these mummies tomorrow.' PAUSE.

- **Now put the Incentive System** on the table and explain it (collecting hairclips on a ribbon). Say, 'When I come to the door I am going to say that you have five minutes to finish what you are doing. I will set my Timer (tool) on my phone. When it buzzes you have to come and put your shoes on.' PAUSE. 'If you can do this we will come home and put a hairclip on the ribbon. The hairclip means that you can go on your next playdate.' PAUSE. 'No hairclip – no playdate. Now when you have collected five hairclips you will get a prize' (this could be having a friend to sleep over). Say, 'Do you understand? What are you

Why is it important for my child to come when asked?

It is important that your child realises that when she is with an adult she does not have the upper hand. When your child comes to you when asked it shows that she respects you and values what you say. It also shows that she has an idea about what might happen if she does not come – the discipline technique that you might use.

going to do when the Timer goes off at a friend's house?' Make the alarm sound on your phone. She needs to respond with, 'Shoes on' or something similar.

ACTION IT!

- **On the morning of the playdate** remind your child of the playdate system. Say, 'Now, remember, I will arrive and set my Timer for five minutes. You finish your game. When the buzzer sounds on the Timer, what do you do?' She needs to answer, 'Shoes on' or 'I come home'. Say, 'Brilliant! And then we put a hairclip on the ribbon. Five hairclips is a sleepover!' PAUSE. 'Remember. What happens if you don't come when I ask?' She might remain quiet. Say, 'You lose your next playdate and no hairclip.' PAUSE. 'But that won't happen. I know you will come as soon as I ask.'

CARRY ON!

To make this process work you need to be able to follow through what happens if she doesn't come. When the buzzer sounds you go to her and make eye contact and say, 'It is time to put your shoes on. Remember what happens if you don't come? No playdate at Maisie's house next week.'

If she still refuses, you know that you are going to have to cancel that playdate. Your child may not believe that you are going to do it, but you must follow through. She will be very upset and it is a hard lesson to learn. We learn from our mistakes and she is not likely to make that mistake more than once. Be strong and remain true to your word. Always have dates in the diary for her to look forward to.

My child continually says 'MINE!'

'My daughter, Tilly, has just turned two. Her favourite word is 'MINE!'. She won't let anyone touch anything that belongs to her. She will often shout at her older brother because he might be playing with something that she classifies as "hers".'

YOUR TOOLS

Shout Spot

See pages 54–71

YOUR SKILLS

You Choose

Ask, Tell, Warn, Act

See pages 72–77

LET'S DO IT!

WHAT TO DO

- **Find a place in your home** for the Shout Spot (tool).
- **Decide what you can ignore.** Consider that some of the 'MINES!' need to be ignored, while others must be addressed. Identify together the situations you do need to tackle. For example, when your child screams at a friend and reduces her to tears this is more serious than when she approaches her brother and takes his toy, shouting 'MINE!'.

WHAT TO SAY

- **Sit down with your child.** She needs to be fully focused on what you are saying. Remove all distractions. Say, 'Now. There is going to be no more "MINE!".' PAUSE. 'You are not going to take toys when other children are playing with them.' PAUSE. 'If you shout "MINE!" you are going to have to go and sit on the Shout Spot until I am ready.' PAUSE. 'Now, we are going to have a nice day. Eva is coming to play and we are not going to take toys from her.' Due to your child's age she will not have a full understanding of what you are saying. She will only fully comprehend when you carry out what you have said and place her on the Shout Spot. The reason you have explained it to her is so that you can hear yourself saying it out loud. Now you have said it, you will have more confidence to follow it through.

ACTION IT!

- **When the friends arrive to play** it won't be long before the 'MINE!' is heard! Give your child a warning, 'Now, I want you to give that to Eva. No more "MINE!" or you will go to the Shout Spot.'
- **The next time she shouts 'MINE!'** and you think it needs addressing use You Choose (skill) and say, 'Choose stop saying "MINE!" or Shout

Why is it important to teach my child to share?

Every child has to go through the learning curve of having to share and some children find it far harder than others.

It is important that your child realises that not everything can belong to her and that it is okay to let someone play with her toy, knowing they will give it back afterwards.

Spot. Give that to Eva. One, two, three.' If she doesn't return the toy, take her to the Shout Spot.

- **If she visits the Shout Spot four or five times** over the three-day period she will start to understand that if she keeps taking toys from others she is going to be on her own on the Shout Spot.

CARRY ON!

Remain consistent and ensure that you Ask, Tell, Warn and then Act (skill) by taking her to the Shout Spot. Don't ignore any behaviour that warrants a trip to the Shout Spot.

TAKE NOTE!

There is pleasure in giving and sharing. This is something that we need to guide a child to discover.

My child hits

'My child, Bella, hits other children when she is on playdates or when we are out at the park. She doesn't like to share or wait and she lashes out. This happens very quickly. Sometimes I catch her in time, but most of the time the other child ends up in tears.'

YOUR TOOLS

Shout Spot

See pages 54–71

YOUR SKILLS

Zero Tolerance

Teacher Tone

See pages 72–77

LET'S DO IT!

WHAT TO DO

- **Your child knows** that hitting, biting and kicking are wrong. You don't need to tell her this every time she commits a violent act. In fact you don't need to say anything to her at all.

- **The only way to deal with violence** is to isolate and ignore your child. This is not an easy thing for a parent to do, but you have to think 'big picture'. You don't want your child thinking it is fine to hurt others.

- **Plan the locations for socialising** over the initial three days: a public playgroup, a friend's house, the playground and playdates at home.

- **In all these locations think of a spot** you can make into a Shout Spot (tool) for your child, where she cannot see what else is going on. Most public buildings have a hallway, as do homes. At a park find a tree in the distance where your child has to sit until you are ready to say she can return to play.

- **Plan at least five social occasions** over the three days and inform your friends what you are going to be doing. Make sure your friends support you and you don't feel judged. Generally in a social environment people understand that children might misbehave. What they do like to see is that parents don't ignore or excuse the behaviour but address and discipline their child. This kind of parenting is to be admired.

WHAT TO SAY

- **Before your friends arrive at your home,** on the doorstep of a friend's home or just before entering the park, give your child a small pep talk. Say, 'Now we are going to have a lovely time playing. You are a very good girl. I just want you to know that if you snatch or push or hit anyone you will have to go and sit all on your own in the hallway/ by the tree on the Shout Spot. I don't want you to have to sit on your own, so let's behave nicely and have fun.'

ACTION IT!

- **You have to stop violence immediately.** It cannot be ignored otherwise your child will think it is acceptable to use force to get what she wants. Use Zero Tolerance (skill).

- **The moment you see your child hurt another child** remove her from the situation.

- **Walk with her slowly and calmly** to the Shout Spot. Don't speak to her until you get there.

- **Bend down and make eye contact.**

- **In your firm Teacher Tone** (skill) say, 'We do not hurt other people. Stay here until I am ready.'

- **In a house you can leave her in the hallway** on the Shout Spot and close the door. Check there is nothing she can hurt herself with.

- **In a park stand close to her** so she can't run away. 'Act busy' with another child/look at your phone. Blank her and do not look/talk to her.

- **It is only when you start to hear that she is annoyed** at being removed from the fun that you know she is beginning to feel the consequence. She needs to shout, even shed a few tears, then quieten on her own. Once she has quietened, go to her, bend down and say, 'All finished. Let's go.'

- **Just before you go back into the room/park** remind her. Make eye contact and say, 'Let's be kind. I don't want you to sit here again.'

CARRY ON!

If, after the discipline, you return to the other children and she repeats the behaviour, you know she wasn't on the Shout Spot for long enough. She needs to feel the consequence and be able to link this in her mind to her violent act. By remaining consistent and really using the Shout Spot a lot over the initial three days you should see a difference.

If the behaviour isn't improving ask yourself if you are using the Shout Spot consistently and for long enough.

Why is it important to stop my child being violent?

A child who pushes, hits and kicks other children can very quickly turn this into a habit: a reflex that she is not even stopping to think about.

Children don't gain friends by bullying them. The sooner you teach your child that if you hit someone you can end up very lonely – the better.

My child won't stay on the Shout Spot

'As soon as I send my child, Lucy, to the Shout Spot she follows me back to the kitchen. She isn't shouting, she's laughing at me!'

LET'S DO IT!

YOUR TOOLS

Shout Spot

See pages 54–71

YOUR SKILLS

Ask, Tell, Warn, Act

The Back

See pages 72–77

WHAT TO DO

- **Make sure you have a safe environment** for your child when she needs to let off steam on the Shout Spot (tool). The hallway (front door locked) is a good place to choose. All doors must be closed.

- **She might go upstairs,** but just ensure there is nothing risky within reach. Put all toiletries and breakables up high or in cupboards.

- **Close the doors to bedrooms, with all lights off.** You don't want upstairs rooms to look inviting.

- **The door to where you will be** needs to shut firmly and be difficult, or impossible, for her to open. It only opens when you are ready, not when she is.

WHAT TO SAY

- **Go into the hallway with your child** at a calm moment.

- **Sit on the bottom step (the Shout Spot)** and have her sitting next to you. Say, 'Now. I have decided that when you are not listening or when you are shouting I am going to ask you to stop. If you don't listen I am going to bring you into the hallway to the Shout Spot.' PAUSE. 'You will stay there until you are quiet and I come and get you. The kitchen door will close and you will not be able to open it.'

- **At this stage show her by leaving her** in the hallway (on the Shout Spot) and you going into the kitchen, closing the door. Say, 'Now, try and open it.' This is when she will try to open it but not be able to.

- **Leave her for a moment until she shouts for you to open it.** This reinforces her understanding of the process.

- **Go back into the hallway with her.** Say, 'Now. You are a good girl and you can listen. I am only going to ask you to come out here when you are not listening or are shouting and cross.' PAUSE. 'When you are quiet and calm I will open the door and you can come back!'

Why should my child go on the Shout Spot?

The reason for excluding your child and placing her on the Shout Spot when she is misbehaving is for her to learn a fundamental life lesson: when life isn't going your way and you feel frustrated and cross, take yourself away from the situation, calm down and come back when you are feeling better.

The best place for the Shout Spot is the hallway. It needs to be a safe and boring environment, with all doors leading off it closed.

ACTION IT!

- **Aim for three consecutive days** where your child ends up in the hallway on the Shout Spot three or four times. She needs to fully understand the process and so do you. Practice makes perfect!

- **When she refuses to listen** use Ask, Tell, Warn, Act (skill). You then slowly take her to the Shout Spot.

- **Remain calm** and when you are in the hallway say calmly, 'You shout away and when all is quiet I will come and get you – when I am ready.'

- **Confidently walk away using The Back** (skill) and close the door. This might have to be a quick action if she is following you, but it is possible if you are prepared.

TAKE NOTE!
Think of the Shout Spot as an 'area' rather than an actual 'spot'.

CARRY ON!

If you open the door and she comes in still angry you know she hasn't let off all her steam. It will not be long before she misbehaves again and you will have to return her to the hallway. If this happens you know that she was not left long enough on the Shout Spot the first time.

If she goes up to her room and starts to play rather than staying in the hallway on the Shout Spot, leave her. This is a good thing. She has found a way to calm herself down. Leave her up there until you are ready. Then you can go and tell her that the kitchen door is now open and she can come down when she is ready.

My child says, 'Mummy do it. Go away Daddy'

'My child, Edie, is two and a half. I am a full-time mum and my husband sees her mainly at weekends due to his long work days. At the weekend he wants to be involved, but Edie pushes him away and demands I do everything. This is exhausting as I never get a break.'

YOUR SKILLS

Teacher Tone

You Choose

The Back

See pages 72–77

LET'S DO IT!

WHAT TO DO

- **Plan a weekend with moments** where your child is just with her father. You can leave the house or send them out to the park. When it is just the two of them there is bound to be a nice bond between them. This is a good thing for your partner to do first thing on Saturday, to set the tone for the weekend – Daddy is involved.

- **Plan how you are going to divide your time.** For example: Mummy has a rest after lunch and Daddy watches a film with your child. Once you have divided your time you need to make your child aware of this.

WHAT TO SAY

- **Sit down at breakfast time together and talk through the day.** Say, 'Right, after breakfast you are going to go and brush teeth with Daddy. When you come down the playdough will be waiting. After playdough Daddy will take you to the park. He is going to push you on the swings.'

- **At lunchtime explain the afternoon** in the same way.

- **At dinnertime explain the bedtime routine.**

- **Now speak in your firm Teacher Tone** (skill) with your partner by your side. Say, 'There is going to be NO MORE "Mummy do it".' PAUSE. 'If you say "Daddy go away" you are going to go and sit on the Shout Spot.' PAUSE. 'I love Daddy very much and you are NOT to tell him to "go away". Do you understand?' Now you have said this, action it.

ACTION IT!

- **After giving this talk to your child,** hug your partner and let her see you doing it. Then have him pick her up and have a family hug.

- **Move on to teeth-brushing.**

- **Your partner needs to make sure he has his assertive, confident voice.** He needs to use the Teacher Tone so that your child knows 'he means what he says'. He needs to say, 'Right, monkey, teeth then playdough. Let's go!'

- **He then holds her hand** and they go to the bathroom. He says, 'You squeeze the paste and I will turn the tap on.' The manner needs to be done in a no-nonsense style.

- **The moment a scene occurs** with 'Go away Daddy' or 'Mummy do it' stand your child on the floor and bend down, make eye contact and speak firmly to her. Using You Choose (skill) say, 'Now, you choose. You go for a bath with Daddy or you sit on the Shout Spot and then go for a bath with Daddy. Bath or hallway?'

- **He then approaches** and uses a no-nonsense approach. He says, 'Let's put bubbles in the water and hide all the animals in it.'

- **If she makes an extreme fuss** he needs to bring her to the hallway and say, 'Okay, you are not ready yet for bubble-bath time. Sit on the Shout Spot until you are ready to come with Daddy.'

- **He should confidently walk away** using The Back (skill) and shut the door. She may scream and shout, but only once she is quiet and this is out of her system should you approach her.

> **TAKE NOTE!**
> Whichever parent puts the child on the Shout Spot must see it through and collect her from it saying, 'Right, bubble time (or whatever). Let's go.' At this stage you know if she is ready to conform or if she needs to shout a little more. You need to make this judgement.

CARRY ON!

It is very important to stand strong together, showing affection to one another in front of your child. Show her that by being unkind she ends up on her own. When she is disciplined ONE of you does it and the other stays well away. Don't overrule one another in front of her – this is when children learn to play one parent off against the other. Consistency is the key. After a long weekend of following through with the process you (both) and your child will all be in tune with one another.

Can't I do as she asks and let Daddy keep his distance?

It is very common for a child to 'tune in' to one parent and the way they do things, taking comfort in this. When the other parent comes into the equation, this can throw her. She then asks the first parent to go away to get a reaction. All children love a reaction, even if it is negative, and a pattern then develops.

It is important that your child sees that her parents are a team. She should not thinks she is in control and needs to adapt to both parents. She can only do this if you reinforce the idea that you're a team on a regular basis.

My child is shy

'My son, Mohammed, is two and a half years old and when we go to playgroups or the playground he stays very close to me. He doesn't run around with the other children. He is very cautious.'

YOUR TOOLS

Bag of Tricks

See pages 54–71

LET'S DO IT!

WHAT TO DO

- **Collect some small items** and put them into a bag called the Bag of Tricks (tool). By playing with this your child will attract other children's attention and they will approach him. A shy child finds it easier to talk about 'objects' than ask to play with other children.
- **Plan to go to the park** every day at times when other children will be there. Take the Bag of Tricks and aim to look in it with your child in a place where children are likely to see and come and look at it too.
- **As children approach,** shuffle to the edge of the rug/bench and let your child have the children around him. If he asks where you are going just say, 'I am here looking at my phone for a minute.' He needs to see that you are busy. This is when he will 'manage alone'.
- **Guide him to take certain objects from the bag** on the swing, down the slide, on the roundabout. Children like the comfort of something in their hand. This is what is looked at by other children (rather than the child) and it really helps him if he feels shy.

WHAT TO SAY

- **Show the Bag of Tricks to your child.** He can look inside, but he should not take any items out. Say, 'Now. This is your Bag of Tricks.' It is something we take to the park or to friends' homes.' PAUSE. Say, 'It is for you to play with and share with other children. You can take these things on the slide, swing and anywhere in the park.'

ACTION IT!

- **Aim to visit friends' homes/parks and playgrounds** over a week. Two trips a day would be ideal.
- **When you arrive at the park** talk to your friends once you have set out your child's Bag of Tricks for him to look at.
- **Encourage the other children** to see what he has.

Is shyness a phase I can just expect him to grow out of?

You do not want to force your child to do things he doesn't want to do, but at the same time he needs a little 'push' to show that you believe in him and he is capable of things.

The key is not to over-focus on the shy behaviour. Do not label him 'shy' in front of your friends. Take little steps to guide him to play with other children.

- **Then stand back** and let him have space.
- **If there are no children around him,** guide him to go on the slide or a swing with a toy. You might have to go with him initially, to break the habit of him just standing by your side.
- **You should start to see little changes** as you guide him. If he wants to remain by your side let him, but don't engage with him too much. Sometimes a child just needs to get to a stage where he is bored before he makes the leap to go and play.

CARRY ON!

The aim is that you regularly socialise and always take the Bag of Tricks for your child to 'show' other children. Guide him to do this and take a step back. Perhaps play 'with him' initially and then step back.

> **TAKE NOTE!**
> Be consistent and you should see his confidence and independence start to grow.

My child demands my ipad/ phone all the time

'My daughter, Chloe, is four years old and whenever she sees me on my phone she demands that she plays the games that I have put on it for her. She will shout and scream, drawing attention to us in public. I give in to avoid having a scene.'

YOUR TOOLS

Screen Rules

Shout Spot

Bag of Tricks

Timer

See pages 54–71

YOUR SKILLS

Teacher Tone

You Choose

See pages 72–77

LET'S DO IT!

WHAT TO DO

- **Create your Screen Rules** (tool – see example below). It's best for your child to know when she can/cannot have the screen. If you don't have a framework of rules to work from she will continually ask to use it.

We do not have the TV/ipad/phone before school.
We do not use Mummy or Daddy's phone to play on. Only when they say I can as a big treat.
TV/ipad/phone time is after dinner. Time is 30 minutes.
On Saturday we have one hour of TV/ipad/phone after breakfast.
On Friday we have 'movie night' in our pyjamas.
We NEVER use the TV/ipad/phone without asking.
We do not use the ipad/phone when we are out.

- **Sit down with your child** and show her the Screen Rules. Stick them up somewhere for everyone to see. Say, 'We are all going to follow these. Look NO more ipad/phone when we are out, so don't ask.'

WHAT TO SAY

- **Bend down and make eye contact** with your child before going out and you think she is likely to ask for the ipad/phone. Say, 'Now, listen. We are going out and we have packed a bag of toys.' PAUSE. 'I am NOT going to give you my ipad/phone.' PAUSE. 'If you decide to shout, I will take you outside to a Shout Spot (tool) and we will stay there until you are ready to go back inside.' PAUSE. 'Do you understand?' Use a confident Teacher Tone (skill). You must truly believe that when she shouts you are going to take her outside.

ACTION IT!

- **Arrive at your destination** (such as a restaurant) and give her the Bag of Tricks (tool) so that she can entertain herself.

- **When she asks for the ipad/phone** initially distract her and say, 'We have talked about this. I am not giving you my ipad/phone now.' Distract her by saying she can go for a walk around, play a game with you at the table or draw a picture.

- **If she starts to raise her voice** and shout, stand up and ask her to 'come with you'. If she refuses use You choose (skill) say, 'Either you come when I ask or I will ask the waiter to tell you to leave.' If you say this you have to follow it through if she doesn't conform.

- **Take her hand and guide her to the bathroom.** Do not talk to her until you are there. Say, 'Now, we are going to stay here. Have a wee if you need one, wash your hands and when you are ready we can go back.' Speak in a calm way.

- **When she claims she is ready** say, 'Let's think of what we can do when we get back to the table'.

- **Suggest something** and then return to the table.

CARRY ON!

If you have set these rules you must stick to them because the next time you hand over your ipad/phone she will expect it whenever you are out and you will be back to square one.

You can always let her use your ipad/phone, say, for 20 minutes at the end of the meal, when the adults are having coffee. This is a clear rule where you set the Timer on your phone. When it buzzes you take the phone away again. This is about you being consistent. Your child will understand clearly when she can and cannot have the device.

Why can't she have my ipad/phone when we are out?

All children love ipads and phones! They all tend to want to spend longer on them than we would like, so the boundaries have to be clearly set.

When you are out socially, this is when your child needs to work on her social development. She needs to talk to adults, play with children and use her manners at the table. These are all life skills that everyone needs. However, you can let her use the screen at the end of the social occasion as a wind-down.

My child refuses to tidy her toys

'My daughter, Millie, is five years old and plays beautifully on her own. She has a wonderful imagination. However when I ask her to tidy her toys she just ignores me. "I don't want to" is often her reply.'

LET'S DO IT!

YOUR TOOLS

Shout Spot

See pages 54–71

WHAT TO DO
- **Let your child play as she usually does** and when it is time to tidy up accept that you are going to guide her by doing it together.

YOUR SKILLS

You Choose

See pages 72–77

WHAT TO SAY
- **Bend down and make eye contact** when the toys have all been played with.
- **Make sure you have her full attention.** Say, 'Now. I have decided that we are going to have a tidy-up dance!' PAUSE. 'We are going to tidy up together. I am not going to ask you to do it on your own. We are a team. Once we have finished we will put the music on and dance before dinner!'

ACTION IT!
- **Start by saying,** 'Now. It is time for dinner and we need to put your toys away ready for tomorrow.'
- **Give your child a box and say,** 'You put all the dolls in there. I will put all the cars in here.'

Why should my child tidy her toys away?

It is good practice for your child to understand that after playing she then needs to tidy away. Often a child will not know where to start when asked to tidy up. So she needs clear direction and tidying is a job you need to tackle together to begin with. You also need to be realistic in what you are asking of her because she might find the job overwhelming at first.

- **Work alongside one another,** say, 'Brilliant work! Now you pop the books on the shelf.' Give her the pile. 'I am going to put this board game away.'
- **Offer a reward at the end of the task.** Say, 'At the end of tidying I think we should put the music on and have a quick song and dance!'

CARRY ON!

If she refuses to help, you need to ask her to make a choice using the You Choose (skill). Say, 'You can help or go and sit on the Shout Spot (tool) on your own until you are ready to help.' PAUSE.

Now continue with your tidying and don't look at her. If she doesn't start to tidy, then take her to the Shout Spot. Say, 'You made your choice. Sit here and come in when you are ready to help.'

Leave her and return to the playroom. Tidy up some of the toys, but not all. Leave two or three types of toy and their boxes for her to tidy. If she comes back in and doesn't tidy you need to take her out again.

Remain consistent with this and you should find that tidying together becomes an efficiently done task at the end of the day.

My child is a bad loser

'When we play a family game Daniel, aged four, cannot bear to lose. He will refuse to continue if he is not winning throughout the game. He will get cross and shout and often accuses his sister of cheating. We have almost got to the stage where we let him win just for the sake of keeping the peace.'

YOUR TOOLS

Shout Spot

See pages 54–71

YOUR SKILLS

You Choose

See pages 72–77

LET'S DO IT!

WHAT TO DO

- **Have a plan** for how you are going to play the game. Decide as a family whether: the winner is the one who finishes first, the winner is the one who finishes last or you play in teams.
- **Have a talk** before the game starts. Make everyone aware of the Shout Spot (tool).

WHAT TO SAY

- **Sit at the table** with the game. Do not open the box yet. Say, 'Right! First we need to decide how we are going to play. Shall the winner be first or last – or shall we play in teams?' Ask your child to choose.
- **Now say,** 'Now, everyone who wants to play the game has to make a pact that they stay and play until the end. You cannot get cross or quit. Quitting is losing!'
- **Everyone has to put their hands on top of one another's** to make this pact. PAUSE.
- **Then say,** 'Now, if there is any shouting/getting cross you will be asked to leave the game and the room. You will go to the Shout Spot (tool) in the hallway or go to your bedroom until the game is over.' PAUSE.

ACTION IT!

- **Open the box** and begin the game.
- **Keep everything upbeat** and talk about other things as well as the game. For example, what you did today while they were at school.
- **The moment your child shows signs** of being cross, give him a warning using the You Choose (skill), 'Choose – calm down or leave the room.' PAUSE. 'That is a warning.'

Does it matter if he is a bad loser?

Many children find the concept of losing difficult. This is because they are very competitive – a quality that is likely to take them a long way in life! However, it is not nice to have a bad loser in the family and we often take a dim view of it. Not always coming first is a quality that comes with maturity so this is not something we can speed up.

- **If he gets cross a second time** you need to decide on a second and final warning or to send him out of the room to the Shout Spot.
- **Once he is out of the room** you close the door and exclude him.
- **When the game is over** you can then call him back, but you don't need to tell him who won. 'You weren't in the game any more so it doesn't matter.'

CARRY ON!

You need to remain consistent with this system so that your child realises that the moment his behaviour becomes unpleasant he is warned and then is out of the game.

The more you play, the easier he will find it to bite his tongue – he won't want to be excluded.

TAKE NOTE!
The bottom line is: your child does need to be able to continue a game through to the end, whether he comes first or not.

My child throws tantrums in public, especially in shops

'My son, Lucas, aged two and a half, will lie on the floor and scream and shout if he doesn't get his own way. I can manage this situation at home, but I don't know what to do when we are out. He often wants me to buy him things at the supermarket. When I say 'no' he will lie in the aisle and scream. The embarrassment of being watched by other shoppers makes me give in and let him have what he wants.'

YOUR TOOLS

Shout Spot

See pages 54–71

YOUR SKILLS

The Back

See pages 72–77

LET'S DO IT!

WHAT TO DO

- **Aim to spend three consecutive days** going to places (shops) that could cause tension and a possible tantrum in your child. The only way you are going to overcome this problem is for him to see that you are not going to change your mind, whether he shouts or not.

- **Think of the shops you are going to go to** and where the Shout Spot (tool) could be if you need one while you are there.

- **Before practising the Shout Spot in a shop,** establish a Shout Spot at home and use it several times before you go to the shops.

WHAT TO SAY

- **Bend down and make eye contact** with your child before you enter the shop. Say, 'Now, we are going to go into the shop to buy the food. You can have a comic at the end, but you are not putting anything else into the trolley.' PAUSE. 'If you start any silly shouting I am going to find a Shout Spot you can sit and shout on and when you have finished we will carry on shopping. It's just like the Shout Spot at home. Understand?'

- **If he doesn't respond** say, 'Let's be quick so we can buy your comic.'

ACTION IT!

- **Go into the shop in a positive frame of mind.** Trust that he will behave and that you can manage a tantrum if he has one.

- **The first time he picks something up** think of how to say 'no' in an upbeat way (see page 19). Try, 'We don't need those fruit yoghurts. Can you put these plain yoghurts in instead?' Pass him two items.

- **Continue walking with confidence.** Don't hover, waiting for a tantrum to start. Carry on with this attitude. Say, 'Pop that back and put this in instead. Two more aisles and we'll be at the comics!'
- **The key is to continue walking.**
- **If he does start to shout** abandon your trolley and take his hand. Act as you do at home. Say, 'Right, if you need to shout, do it here.' Sit him in the corner, out of the shoppers' way. This is the temporary Shout Spot. Say, 'When you are quiet we can find our trolley and finish our shopping.'
- **Have the confidence to stand close to him,** but have your back to him using The Back (skill) and look at your phone (act busy). He needs to get out his frustration. It is hard for a child to accept 'no', especially if he has always got his own way by shouting before.
- **Once the noise subsides** and you can hear the frustration has passed, bend down and say, 'Okay, let's go and find the trolley together.'
- **If he starts to shout again** you know you need to leave him longer. Eventually the shouting will stop. You will finish your shopping and buy the magazine.

CARRY ON!

It is hard when other shoppers walk past and see this scenario going on, but this is not something you will be doing every time you go shopping. Remain consistent and do the same two or three times and your child will understand that shopping is about you buying and choosing, not him.

Make sure that you do not find yourself some weeks letting him choose the shopping and then other weeks saying 'no'. You must remain consistent for him to fully understand. Set the rules before you go into the shop. Say, 'Today you can choose a fruit, a yoghurt and a comic' or 'Today you can choose a bubble bath, toothpaste and loo-roll colour!'

> **TAKE NOTE!**
> He shouldn't lose out on his comic. That was part of the shopping trip, not part of his punishment.

Why is it so important to be consistent?

The key to parenting is to remain consistent. It is very hard for your child to abide by a different set of rules at home to when he is out. You do not want to be in a situation where your child believes that whenever he is out and he wants something all he has to do is scream and shout and he will get it.

It isn't easy to stick to your usual parenting tactics and be consistent (especially when they involve your child being noisy) when you feel watched by others, but your primary concern is your child, not what other people think.

My child is happy to go and sit on the Shout Spot!

'My daughter, Erin, aged three, rarely listens to what I say. I send her to the Shout Spot and she happily sits there and then comes and says "sorry". She then misbehaves all over again. The Shout Spot clearly isn't working.'

YOUR TOOLS

Shout Spot

See pages 54–71

YOUR SKILLS

Ask, Tell, Warn, Act

See pages 72–77

LET'S DO IT!

WHAT TO DO

- **Make the Shout Spot (tool) in the hallway,** away from any entertainment. It needs to be a boring place to sit.
- **Be prepared to leave your child** there for as long as it takes her to calm herself down and learn from being there.

WHAT TO SAY

- **Go into the hallway and sit together** on the Shout Spot. Say, 'Now, this is where our Shout Spot is. When you are not listening or are shouting I am going to ask you to stop. If you don't, then we will come out here into the hallway to the Shout Spot.' PAUSE. Say, 'You will sit on the Shout Spot until I am ready for you to come back into the kitchen.'

ACTION IT!

- **Aim for there to be challenges** for your child over three consecutive days that could cause her to need to visit the Shout Spot.
- **Follow the Ask, Tell, Warn, Act** (skill) and then calmly take her to the Shout Spot in the hallway if that doesn't work.
- **Close the door behind you** so she is left alone. The environment must be safe and boring. Ensure the front door is locked.
- **Now be prepared to wait.** Your child may start with silence, but then expect the 'old way', in which you go and get her because she is quiet.
- **She will then start to call for you** and moan and groan. This could build to a shout and a bang on the door.
- **Now you know the Shout Spot is working.** She has now realised you are in control – not her.

Why isn't the Shout Spot working?

Some children are very smart and know that they are going to be on the Shout Spot for only a short time. They just sit quietly and wait for the time to be over. However, the fact is that you haven't left your child there for long enough.

She needs to get to a stage where she is bored, feels she is missing out and wants to be back in the room with everyone else.

For some children this can be 20 to 30 minutes of silence before they start showing signs of not wanting to be on the Shout Spot any more.

- **She will shout and then you will hear her calm down** to a whimper and a moan. At this stage, open the door and say, 'All finished? You can come into the kitchen when you are ready.'
- **When she comes in and engages in play** that you have set up for her, simply say, 'Next time Mummy asks you to (name task), please do it and then we don't have to visit the Shout Spot.'

CARRY ON!

It is so important that you remain consistent and leave her to sound frustrated at being in the hallway on the Shout Spot. If you find that at times you let her back in before she has felt the pain of the consequence it will break the rhythm of the Shout Spot working.

Over time she will shout and show her frustration more quickly and the process will become far shorter. Eventually the Shout Spot will be visited once in a blue moon!

> **TAKE NOTE!**
> It is vital that the Shout Spot is away from the rest of the family.

My child swears

'My son, Simon, aged four, attends nursery school five days a week. To my dismay, he has recently come home using the f*** word. He says it when he is cross or if we have asked him to do something he doesn't like. He also says it to get a reaction from us. Our concern is that he says it when we are out and about or socialising with friends.'

LET'S DO IT!

YOUR TOOLS

Shout Spot

See pages 54–71

WHAT TO DO

- **First of all, ignore it when your child swears.** Walk away and act as if you haven't heard him. This means that you are not to say anything to him. He may just be doing it to get a reaction from you.

- **After a while** he will get bored swearing and not getting a reaction. Hopefully he will stop swearing altogether at this point.

- **If the bad language continues** you need to take more serious action. If he is using it increasingly, let your child know that he IS allowed to use this word, but only when he is on his own in his bedroom. This is going to be the Shout Spot (tool).

- **Each time your child says the word,** take his hand and take him to his bedroom and close the door. Do NOT say anything to him as you are doing this. He might be shouting, 'I won't say it. I am not saying it now', but you need to continue to take him to his room.

WHAT TO SAY

- **Sit down with your child and make eye contact.** Say, 'Now. I have something to ask you.' PAUSE. 'You keep saying f***. What is it? What does it mean?' PAUSE. He is likely to look at you without an answer. Now say, 'Well. I don't like you saying it, so I have decided that you can say it in your bedroom on your own.' PAUSE. 'When you say it, I am going to take you to your bedroom. You can say it there. I will close your door and you can come downstairs when you have finished.' PAUSE. 'Do you understand?' He is likely to remain quiet.

- **Now move onto doing something else** and leave him to digest what has been said to him.

Why is it important for my child to stop swearing?

Most parents hate to hear their child swearing – it reflects badly on them as it makes it seem as though swearing is part of their vocabulary too. It's embarrassing! Your child is probably intrigued by this new word that he has heard in the playground and even though he has no idea what it means, he enjoys the reaction and attention he gets from adults when he uses it. Your child needs to be corrected in this because he has to learn that he can't just go around saying what he likes and upsetting people.

ACTION IT!

- **At first ignore the swearing.**

- **If it then seems to be increasing,** talk to your child about what you are going to do each time he uses this word (see opposite).

- **It is now important that you follow through** with what you have said. Every time he uses the word, either ignore him or silently take him to his bedroom. He will not like going to his room, but you must follow through and do what you said you would do. The message is that you CAN swear – just do it away from others in your own space.

CARRY ON!

The key to success is to remain consistent. You can either ignore your child or react to his swearing in a calm way. If you find yourself saying, 'Don't say that' you can be sure that the swearing will continue because the main reason your child is speaking this way is to get you to react.

My child lies

'My daughter, Sadie, aged three, has started to tell lies. She will take a biscuit from the cupboard but deny it was her. She will spill something and say that she didn't do it. Last week she hit her younger brother over the head with a toy, which I saw, but she said, "It wasn't me".'

YOUR TOOLS

Incentive System
(fill-it-up marble jar)

Shout Spot

See pages 54–71

YOUR SKILLS

The Back

See pages 72–77

LET'S DO IT!

WHAT TO DO

- **Ignore the smaller 'lies'.** You might find that by ignoring them they go away and you do not need to say anything about them. You don't even need to look at her in a strange way. Turn your back using The Back (skill) and continue doing something else.

- **If the lying becomes dramatically worse,** it is time to sit her down and talk to her.

- **Create an Incentive System** (tool) to help stop your child lying. The fill-it-up marble jar is a good one to try, but devise one that works best for your child.

WHAT TO SAY

- **Find a time when it is quiet** with just the two of you. Say, 'Now. I want to talk to you about telling the truth.' PAUSE. 'You can tell Mummy anything and she will not be cross.' PAUSE. 'I have decided that every time I ask you a question and you tell me the truth I am going to give you one of these marbles.' PAUSE. 'The marble goes in this jar and when it is full you will get a prize for telling the truth.' PAUSE. 'This means no more lies and story-telling.' PAUSE. 'If I do ask you a question and you answer with a lie I am going to ask you to spend time sitting on the Shout Spot (tool).' Take her to the bottom stair or hallway and show her where you mean.

ACTION IT!

- **Find the marbles and the jar** and start the process straight away.

- **Ask her several questions** that involve a clear answer. For example: 'What did you have for breakfast?', 'Did you wash your hands after going to the loo?' or 'Did you have a wee before getting into the bath?' The more you ask questions and the more marbles she can receive the faster she will correct her lying.

Why is it important for my child to tell the truth?

No one likes a child, or indeed a grown-up, who seems sneaky and is always trying to get out of things by telling lies – no matter how small. All parents want to bring up their child to be 'nice', to have integrity and be honest. So the sooner you jump on this issue and nip it in the bud, the sooner your child will get the message that lying is a very poor habit to get into and not worth the trouble.

- **Be consistent** and when she does lie take her to the Shout Spot and say, 'Stay there until I am ready. I don't like it when you tell a lie. I cannot give you a marble when you do that.'

CARRY ON!

It is very important that you remain consistent – you either praise her and persevere with the fill-it-up marble Incentive System or take her to the Shout Spot. The moment you stop reinforcing your words, your child will think that you do not mean it any more and you risk the lying returning. You will be back to square one.

My child hits both me and my husband

'Our son, Adam, is aged three and a half. He is very well behaved with our extended family and at nursery, but at home he lashes out at me and my husband if we say "no". He will come up behind me and hit my back and if I bend down to talk to him he might slap my face.'

YOUR TOOLS

Shout Spot

See pages 54–71

LET'S DO IT!

WHAT TO DO

- **Act immediately.** This behaviour is your child being violent and you must do something straight away when it happens.
- **When you have to say 'no' to him,** do it in a positive way and then walk away. For example say, 'Dinner is in 15 minutes. You can have a biscuit after dinner, not now.'
- **Don't stand and wait for him to react.** Walk away and continue doing something else.
- **If he does hit you** take him to the Shout Spot (tool) in the hallway or his bedroom. He must remain there until you go and get him.

WHAT TO SAY

- **Sit down with your child** and let him know what you are going to be doing every time he hits you or your partner.
- **Say,** 'You are a very good boy and we love you very much.' PAUSE. 'We don't like it when you hit. This is a horrible thing to do and you are not a horrible boy.' PAUSE.
- **Now go on to say,** 'We have decided that if you hit us you are going to be taken to the Shout Spot until we are ready to come and get you.' PAUSE. 'It would be much nicer if you just didn't hit.' PAUSE. 'Do you understand? Hitting? You are on the Shout Spot.'

ACTION IT!

- **It is important that you have a Shout Spot** where you can take your child if he hits you and you can close the door on him. This door, ideally, remains shut until you are ready to open it.

Why my child should never hit other people

If your child is continually hitting you to get his own way, he sees this as 'normal' behaviour. It is something he does without thinking about it and it is a strong sign that he is in charge of the situation, not you.

It is highly undesirable to think that this is 'normal' – and he might start to behave with his friends this way.

You need to teach your child that life is about compromise and that he mustn't believe that being physical will get him what he wants.

- **Give it time.** He needs to sit out on the Shout Spot and you need to hear him protesting and being cross that he has had to be on his own.

- **Only open the door** once he is quiet and calm. Simply open the door and say, 'All finished? You can come in here when you are ready.'

- **Don't wait for a reaction.** Simply have something for him to play with when he comes back into the room.

CARRY ON!

It is important to be consistent when you are dealing with this issue and to ALWAYS remove your child from the room you are in when he hits you. DO NOT ignore him sometimes but then react at other times. It is important for your child to realise that violence leaves him on his own. Very soon you will see an improvement in his behaviour.

My child won't let me cut her nails

'My daughter, Lily, aged three, will scream and shout, refusing to let me cut her nails.'

YOUR TOOLS

Incentive System
(paper flower)

See pages 54–71

LET'S DO IT!

WHAT TO DO

- **First, teach your child to use** scissors and get used to cutting different things (paper, cardboard, fabric, etc).
- **Sit and cut your nails in front of her,** both fingers and toes.
- **Create a Incentive System paper flower** (tool) to help her with having her nails cut. Every time you cut a nail she cuts off a petal. When all the petals are gone, she wins a prize (20 petals for 20 nails).
- **Think of a song** that you sing while her nails are being cut. This makes her aware that the cutting will stop when the song comes to an end.

WHAT TO SAY

- **While you are sitting with her at the table** and she is cutting paper, say, 'Now you are brilliant with scissors and so am I. I have got a great idea here for cutting your nails.'
- **Produce the paper flower Incentive System.** You could make it flat (on paper) or standing in a pot made of cardboard. Use your creativity to engage your child. Say, 'Now, I have my nail scissors and you have your scissors. I will cut one of your nails and then you can cut a petal off the flower.' PAUSE. 'When all the petals have been cut off you get a prize! Choose which nail and then which petal.'

ACTION IT!

- **Try and act on this** as soon as you have given your speech, so have your nail scissors in your lap.
- **After saying,** 'Choose which finger', strike while the iron is hot. Take her hand and say, 'Look at the flower! What colour petal are you going to cut off first?'
- **As she looks at the flower,** cut the nail! Praise her enormously and let her cut a petal and then repeat the process.

Why are some things not worth battling over?

There are certain things that are not worth the battle and these are the situations where you cannot win! If your child refuses to eat, use the loo, have her hair/nails cut there is no way you can force her because she is in control of her body. The best course of action is to teach her to do these tasks by herself.

- **Move from the fingers to the toes.**
- **Have a small prize** wrapped in foil that you can hide somewhere in the house. She has to find it!

CARRY ON!

It is important not to force your child to cut her nails. If she protests, immediately say, 'Fine. I will put the flower up here on the fridge/window sill and when you are ready we can win a prize!'

If you find the Incentive System is not getting you anywhere, remember that this is not an issue to create a battle over. Instead, you could aim to cut her nails when she is in a deep sleep at night – the ideal time being at least one hour after she has fallen asleep. Alternatively you can file down her nails or use clippers not scissors.

BEHAVIOUR SCENARIO **48**

My child is a thumb-sucker!

'My child, Finn, sucks his thumb at every opportunity. I am worried that it is affecting his speech and teeth development.'

LET'S DO IT!

WHAT TO DO
- **Talk to your partner** so that you know you are both 100 per cent dedicated to making this change. Consistency is the key.

Continued ▶

- **Establish a Sucking Spot,** which is a place where your child goes to suck his thumb. He does not suck his thumb anywhere else. His bedroom is probably the best place to choose.

WHAT TO SAY

- **Get down to your child's level** and say, 'Now. We know you like to suck your thumb, but we have decided that you are now old enough to understand that it is not something you do in front of other people. When you are home and wanting to suck your thumb we are going to guide you to your bedroom. This is going to be the Sucking Spot. You can suck your thumb all you wish there, but not downstairs.' PAUSE. 'You will have to try hard when the TV is on. You can sit on your hands or put gloves on!' Say, 'If you put your thumb in your mouth during TV time we will have to turn it off.'

ACTION IT!

- **You are not telling your child** that he cannot suck his thumb, you are simply saying that it can only take place on the Sucking Spot in his bedroom.

- **Remain consistent** and every time you see the thumb go to his mouth guide him to his room. He will say, 'I have taken it out now', but simply say, 'You might change your mind. Go and have a little suck and then come down when you are ready.' You are kindly excluding him.

- **At times you will have to lift him** from behind to take him to the Sucking Spot if he does need to visit it regularly. Eventually you will see a change.

TAKE NOTE!
You can use this process for other unappealing habits such as nose-picking. or hair-twiddling.

CARRY ON!

Be consistent. Support one another and watch him to ensure the thumb is not going in while you are not looking. This is a process of retraining his brain, so keep on going and use his bedroom and the Sucking Spot!

Some habits you have no control over

Your child's thumb is connected to him so ultimately there is nothing you can do to stop the sucking. This is something your child will decide to stop when he is ready. All you can do is restrict your child about where he can do it.

Potty-training scenarios

Many parents worry about potty training – usually quite unnecessarily as most children train themselves when they are ready. However, there are a few tips you can try to encourage your child along the right path – he or she will get there in the end.

Importance of routine
Setting up, and sticking to, a good daily routine will help with potty training. For example, you can start the habit of always getting your child to go to the loo before leaving the house or going to bed.

Don't force the issue
Potty training is not something that you can force to happen. It will happen, sooner or later, whatever you do. So it's best not to worry about it and better not to make a big deal about it. Never punish your child for having accidents.

Get some good habits going
Good hygiene habits are things that can be taught – the most important being hand-washing, so this is definitely something that you can encourage you child to adopt. This section gives you plenty of good Tools and Skills to help you achieve your ends.

My child always refuses the loo when I ask him to go

'No matter how many times I ask Carlo if he needs the loo, he always says 'no'. He doesn't tend to have accidents, but he dashes to the loo right at the last minute, which can be very annoying.'

LET'S DO IT!

WHAT TO DO

- **Aim to get your child** to think for himself. If this means he has a few accidents along the way, this is fine. After all, we learn from our mistakes. Remember that your child's bladder can probably hold for two and a half to three hours. Some children can last even longer.

- **STOP asking him** if he wants to 'go'.

WHAT TO SAY

- **Bend down to your child's level and say,** 'Now. I have decided that I am not going to ask you if you need the loo any more. You are going to go when you are ready and if you need some help, just ask me.' PAUSE. 'The only time we are going to use the loo is before we leave

Why should I NOT ask if my child needs the loo?

Using the potty/loo is something your child decides to do when he is ready. It is a huge step in his development because he is learning how to read his body. However, this can be exhausting for you in the initial stages.

If you continually ask your child if he needs the loo you are doing two things:

1. You are preventing him from thinking for himself. He needs to make the decision about when he needs to 'empty'. A child who uses the loo because he is told to is not thinking for himself. This is

not being 100 per cent potty trained because if you don't take him to the loo, the chances are he will forget and have accidents.

2. You are putting pressure on him and focusing on something he doesn't want you to focus on, so there is a very high chance that when you ask, 'Do you need the loo?' he is likely to say, 'No'. If you put yourself in his shoes and you were frequently asked if you needed the loo, you would probably reply with more than just 'No'!

the house and when we first get home after being out.' PAUSE. 'Do you understand? I won't ask you any more. You can do this. You know your body best. You know when wees or poos need to come. Now go off and play.'

ACTION IT!
- **This is simple.** The action is to do nothing!

CARRY ON!
Accidents are likely to happen and this is all part of the learning process. If after three days there are more accidents than successes, you need to ask yourself whether your child is truly ready for potty training. Don't get anxious if he is nearer to three than two years of age before success is in the air. He will do it when the time is right for him. When he is ready, it all happens very quickly. Pop the nappy back on and if he doesn't protest, you'll know he wasn't ready in the first place.

POTTY-TRAINING SCENARIO **2**

My child insists on standing to wee, but he tinkles on the tiles

'My child, Arthur, has been potty trained for six months. He now wants to stand like Daddy. But this is causing a real mess.'

LET'S DO IT!

WHAT TO DO
- **Ensure your son knows** where his tummy button is.
- **Buy a ping-pong ball** to be used as the Ping-Pong Face (tool) and draw a face on it in waterproof ink. Or buy some colourful hundreds and thousands for the Wee a Rainbow (tool) – you sprinkle them around the toilet bowl and your child can flush after weeing 'a rainbow' and see all the colours merge.

YOUR TOOLS

Ping-Pong Face

Wee-a-Rainbow

Incentive System chart (optional)

See pages 54–71

YOUR SKILLS

Tummy Push

See pages 72–77

Continued ▶

Why can I let my child have a few accidents?

Initially, the only way your child learns about potty training is to have a few accidents. He needs to have the experience and know that this is an uncomfortable feeling that he wants to avoid in the future.

It is different, however, when your child has learnt how to use the loo but is getting most of it on the floor due to poor aim. This is when the lessons of hygiene need to come into play.

WHAT TO SAY

- **A good time** to have this conversation is towards the end of breakfast, while your child is still sitting. Say, 'I've got something to show you in the bathroom. Just tell me when you need a wee.'
- **Now wait** for the time to come!
- **Take him to the loo** and point into it. Say, 'Now. This little man is the Ping-Pong Face who lives in our loo. He's quite strange because he likes to be washed with wee. He is called Mr Wee Head!' PAUSE. 'Aim at him so we don't get wee on the floor.' PAUSE. 'Now after a wee what's really funny is that when you flush he never goes away, but he gets a wash ready for the next wee shower!' PAUSE. 'Then wash your hands and get ready for your next visit to the loo.'

TAKE NOTE!
Yes, you can poo on the Ping-Pong Face! Boys love to know this!

ACTION IT!

- **While you are standing at the loo** and have just explained the Ping-Pong Face and/or Wee a Rainbow, show your child how, if he pushes his tummy just below his tummy button using the Tummy Push (skill), this will cause his willy to point in the right direction.
- **Bend over from above him** and push on his tummy. You will see the effect. By teaching him this and giving him something to aim at your tiles will be saved!

CARRY ON!

Each time your child visits the loo, quietly visit afterwards to ensure the floor is dry, that the loo has been flushed and that there is evidence of some form of hand-washing. If he needs a stronger incentive, you could start an Incentive System chart (tool) where he gains a sticker after each successful visit to the loo.

My child refuses to wipe her own bottom

'My child, Elsie, is five and is capable of wiping her own bottom, but at home she shouts for me, saying, "It might not be clean enough".'

LET'S DO IT!

WHAT TO DO
- **Ensure you have plenty of loo roll** in the house.

WHAT TO SAY
- **When the time comes for wiping,** guide your child to remain on the loo and lean forward with paper in her hand. Explain, 'Now, bring the paper from front to back.' PAUSE.
- **Teach her the Wipe Till White routine** (skill). 'Wipe! Note the poo/put paper down the loo. And wipe! Note the poo/put paper down the loo. Until it's white! Once the paper is white the job is done!'

ACTION IT!
- **Be firm and clear with yourself.** Now you have made the decision NEVER to wipe your child's bottom again – remain consistent.
- **Give your child the little talk** when she next calls you for assistance!
- **Once the job is done** bend down and say, 'Now, you can do this on your own. If you do call, I am not coming.' PAUSE. 'You are grown up.'
- **Move on to another activity.** Leave her to think.

CARRY ON!
Next time your child calls you from the loo, ignore her. She can do it.

YOUR SKILLS
Wipe Till White

See pages 72–77

TAKE NOTE!
Teach your daughter to wipe from front to back and your son to wipe from back to front.

Why is it important for my child to wipe herself?

This tends to be the last potty-training stage and it may be one your child resists. It is the final task to independence in the loo but once taught, your job is done! The sooner she is self-sufficient the easier it is on everyone and it is a wonderful feeling when your child realises she doesn't need adult help.

My child takes all his clothes off when he goes to the loo

'We know when our son, Luke, has been to the loo because suddenly he is naked! He then sees no point in getting dressed again!'

YOUR TOOLS

Incentive System
(fill-it-up pasta jar)

See pages 54–71

YOUR SKILLS

The Back

See pages 72–77

LET'S DO IT!

WHAT TO DO

- **Find a glass jar to make into an Incentive System fill-it-up pasta jar** (tool) and enough pasta (in a tub) to fill it.

WHAT TO SAY

- **Sit down with your child** at a time when he is not needing the loo.

- **Show him the empty jar** and the tub of pasta. He should not touch the pasta at this stage. Say, 'Now. Every time you go to the loo I am going to give you a piece of pasta and you are going to put it in the jar.' PAUSE. 'When the jar is full there is going to be a prize!' PAUSE. Say, 'One piece of pasta for going to the loo.' Give him a piece to put in the jar. Now say,'Two pieces of pasta for keeping your clothes on!' Give him two pieces. Say, 'Two pieces for a flush and washing your hands. That is five pieces of pasta altogether.'

ACTION IT!

- **As your child goes to the loo,** follow him and simply say, 'Great. You are going to the loo. That is a piece of pasta. Remember to keep your clothes on. That's two pieces of pasta!'

- **Walk away and trust him.** If he comes out naked you need to take him back to the bathroom.

- **Bend down** and make eye contact. Say, 'Now, I forgot to say. If this happens, you then need to get dressed. Clothes on and you get three pieces of pasta!' PAUSE. Say, 'You are to stay in here and get dressed. You can only come out when your clothes are on.'

- **Now confidently close the door** using The Back (skill) and leave him in there.

- **If he comes out shouting** you need to simply take him straight back. Whatever he asks you for, say, 'Yes, we can do that/have that/talk about that when we are dressed.'

TAKE NOTE!
It should take a week to fill the jar. Calculate this beforehand, so you know roughly the amount of pasta and size of jar you need.

Does it matter if my child removes all his clothes?

There is no need to worry about your child removing his clothes – it's quite common for a child to think he might dirty his clothes while he is going to the loo. The challenge is that he won't put them on again! You do not want him to make this part of his daily routine, so the sooner you help him correct it the better.

CARRY ON!

You must remain consistent and after three or four days your child will understand that he is not going to be able to leave the loo until he is dressed. He will shout initially, but let him do this. This is part of the realisation that things are changing and he has to conform.

Stay strong. It's worth it!

TAKE NOTE!
You can always look at things like this as a phase, but you have to decide how long you want to wait to see if it passes without guidance.

My child refuses to let me in when he needs the loo

'When my child, Hamish, aged four, goes to the loo he insists he shuts the door. I can't see what he's doing. He doesn't have accidents.'

LET'S DO IT!

YOUR SKILLS

Sniff Soap Test

See pages 72–77

WHAT TO DO
- **Buy a pump-action soap** – enjoyable and easy for your child to use.

WHAT TO SAY
- **Find a moment when your child is not due** to visit the loo. Say, 'I am not going to come with you to the loo any more. I trust you to flush and wash your hands after you have been.' PAUSE.
- **Explain the Sniff Soap Test** (skill). Say, 'The only thing I am going to do is the Sniff Soap Test. When you come out of the bathroom and I have heard the loo flush, I am going to ask you to come to me so I can sniff your hands.' PAUSE. 'If they smell of soap I know you have done a perfect job. If they don't, I will ask you to go and give your hands a proper wash.' PAUSE. 'Is this okay? That's what I am going to do.'

TAKE NOTE!
You know in your heart of hearts that there is no need to escort your son to the loo. Think yourself lucky. It's a job that you no longer have to do!

ACTION IT!
- **Start the process of listening** for the flush and then sniffing his hands. Sometimes you can just go to him and sniff them. Don't always make it that he has to 'report to you' as this shows you don't trust him.

CARRY ON!
Remain consistent. Try not to return to old ways of policing him in the loo. Your child is independent – let him do what he can on his own.

Why should I trust my child?

By trusting your child to deal with everything by himself when he goes to the loo you allow him to be independent and to feel grown up. The Sniff Soap Test is a way to start trusting him to do what he needs to do.

My child refuses to wash her hands after going to the loo

'Kitty is three and is great at using the loo, but refuses to wash her hands afterwards. I rub her hands with a hand wipe before she plays.'

LET'S DO IT!

WHAT TO DO
- **Buy some toy fish** and put them in a sink of water with some bubbles.
- **Place a bucket next to the sink** to make into the Ocean Sink (tool).

WHAT TO SAY
- **Take your child into the bathroom** and ask her to look in the sink. Say, 'Now, every time you come for a wee or a poo, once you have finished and wiped your bottom you are going to wash the fish.' PAUSE. Say, 'Rub the fish in the bubbly water and then put them in the bucket.' PAUSE. 'Then dry your hands and come out to play!'

ACTION IT!
- **Once you have given your child the talk,** guide her out to play. It is only a matter of time before she visits the loo.
- **When she comes out,** rather than say, 'Hands!' ask, 'Have you put the fish in the bucket?' If she replies 'no' guide her back to wash the fish.

CARRY ON!
Be consistent. When the novelty of the fish wears off, put toy spiders, snakes or tiny dolls into the sink. If resistance is still strong start an Incentive System (tool), such as a chart. The key is for your child to realise that she cannot come out of the loo until the fish are clean. Keep returning her and eventually she will get bored of being asked and she will just do it.

YOUR TOOLS

Ocean Sink

Incentive System (optional)

See pages 54–71

Does it really matter if she doesn't wash her hands?

It is good practice for children to understand about germs and how they can make us ill. Washing hands regularly can keep germs away and stop us becoming unwell. Children from age two can understand this concept.

My child will not poo in the loo. She asks for a nappy

'My daughter, Zoe, was toilet-trained at two years of age, but six months on she is still not using the loo to poo. She opens her bowels during her lunch nap or at bedtime.'

LET'S DO IT!

WHAT TO DO

- **Don't be in a rush.** Your child is only two and a half years old, which is young to be potty trained, so you can leave her for a while to just poo in her nappy during her rest period.
- **In time you can progress** to placing the nappy on the potty before rest time and leaving her to sit there with a book for a time without you in the room.
- **After doing this for three days** you will know whether there is progress or whether she isn't yet ready to take this step.
- **If she isn't ready,** simply return to her pooing in her nappy at rest time.

WHAT TO SAY

- **There isn't anything to say** to your child. She will make the change when she is ready. It is important not to focus on this issue too much, otherwise you could make a problem out of something you have no control over.

ACTION IT!

- **Best to ignore this issue.**
- **If, after two months** you wish to place the nappy over the potty, do so, but remember to read your child accurately. If she isn't ready, then stop and return to your usual system.

CARRY ON!

This is a delicate subject, but if you do not make an issue of it and you ignore the behaviour, it will correct itself.

Is pooing only in a nappy a common problem?

Most children tend to grasp the urinating part of potty training long before the opening of bowels. This is due to the fact that your child can see what is happening when she wees because it takes place around the front, whereas the idea of something substantial leaving her body at the back can cause her slight concern.

This doesn't mean that your child is distressed; she is just thinking about it.

It is important not to focus too much on the issue because this can cause your child to start withholding her stools, leading to discomfort and severe constipation. The important issue is that she is opening her bowels daily – or every other day.

TAKE NOTE!
Your child won't be heading off to school at age five in a nappy – relax!

My child still has one or two accidents a week

'My child, Susie, is fully potty trained, but when excited or distracted she will wee. She stops what she is doing and dashes to the loo.'

LET'S DO IT!

WHAT TO DO
- **Sit with your child** (not during a loo visit) and discuss 'little accidents'.
- **Reassure her** that you are not concerned, upset or worried about them. Make her aware that it does happen to other people.

WHAT TO SAY
- **Explain what you are going to do.** Say, 'Now, I don't want you to worry if you have a little accident.' PAUSE. Say, 'I am going to leave a basket of clean knickers in the loo and if you need to change them, do.' PAUSE. 'If we are out, I will have some spare knickers in my bag.'

ACTION IT!
- **Place the basket of knickers** in the loo. Show them to your child and say, 'I won't talk about it. I trust you that if your knickers are wet you will change them'. PAUSE. 'If you need me you can always ask.'

CARRY ON!
Once you have made this arrangement you must stick with it. Ensure that the accidents are only one or two times a week. Remember that she doesn't want to wet her knickers and doesn't mean to do it.

Should I be concerned about a weekly accident?

The answer to this is 'not at all'. If a child is potty trained the majority of the time yet on occasion excitement gets the better of her it is not something to be concerned about.

Simply give her some fresh knickers and send her to the loo to change. Say, 'Not a problem. These things happen. You are not the only one.'

It is important not to make a fuss or ask her about this. Gloss over it because it is not a major concern.

My child always has damp pants at the end of the day

'Lewis has just turned three and since going to nursery at two and a half he comes home with slightly damp pants. This doesn't tend to happen so much at home.'

LET'S DO IT!

WHAT TO DO
- **Ignore the fact** that on nursery days your son's pants are slightly damp. Nursery is a busy place with a lot to remember. Going to the loo is something most children rush because they want to return to play.

WHAT TO SAY
- **Don't say anything at all.**

ACTION IT!
- **When he arrives home** from nursery you can suggest changing clothing due to them being 'nursery clothes' or slightly dirty. This is your chance to change the pants.
- **If you can see that your child's skin** is irritated, put some barrier cream on him before he attends school and when he returns home. If he asks you about this simply say, 'Sometimes your pants are a little wet and your skin goes red because it doesn't like it.' PAUSE. 'This cream should stop the redness.'

CARRY ON!
Be consistent and continue to ignore it and change clothing after school. In time this issue will correct itself – after all, it only happens at nursery.

Why should I ignore slightly damp pants?

There are certain things that are not behavioural traits, but phases that will eventually pass. If you focus on such traits too much you will turn them into an issue. This is one of those things.

My child always has an accident when we are out

'No sooner have we arrived at the park or café than Matthew has done a wee!'

LET'S DO IT!

WHAT TO DO

- **Get a stool** and leave it on your doorstep so that your child can reach the doorbell to use the Family Loo Stop Bell (tool).

WHAT TO SAY

- **Before heading out** on a family trip sit down with your child and his siblings and explain that there is a new house rule. It is important that you have eye contact with the children. Say, 'Now, before we go out, everyone, Mummy and Daddy included, has to visit the loo.' PAUSE. 'Everyone is to do a wee. Even if it is very, very small.'

Why must I keep calm when my child has an accident?

Getting angry can really lower your child's self esteem and it doesn't achieve anything positive. You need to remember that most of the time your child does not want to have accidents – he's not doing it on purpose or just to annoy you.

You might even find that your child thrives on the attention and continues to do it to see your reaction.

PAUSE. 'After visiting the loo put on your coat and shoes, stand on the doorstep and ring the doorbell!' PAUSE. 'Once everyone has rung the doorbell, it is time to go.' PAUSE. 'The rule is you can only ring the bell if you have had a wee.' PAUSE. 'Does everyone understand?' You need to hear a response. Ideally you want to leave the house 30 minutes after this.

> **TAKE NOTE!**
> Keep calm and remember – all children get there in the end!

ACTION IT!

- **When it is time to go out** announce, 'Doorbell-ringing time. Can everyone visit the loo, please?'
- **At this stage** you need to take your child (Matthew) to the loo.
- **Stand him/sit him by/on the loo** and say, 'Wee now and it won't happen when we are out. That would be great!'
- **Stand outside the door** and leave him to wee. He needs to be alone to focus on what he has to do.
- **If he claims he cannot go** say, 'Wait a minute and one will come.'
- **Once he has been,** have him put on his coat and shoes and ring the bell. Ideally you want him to be first – to boost his confidence. Say, 'Okay, everyone, Matthew has done as he was asked. Let's visit the loo and get going.'

CARRY ON!

It is important that you remain consistent with this process. The chances are that if your child empties his bladder before leaving the house he should be fine for two to three hours.

You can follow the same principle if you want him to use the loo once you are out, before returning to the car. He can push the horn of the car when he has had a wee and it is time to go!

The key is to persevere in getting him to use the loo before leaving the house.

My child won't use the school loo and wees on the way home

'Our daughter, Holly, is quite shy and doesn't like to ask to leave the classroom to use the loo. She holds it in all day, comes out of school and "explodes" on the journey home.'

YOUR TOOLS

Incentive System
(wee routine chart)

See pages 54–71

LET'S DO IT!

WHAT TO DO

- **Sit down with your child** one day after school and let her know what you are going to do. Explain the Incentive System wee routine chart (tool). See an example chart below:

Day	Before school	At morning break	After lunch time play	Before leaving school	Total
Monday					
Tuesday					
Wednesday					
Thursday					
Friday					

WHAT TO SAY

- **After school when an accident has occurred** sit down with your child on her own and explain the change you are going to make. Show her the wee routine chart. Say, 'Now. I was the same as you at school – I didn't want to leave the class to go to the loo. This is how I stopped myself needing a wee in class.' PAUSE. Point at the chart and say, 'These are the times in the day to go and have a wee.' PAUSE. 'Your bladder is a bag that holds all the waste liquid in your body. It is important that we don't let it get too full. That's when we have an accident.' PAUSE. 'It is best to empty it little and often. Now, do you think you could use the loo at these times? List them. When you get home from school you can put a sticker in each box if you used the loo.

Why guide my child to use the loo during breaks?

Many children find it hard to ask to leave the classroom if they want to go to the loo. This is often due to the fact that they don't want to miss out on anything. They enjoy learning.

Rather than guide her to put up her hand and ask (which she is unlikely to do anyway), guide her to use the loo at breaktime and lunchtime. Tell her, 'When the bell rings for afternoon lessons – go to the loo'.

- **When the wee routine chart is finished** after one week give your child a prize and then begin again the following week, if necessary. PAUSE. Say, 'I think this is something you can do.' PAUSE. Say, 'At the end of the school day when I pick you up you can run back into school to use the loo if you wish. This means you won't be uncomfortable when we are walking home. This will stop the distressing end-of-day accident happening.'

ACTION IT!

- **Start the day after you have explained it** and ensure a sticker is on the wee routine chart before she leaves for school (for visiting the loo before leaving the house). You now have to trust her. Say, 'Try your best to use the loo at morning break and after lunch break. I will remind you quietly when I collect you from school.' PAUSE. 'Using the wee routine chart is fun and it leads to a prize!'

CARRY ON!

It is important that you continue with the wee routine chart for the full week. The aim is not that she has to visit the loo both at morning break and at lunch, but that she doesn't have an accident on the way home from school. If she only goes to the loo at the beginning and end of school but manages to concentrate in class and her body is fine then this is wonderful and deserves a prize.

After two weeks of following the wee routine she is very likely to have found her pattern for visiting the loo – so she is not uncomfortable.

> **TAKE NOTE!**
> If you need to ask your child's teacher to quietly prompt her at morning break and before afternoon class, do so. It could be helpful for your child to know that this is something you are all quietly supporting her on together.

My child wets the bed every night

'My daughter, Betsy, has just turned four years old and doesn't want a nappy at night. But every night we have to change her sheets.'

YOUR TOOLS

Dry Night Wheel

See pages 54–71

LET'S DO IT!

WHAT TO DO

- **Make a Dry Night Wheel** (tool) by getting a paper plate and putting an arrow in the middle that can rotate.
- **Colour each third** of the plate a different colour, with the numbers one, two and three in each section.
- **Buy some pull-up pants.**

WHAT TO SAY

- **Explain the new system.** Say, 'Now Mummy and Daddy have made a decision that you are going to wear pull-ups to bed at night. Never during the day. Just at night.' PAUSE.
- **If she instantly protests,** ask her to wait and listen to the fun bit.
- **Show her the wheel.** Say, 'This is the Dry Night Wheel. Now each night before I go to bed I am going to wake you up and take you to do a wee. We want to keep the pull-ups dry.' PAUSE. 'In the morning when you wake up you need to go straight for a wee and then jump back into bed. If the pull-ups are dry in the morning we are going to move the arrow onto "one". If we can then have another dry night we will move it onto "two" and then onto "three". If you have three dry

nights in a row that is when your body is ready to throw the pull-ups away. Your body has to be ready first. This is what all children do first before they go to bed with a bare bottom. After three dry nights you will get a prize.'

ACTION IT!

- **Don't give your child drinks less than two hours before bed.** The last drink should ideally be at dinnertime (17.00).
- **Have her visit the loo** before bedtime.
- **Lift her at 22.30/23.00.** She must be fully awake and walk to the bathroom.
- **If she is dry in the morning** you know you are getting somewhere. Two wet mornings in a row and you know her body isn't ready and you need to put the wheel away for a while.
- **Each morning the arrow moves on** or returns to zero. Returning to zero should not happen continually. Use the wheel once more and if she doesn't get to three consecutive days, just say, 'Do you know what? Your body isn't quite ready yet. We are going to leave it for a while and try again after Easter/Christmas/your birthday.' Leave it for at least two months more.

CARRY ON!

You only carry on for three consecutive nights and after this you decide whether it is now 'bare bum' at night or 'try later'. It is important that you are consistent with no fluids at bedtime and lifting before you go to bed. These two factors give your child the most chance of success. You cannot do more. It is up to her to know when her body is ready.

> **TAKE NOTE!**
> Staying dry through the night is not something you are in control of as a parent. Your child's body will do it when she is ready.

When is my child ready to go dry through the night?

There is no set age for this stage to take place. Some children are ready before others. It all depends on their bladder control. Lifting your child at night (wearing pull-ups), walking her to the loo (at 22.30 as a rough gauge) and then seeing whether she is wet or dry in the morning is all you have to do and this technique will tell you whether she is ready or not. If she still cannot hold her bladder for eight hours (23.00–07.00), she is not ready.

Don't let her drink anything two hours before bedtime – and she needs to have a final wee before jumping into bed.

My child is having accidents after three weeks in pants

'My son, Ryan, aged two years and two months, showed all the signs of wanting to potty train. It started very well, but gradually he began to have more and more accidents. He is now having two or three accidents every other day. Do I put him back in nappies?'

LET'S DO IT!

WHAT TO DO
- **Stop and try again** in two or three months' time or when you can see that he is showing signs of being more ready. Your child is still young.

WHAT TO SAY
- **Explain what you're doing.** Say, 'Now your body is not yet ready to use the loo/potty. We're going back to nappies. We'll try again another day.' If your child isn't ready he will happily return to nappies.

ACTION IT!
- **Explain to your child** that his body is not yet ready. Do this at the start of the day when he is still in his pyjamas – just before getting dressed.
- **From that moment on,** dress him in a nappy and don't look back. You have done the right thing. You have put your child first.

CARRY ON!
Only try potty training again when you believe he is truly ready. This might be nearer to age three than two.

Should I keep on potty training if he has accidents?

Don't be pressured by others around you. Be honest with yourself. Is he truly ready? The chances are you are going to say 'no', so pop him back in nappies.

Potty training is all about timing. You tried and learnt that he wasn't ready.

Take that as a positive. If anyone asks, simply say, 'We gave it a try but my son's bladder isn't ready to take control!'

A good parent doesn't push their child, but encourages him when they can see he has the capacity to achieve the goal.

Out and about scenarios

Taking your child out – whether to the shops, to friends' or relations' homes can be a pressure. You may not feel that you can impose the same strategies when you are out as you can at home – it almost seems as though the world's eyes are on you! However, it's important to remain consistent in your parenting – put your child first and behave as you do at home. And don't forget, being out poses fresh challenges, especially safety!

Your child is on show

Your child reflects on you and your parenting skills: a well-behaved child lets you bask in a warm glow of pride while a child throwing a tantrum in public makes you want the ground to swallow you up. You feel judged. Don't worry! A few helpful tips and you'll be able to deal with anything that crops up with aplomb.

Fresh challenges

Getting around safely poses fresh concerns for parents of toddlers and safety concerns need to be a number-one priority. Your child must hold your hand at certain times (especially when you are crossing the road), he must stay within sight and avoid getting lost – not always straightforward.

My child refuses to hold hands when we're walking along

'As soon as we leave the house my son, Archie, aged two and a half, runs ahead of me. He will not hold my hand and I worry about the busy roads.'

LET'S DO IT!

YOUR SKILLS

You Choose
(hand or sit)

You Choose

See pages 72–77

WHAT TO DO

- **Plan three days** when you are going to go for a walk both morning and afternoon. These walks can be short – around the block or to the letter box. You do them holding hands.

WHAT TO SAY

- **Ask your child to sit on the bottom stair** – once you have put on coats and shoes and are ready to leave.

- **Bend down and make eye contact.** Say, 'Now when we go for a walk today, we are going to post this letter. We are going to hold hands.' PAUSE. 'If your hand comes out of my hand you will sit on the ground until you are ready to stand up and walk with me, holding my hand.' PAUSE. 'Now, are you ready? Hand time!'

ACTION IT!

- **Leave the house together** and immediately hold your child's hand. DO NOT say 'hold my hand' because this is likely to make him not want to! The moment he pulls his hand out of yours, you need to try and hold it again but without mentioning it.

- **If he refuses to hold hands,** then sit him on the ground and use You Choose hand or sit (skill). If the weather is wet, take a plastic bag for him to sit on. Say, 'Now, you sit there for a while.' PAUSE. 'When you are ready we can go and post our letter.'

- **Now act busy,** take a look at your phone or start to rummage around in your bag. Be patient. Do not say anything. Wait.

- **It will be a matter of time before he stands up,** but when he does, just take his hand and focus on something ahead. Using the You Choose (skill) say, 'Shall we run to that tree? Or shall we go and see what is parked around the corner? A blue or red car?'

> **TAKE NOTE!**
> Holding hands allows you to enjoy the journey together far more. You are a team working as one.

Why should my child hold my hand when asked to?

There is nothing more unnerving when walking with a child along a busy road than not knowing whether he is going to walk, run or trip and fall into the oncoming traffic. The chances of any of these things happening are slim, but it's a risk you never want to take.

It is important that your child respects you when you ask him to hold your hand.

It also means that he can fully focus on his surroundings without having to think about all the danger elements.

A child is capable of walking down the street without holding hands if he knows that he must stay by your side. The fast-paced, independent child who wants to run ahead is the one we need to be most worried about.

- **If he pulls away again,** repeat the process. If you are finding that he is pulling away a lot you need to leave him sitting on the ground for longer periods.

CARRY ON!

When you dedicate three days to curing this problem, don't arrange any outings where you have to arrive at a certain time. The aim is that you teach your child that he will be sitting down on the cold ground unless he holds hands and this could delay your trip.

Most children fight this until they realise that their parent is going to be consistent and not relax this boundary. If you let your child run sometimes, you need to make it quite clear that it was a one-off treat, or that you were away from the road and traffic, or that you trusted him to stop at the corner. You do not want to insist that he walks holding hands sometimes and not explain the times when he doesn't. Consistency is the key to success with this rule.

When we're out my child tends to shout to get what he wants

'If my child, Percy, asks for something when we are in a shop or restaurant, he will raise his voice and shout, knowing my embarrassment will get him what he wants. He is five years old.'

YOUR SKILLS

You Choose
See pages 72–77

LET'S DO IT!

WHAT TO DO
- **Plan three days** where you are going to enter a social situation every day. This can be shops or a restaurant.

WHAT TO SAY
- **Before entering** the shop/restaurant you need to bend down and make eye contact with your child. Say, 'Now. We are going to put on our quiet voices before we go into this shop.' PAUSE. 'I am going to be so proud if we can be calm. We are going in here to buy (state item). Nothing else.' PAUSE. 'If we can be quiet in the three shops we are going in there will be a little treat for you at the end of the trip.'

TAKE NOTE!
The treat can be a comic, ice lolly or a new toothbrush and paste. It doesn't have to be huge!

ACTION IT!
- **Aim to enter three shops in succession,** each time giving your child a little talk about quiet voices.
- **Praise him each time you leave the shop** if he has achieved his goal.
- **If he does become loud,** just bend down and look in his eyes using You Choose (skill). Say, 'Little voice or we leave. Now try again.'

Why should my child have to speak quietly?

When out in public it is important to teach your child that he has to consider people around him. The simple message is, 'Not everyone wants to hear your voice'. It is also an important lesson to teach him before he starts school.

Teachers find that loud children are very distracting for others in the class. They can slow down the learning process for everyone, including themselves.

All children need to know that they are part of a bigger picture.

- **At this stage** you need to speed up your shopping so you can have a change of scenery.
- **After day one and three shops,** try a restaurant or a café for an afternoon snack. Or go to the library, use a bus or a train.

CARRY ON!

The more you practise with your child the faster he will learn. It is so important that he understands the importance of respecting other people around him. You can always stop in the middle of a busy area and say, 'Quiet! Let's listen. Is anyone shouting? You see, we can all talk but we do not need to shout at one another.'

For older children, nearer to five years of age, try explaining the concept of 'disturbing the peace' and how it is a 'law of the country'.

My child runs off when I ask her to 'come here'

'My two-year-old, Elena, will purposely run in the opposite direction when I ask her to "come here". This involves me sprinting after her.'

LET'S DO IT!

WHAT TO DO

- **Saying 'come here'** triggers her to run, so stop saying it.
- **Create a Bag of Tricks (tool)** to keep under the buggy. This bag needs to have items of interest in it that you continually rotate.
- **Work on stopping the running** before it starts. For example, when it is time to leave the park approach your child and take her hand. Say, 'Let's go and see what we have under the buggy for you. We need to make our way home now.'
- **When you are in a shop,** always hold her hand. Ask her to hold something you are going to buy to make her feel that she has a role. Let her have a purse of coins to 'pay' with.

YOUR TOOLS

Bag of Tricks

See pages 54–71

Continued ▶

Why it is important not to chase my child

Obviously if your child is running towards danger, you have to chase her. This is a natural instinct and it would be vital. However, if you are in a park and your child starts to run you can stop and make it seem as though you are not focusing on her. View her out of the corner of your eye, but don't let her think your attention is 100 per cent on her.

Walk at speed in her direction but don't 'chase' – it becomes a game and once your child sees it as fun she will continue to do it.

WHAT TO SAY

- **Due to your child's age** there's no need to say too much. If you draw attention to the 'chase' by talking about it you encourage it even more.

ACTION IT!

- **Have the Bag of Tricks under the buggy** with a bottle of water and a healthy snack.
- **Aim to go out for three consecutive days** to work on preventing the sprint-and-chase situation.
- **In the park** guide her to the buggy at the end of play.
- **In the shops** hold her hand and give her a purpose.
- **Always approach her when it is time to go.** Don't say, 'Come here'. This is her trigger to run off.
- **If she runs in the park** and it is safe, let her run and wait on a bench. Say, 'I am on this bench with a snack. Come back when you are ready.'

CARRY ON!

You need to be consistent with this. If you start to chase again the running away will start all over again. Remain consistent in approaching and guiding your child with the Bag of Tricks.

My child screams every time I have to apply sun cream

'I have tried several sun creams and I am sure they don't sting my child, Rachel's, skin. She is fine when it is put on her at nursery! She is three years old and wriggles and whines and screams when her sun cream is applied by me.'

LET'S DO IT!

WHAT TO DO

- **Explain the importance of sun cream** and what will happen if she doesn't wear it.
- **Buy a cream that is easy to apply.**

WHAT TO SAY

- **When you want to apply the cream, say,** 'Now, we are going to do Slap Slip Do Your Bit (skill) and put this cream on together. I am going to squeeze some into your hands and you choose where you are going to put it.' She is likely to put it on her arms. Say, 'Brilliant work. I am so proud of you. I cannot wait to tell Mrs Jones at nursery!'

ACTION IT!

- **While your child is rubbing her arms** with cream you can quickly rub some into the back of her neck and onto her face.
- **If she makes a noise** or starts moaning, ignore it. She knows why she has to have it on. There is nothing more for you to say. The less fuss you make the less likely she is to make a fuss herself. Children will only create a scene if they think they will get a reaction.

Continued ▶

YOUR TOOLS

Shout Spot

See pages 54–71

YOUR SKILLS

Slap Slip Do Your Bit

See pages 72–77

Why my child needs to wear sun cream

Sun cream is so important and needs to be explained to children. If you want to use shock tactics, hold a chicken breast with skin on it over a flame and ask your child to watch it burn. This is what the sun does to your skin. If necessary, find some images of sunburn on the internet.

CARRY ON!

If she totally refuses to have her sun cream applied and is running away, place her on the Shout Spot (tool) in the hallway. Say, 'You can sit there and have a shout until you are ready for this sun cream.' PAUSE. Say, 'We want to get into the garden to fill the paddling pool!'

- **Remain consistent** with this.
- **She puts some on,** you put some on.
- **She moans** and you ignore it.
- **She runs away** – she goes to the Shout Spot!

OUT AND ABOUT SCENARIO 5

My child keeps removing his sunhat

'My son, Joseph, is just two years old and he keeps taking his hat off.'

YOUR TOOLS

Shout Spot

See pages 54–71

YOUR SKILLS

You Choose

See pages 72–77

LET'S DO IT!

WHAT TO DO

- **Before leaving the house** explain to your child that if he removes his hat at the park he is going to have to sit under a tree, which is your outdoor Shout Spot (tool), to stop his head getting hot and burnt.
- **Once this has been said** you have to action it.

WHAT TO SAY

- **Just before leaving the house** sit down with your child and make eye contact. Say, 'Today is a hat day. It has to be worn. If you take it off on the way to the park we are going to stand still and not move until you have put it back on.' PAUSE. 'I am sure you are going to wear it the whole time we are outside.' PAUSE. Say, 'If you take it off at the park you need to sit under the tree in the shade. I will take some books to look at if you want to do this.'

Why my child should wear a sunhat

A burnt head or tops of the ears is so painful that a hat is vital for a child to wear outside, whether it is actually sunny or overcast.

As a parent, it is an awful feeling if you see, at the end of the day, that your child is burnt – all because you didn't remain consistent about him wearing the hat.

ACTION IT!

- **Make sure you 'freeze'** if the hat comes off in the street.
- **Don't move** until he is ready to put his hat back on.
- **If he takes the hat** off at the park, simply go to him with the hat and say, using You Choose (skill), 'Under the tree or hat?'
- **Put the hat back on,** but the moment he removes it take him to the tree.
- **Don't be concerned if he shouts.** This shows you that the discipline is working. He is frustrated that he cannot play until his hat is put back on.
- **Ignore the noise** and once all is quiet simply pop the hat on his head and guide him back to play. Say, 'Look at that little boy on the roundabout. I think he would love a strong boy like you to push him.'

CARRY ON!

Remain consistent and each time your child removes the hat remind him of his options. Use You Choose and say, 'Hat on or sit in the shade of the tree?' By doing this for three consecutive days, by the third day he should have full understanding that play cannot take place without wearing a hat!

My child doesn't stop on his scooter/bike when I ask

'My son, Louis, goes like a rocket on his scooter. He cannot hear me calling to him because he gets so far away.'

LET'S DO IT!

YOUR TOOLS

Landmark Spots

See pages 54–71

WHAT TO DO

- **Plan three consecutive days** where you head out on the scooter twice a day. You will use the Landmark Spots (tool) on each journey. Teach your child local landmarks. When he has learnt them you will find that he naturally stops at them.

- **Buy several 'spot' stickers** that you can easily get to in your pocket.

WHAT TO SAY

- **Before your next journey out on the scooter,** sit your child on the bottom stair at home and bend down in front of him and make eye contact. Say, 'Now. I have decided to play Landmark Spots when we are out with the scooter. This means that you listen to where I want you to scoot to and I meet you there.' PAUSE. 'I might say, "Meet you

Why can't he just scoot until he decides to stop?

Scooters are a wonderful creation and give your child a true sense of freedom. They go at great speed – at times they seem to go faster than a child's brain!

Your child needs to always be able to hear you and focus on you as well as being able to scoot ahead.

This is simple safety, especially when, more often than not, he is scooting alongside a road.

at the post box." And I meet you there. Or I might say, "Meet you on the corner." And I meet you there.' PAUSE. 'When I arrive I put a spot on your scooter. When you have spots from the top to the bottom of the handle you get a prize!'

ACTION IT!
- **Now leave the house** with full confidence that he is going to listen to you calling to him and will do as you ask.
- **Work fast and name the landmark** before he gets bored and scoots ahead each time.
- **At every landmark** you need to quickly think of the next one. The scooting needs to flow smoothly.
- **You can add up the spots** at the stops and give them to him at the end of each journey, if you wish.

CARRY ON!
This is something you must remain consistent with. If your child finds that you let him scoot off sometimes and not others he will not know when to do what you say and when to just do what he likes.

Remain consistent with naming the landmarks and asking him to stop. This way you know that he is safe.

I can't shop without my child insisting I buy him something

'I find it so difficult to shop without my child, Joel, buying as much as me! I do this to keep the peace, but realise I have now made a rod for my own back.'

YOUR TOOLS

Plan Ahead

Money Purse

See pages 54–71

LET'S DO IT!

WHAT TO DO

- **Plan your trip using the Plan Ahead (tool)** and write it down on a piece of paper. For example: post letter, buy a birthday present for Christopher, buy milk and bread, collect dry-cleaning.
- **Have a purse (Money Purse tool)** for your child to use to buy some items with.

WHAT TO SAY

- **Sit down with your child** just before starting the shopping. This might be in the car in the car park, at the bus stop or before leaving the house. Say, 'Now, we are going to go to four shops.' PAUSE.
- **Give your child the purse.** Say, 'It's your job to carry the money. You will pay for the things. Now at the shops we are going to buy a present for Christopher and then go to the supermarket for some bread and milk.' PAUSE. 'We are not buying anything for you or me.' PAUSE. 'Do you understand? You can buy the things with the money in your purse and I will put them in my bag.'

ACTION IT!

- **Go into the shops** and aim to shop quite quickly.
- **Go directly to the till** and let your child empty the purse out onto the counter.
- **Praise him when you leave the shop** for being so grown up.
- **In the last shop you visit,** you can decide if you want to praise him further by letting him choose something to have for dessert, a comic, a new toothbrush.

Does it matter if my child shops till he drops?

It would be the easy option to let your child simply pick up and buy what he wants, but this isn't real life.

We all have limits and the sooner your child realises this the better.

All children want things, but unless they regularly hear 'no' said to them in shops they do not accept this as an answer. The more you say it, the easier it is for them – and for you.

CARRY ON!

Always state the shops you are going in and what you are going to buy. Aim to go to three or four shops maximum. Praise your child when he does well. If he does start to make a fuss about not buying things for him simply bend down to his level and say in a calm voice, 'We are not allowed to make this noise in their shop. Let's make it outside and we can then go to the next shop.' Once he is calm, you can say, 'Right, last shop. You pay and then we will go home and watch some TV.'

Remain consistent. Don't be nervous of the shouting. He can do this and then realise that it achieves nothing. Once he realises this, your child will tend to give up.

My child will refuse to walk and insists I carry him

'My two-and-a-half-year-old, Nathan, will start to walk when we are out, but it's not long before he wants to be carried. This is fine at the weekend with my husband but at other times he's too heavy for me.'

YOUR SKILLS

You Choose

See pages 72–77

LET'S DO IT!

WHAT TO DO
- **Set aside three days** when you go out of the house twice a day, telling yourself that you are not going to carry your child.

WHAT TO SAY
- **Sit with your child** just before going out of the house. Ensure you have eye contact and that he is fully focused on you. Say, 'Now listen. I have decided that while we are out I am not going to pick you up. There is going to be NO carrying.' PAUSE. 'If you want to rest your legs we can stop at a bench or you can sit in your buggy and look at some books.'
- **Now show him** the books under the buggy. Say, 'Now, let's start by leaving the house holding hands.'
- **Now tell him where you are going.** Say, 'We are going to post a letter. After that we will go to the library to change our books and perhaps do some colouring.'

Why it is important not to carry my child everywhere

Children can be very crafty at using their parents as modes of transport! It is far easier to see the world from a higher level and not to have to think about walking and staying safe. To be carried is the easy option on both accounts, but it is stunting your child's development.

A child will strengthen his muscles by walking and also build up his stamina. He will have to be aware of the world around him and listen to you and pay attention to holding hands, road-crossing and generally be more involved in everything. These are all skills a child needs – to grasp the concept of 'the big wide world'.

ACTION IT!

- **Confidently leave the house** with the buggy, but have him walk, holding his hand.
- **Point out things** that you pass and chat about what books you are going to get at the library. The moment he asks to be carried, simply bend down and, using You Choose (skill), say, 'You choose: walking or buggy and books?'
- **Place a book** on the seat of the buggy. If he starts to shout, simply stand up and let him do so. He has just gained the realisation that you meant what you said when you were at home.
- **Stand patiently,** acting busy – look at your phone as a distraction.
- **Only when he has quietened** and you can hear he has 'finished' do you take his hand and continue walking. He will either conform, shout or want to get in the buggy.
- **If the shouting begins,** do as you did before but ensure you leave him long enough to get the frustration out of his system.

TAKE NOTE!
Don't think that you cannot ever pick your child up, just don't revert to being his 'mode of transport'!

CARRY ON!

This process needs to be repeated at least twice a day for three consecutive days before you are likely to see a change and know your child will adjust to the new system. Remain consistent and plan to go on outings that aren't constrained by time. If you happen to pick your child up on day two and walk with him on your hip he will expect this to happen from that moment on and you will have to go back to square one.

My child refuses to wear her coat/hat/gloves

'My child, Polly, refuses to keep warm in the winter. This drives me mad. We have a stand-off every time we leave the house and when she does put on her coat we get to the end of the road and she takes it off again.'

YOUR SKILLS

Freeze Rule

See pages 72–77

LET'S DO IT!

WHAT TO DO
- **On the days when it clearly is too cold to leave the house** without a coat you need to insist that it is worn. Use the Freeze Rule (skill).

WHAT TO SAY
- **Before leaving the house** and the battle beginning give your child a warning. Say, 'We are leaving the house in ten minutes. I have just been outside and I am telling you now that it is a coat day!' PAUSE. 'You don't have to wear gloves or a hat, but you MUST wear a coat.'
- **When it is time to leave the house,** bend down and make eye contact with your child. Say, 'This coat is staying on for the entire outing. If you take it off we will stop in the street and not move until you put it on again.' PAUSE. 'We want to get to where we are going quickly, so I know you will be sensible and keep it on.'

ACTION IT!
- **Leave the house with the coat on** and the moment it is taken off say, 'Right, I am standing here until you are ready to put your coat back on.'
- **Make sure you do not hold the coat** or take it from her when she removes it.
- **Now act busy** on your phone and ignore her. Act as though you would happily stand and wait all day.
- **You need to stand there** for as long as it takes.
- **Eventually she will put on her coat,** but probably not fasten it up. Leave this for now. She has done well to put it back on.

Why insist on a coat if she claims she doesn't need it?

It is both your judgement and your child's as to whether she needs a coat. Many children go through the 'no coat' phase. If it clearly is a day when a coat is needed then it is important to insist, but be aware that children don't feel the cold the same way as grown-ups do.

A 'skin' thermal top under a top and a jumper can sometimes be enough.

This is a subject where you probably need to keep an open mind.

CARRY ON!

If she tries to walk away from you without her coat on you need to take her hand/arm and bring her back. Say, 'We will stand here until you are ready to go. Put your coat on and then we are off!'

Remain consistent. When leaving the house always state whether it is a 'coat' or 'no-coat' day. Insist the coat goes on if the weather is cold. If and when she removes her coat use the Freeze Rule on the street. Remain still, don't move until the coat is on her back once again.

My child refuses to sit down when we go to a restaurant

'As soon as we enter a restaurant my child, Jade, wants to run around. She will only briefly come to the table.'

YOUR TOOLS

Bag of Tricks

See pages 54–71

YOUR SKILLS

Teacher Tone

See pages 72–77

LET'S DO IT!

WHAT TO DO

- **Gather up a Bag of Tricks** (tool) to entertain your child at the table. Ideas for what to include are: mini Lego kit, lump of playdough, slinky, old calculator, colouring book, felt-tip pens, stickers, mini cars/trains, beads and thread. This is a bag that only gets opened in restaurants or cafés and is not played with at home. Try to rotate the items and put fresh things in it so that you can keep her interest going.

- **Aim to take one thing out of the bag at a time.** You will want to pace the activities.

WHAT TO SAY

- **When you arrive at the restaurant,** before you walk inside, bend down and make eye contact with your child. Say, 'Now, we are going to go in and find our table and put our bag down.' PAUSE. 'Then we are going to have a walk around the restaurant together and go and find the loo to wash our hands.'

- **Now use Teacher Tone** (skill). Say, 'There will be NO running around in here or we will be asked to leave. It's very dangerous for waiters carrying hot food around.' PAUSE. 'Are you ready? Let's go.'

ACTION IT!

- **Go into the restaurant** holding your child's hand.
- **Choose a table in a corner** where your child can be 'boxed in' and find it hard to just get down whenever she wants.
- **Place the Bag of Tricks on** the table.
- **Calmly take your child's hand** and go for a walk around the restaurant, pointing things out to her.
- **Visit the loo.** Here bend down and give her a firm chat before returning to the table. Say, 'Now, we are going to have a lovely lunch.

We will go and sit at the table, choose our food and then see what we have in our Bag of Tricks to play with.' PAUSE. Say, 'If there is any silly behaviour or running around we will come straight back here! To the loos. We will stay here until you are ready to behave.' PAUSE. 'Are you ready to go and choose your food? Come on. Let's go.'

- **Hold her hand** to show you are in control of the situation and that she can't run around.
- **Choose what you are going to eat** and then sit and chat. Don't feel that you need to immediately open the Bag of Tricks.
- **Open the Bag of Tricks** and take out one of the activities. Use them one at a time at the table. Make them last.
- **After the main course** take your child for a restaurant stroll and hand-washing again. Tell her how well she is doing.
- **Return to the table** and choose dessert.
- **Get the Bag of Tricks** out again and find something new in it.
- **After dessert** you can tell whether your child is engaged in an activity or whether it is time to collect the bill and leave.
- **Praise her** for her behaviour and tell her you enjoyed lunch with her.

CARRY ON!

Continue to go into restaurants regularly. This is the only way your child will get used to the atmosphere and be able to manage it. Divide the occasion up so that it doesn't feel so daunting: restaurant stroll, loo chat, choose from menu, two or three activities from the Bag of Tricks, put the Bag of Tricks away when the food arrives (no toys on table), restaurant stroll, loo visit – hand wash, look at menu – choose dessert, two activities, eat dessert, complete activity, collect the bill!

Why should my child sit nicely in a restaurant?

You probably like to eat out as a family and the outing should be enjoyable for everyone. Your long-term aim should be that your child can behave nicely in a restaurant and manage the outing easily. However, you need to have realistic expectations: she won't be able to sit at a table without entertainment, so she needs to be busy while waiting for the food to come. The same applies when she has finished her meal – at home she may be used to leaving the table as soon as she has finished. With a Bag of Tricks, your child should be able to sit for one to one and a half hours, with intervals of strolling around.

My child can be very loud in social situations

'My child, Dotty, talks very loudly. She is not necessarily misbehaving but she is drawing attention to our family in social situations.'

YOUR TOOLS

Shout Spot

See pages 54–71

YOUR SKILLS

Teacher Tone

See pages 72–77

LET'S DO IT!

WHAT TO DO

- **Start to correct your child** when she talks too loudly at home. It will then be easier for her to adapt when she is out of the house.

WHAT TO SAY

- **Ensure you have eye contact** and your child's undivided attention. Say, 'Now. I have decided that I am going to help you with your lovely voice. You speak too loudly and it has to stop.' PAUSE. 'When you talk too loudly I am going to say "volume" or I will show you my hand and lower it like this.' PAUSE. 'If you see this (hand movement) or hear me say, "volume" you need to talk more softly.' PAUSE. 'I will only listen to you when the volume is right. If you continue to shout I will not listen.' PAUSE. 'Do you understand?' This needs to be delivered with a firm confident Teacher Tone (skill). It's something you are telling her is going to change; you are not asking her.

Why can't my child talk loudly?

Just to make sure, first get your child's hearing tested to confirm that she is hearing clearly and that this is not the reason why she is shouting.

It is important for your child to realise that when she talks, not everyone around her needs, or wants, to hear her.

This is a simple lesson in learning to respect others and realising that she is not the centre of the universe.

ACTION IT!

- **As soon as you have delivered this speech** to your child you have to follow through and remain consistent.

- **At home you can use your hand** to show her she must lower her voice and if she doesn't adjust it you can walk away and just say 'volume' over your shoulder. She should start to adjust over the course of the three-day process.

- **On day one** visit a restaurant at dinnertime – not too late as you don't want her to be too tired to be able to conform.

- **Before you go into the restaurant** bend down and make eye contact. Say, 'Remember "volume". If you see me do this with my hand you know what you have to do. Come on! Let's go and get our dinner.'

- **Throughout the meal remind her,** when necessary, to lower her voice.

- **If you are constantly having to remind her** and she keeps returning to her usual high volume, take her hand and go and talk to her in the loo. Just calmly say, 'Let's go for a little walk and take a trip to the loo.' Use your firm Teacher Tone. Say, 'Now listen. This is the last time I am going to ask you to turn the volume down. You know how to talk quietly.' PAUSE. 'If the volume goes up again we are going to come back here and we will be in here for a long time. Or we will just go home. No dessert.' PAUSE. 'Now. Think soft voice and let's go!' Take her hand and confidently walk back to the table.

CARRY ON!

You need to remain consistent and correct her volume every time it seems too loud, whether you are at home or out. If she is still being too loud and refusing to listen to you, she should visit the Shout Spot (tool) or go to her bedroom. She needs to understand that it is not socially acceptable to shout and that if you want to shout you end up on your own. Use consistency and she should start to correct herself.

My child asks, 'Can we go now?' when we visit Grandma

'It is so embarrassing. No sooner have we arrived at my mother's house than my son, Joe, aged four, pipes up that he wants to leave!'

YOUR TOOLS

Box of Activities

Bag of Tricks

Shout Spot

See pages 54–71

YOUR SKILLS

Teacher Tone

See pages 72–77

LET'S DO IT!

WHAT TO DO

- **Put together a Box of Activities** (tool) to keep at Grandma's house. These are activities you can do at the kitchen table (for example: paint your own mini teaset, bead-threading, paint your own moneybox, biscuit-decorating kit or playdough).
- **Create a Bag of Tricks** (tool) to take to Grandma's house.
- **Be realistic.** A visit to Grandma's needs three or four activities to be stretched over a two-hour period. The time can also include a snack and some TV.
- **After two hours** a child needs a change of scene, whether this is digging in the garden or a trip to the shops/park and then return to Grandma's for another activity.

WHAT TO SAY

- **On the morning of the day** you are going to Grandma's, sit down with your child. He needs to have his full attention on you. Make eye contact. Say, 'Now. I have a plan for what we are going to do when we go and visit Grandma today.'
- **He might start to moan,** but just wait until he stops and then continue. Say, 'You are going to like this. Now. Last night I put a box in the car full of fun things to do. It's called the Box of Activities (tool). We are going to leave it at Grandma's house and every time we go there we will take something out and have fun with it.' PAUSE. 'We are also going to take a bag with things to do called your Bag of Tricks (tool).' PAUSE. 'We will never go to Grandma's house without the Bag of Tricks.'
- **Now produce your Teacher Tone** (skill). Say, 'Now I DO NOT want to hear "I want to go home" when we are at Grandma's house. If you do, I am going to sit you on the Shout Spot (tool) just like we do at home. You will stay there until I am ready to come and get you.' PAUSE.

Why should children go to places they don't want to?

Children need to understand from an early age that some things are done for them while some things are done for other people.

This builds on the understanding that the world doesn't revolve around one person (them). We are all part of a bigger picture.

'Do you understand?' He doesn't have to reply. 'So, this morning we are going to Grandma's house to show her our Box of Activities and we will take our Bag of Tricks. We will have lunch with her, then watch some TV. You can take one of your DVDs to watch. Then after the DVD we will come home.'

ACTION IT!

- **Let Grandma know** about the plan.
- **Have the Box of Activities ready.**
- **Pack up the Bag of Tricks.**
- **Let your child choose** a DVD for after lunch.
- **When you arrive at Grandma's house** bend down on the doorstep and make eye contact with your child. Say, 'We are going to do some great things at Grandma's kitchen table. You are not to say, "Can we go home" – remember? Don't forget, please. I don't want you having to sit on the bottom step (Shout Spot). Let's go and show Grandma this Box of Activities.'

CARRY ON!

You need to be consistent and remember that if he does say, 'I want to go home' he is to sit on the Shout Spot. Ensure there is plenty for him to do at Grandma's to prevent that from happening. Praise him for behaving well. Encourage him to draw pictures for Grandma and to put them in the post to send to her. This will help him to build up his relationship with her.

My child is pushing other children at the playground

'My son, Stephen, is very impatient and if someone is on playground apparatus that he wants to go on he will push them out of the way. He is two and a half years old and I feel he should know better.'

LET'S DO IT!

YOUR TOOLS

Shout Spot

See pages 54–71

YOUR SKILLS

Teacher Tone

See pages 72–77

WHAT TO DO
- **Note where there is a tree** away from all the children and apparatus. This is going to be your outdoor Shout Spot (tool).

WHAT TO SAY
- **Before you go into the playground** bend down and make eye contact with your child. Say, 'Now. We are going to have a lovely time in the playground. There is going to be no pushing.' PAUSE. 'If you do push anyone, I am going to sit you under that tree and you will stay there until I am ready – just like when you are at home and sit on the Shout Spot.' PAUSE. 'Now. What shall we play on first? Let's go.'

Why it is important for children to wait

We all detest waiting. Therefore it is quite understandable how hard it is for a child. However life is full of moments spent waiting, so the sooner your child learns to wait the better. The simple lesson is that you will not always be first. Once he accepts this, he will find it far easier to wait patiently.

ACTION IT!

- **Now that you have said it,** you need to action it. He has a full understanding that it is wrong to push and hurt others. It doesn't need to be spoken about any more.
- **The moment he pushes,** act and take him to the tree (Shout Spot). Walk him there calmly. Do not act angry in any way.
- **Once you reach the tree** put your Teacher Tone (skill) on. Say, 'We do NOT push. Stay here until I am ready.' Let him sit down.
- **Stand close to the tree,** but don't look at him.
- **If he stands up and starts to walk away** put him back by the tree.
- **This needs to continue** until he has become angry and then has calmed down.
- **Bend down** and make eye contact. Use a calm voice now (the 'discipline moment' has passed). Say, 'So, push anyone else again and you stand by the tree for a long time. Now, let's go and play nicely and we have to wait, remember. No pushing. You are my good boy.'

CARRY ON!

Your child will soon realise that there is no benefit in pushing if he is going to be removed from the fun. Remain consistent with this and hopefully after three or four 'tree visits' the pushing should reduce and then cease altogether. The key is to act decisively every time he does push – to get in there first.

> **TAKE NOTE!**
> Children do have little disagreements and push one another. If it is a 'tit for tat' situation ignore it. This is something they should resolve together as long as it isn't too rough (in which case it needs breaking up).

My child always wants the same snack as other children

'Whenever I am out with friends and the time comes for the children to have their snacks, my child, Maya, instantly wants what the others have. She then sulks when she can't.'

YOUR TOOLS

Snack Menu

Shout Spot

See pages 54–71

LET'S DO IT!

WHAT TO DO

- **Create a Snack Menu** (tool) on a piece of paper and decorate it with your child. This needs to contain between five and eight snack choices (any more and it will be too hard for her to choose). You need to be happy with anything she chooses, so don't put 'chocolate muffin' on the list if you don't want her to choose it!

WHAT TO SAY

- **Once you have decorated the menu,** explain it to your child. Say, 'Now, this is our family snack menu. When we are packing up a snack to take out we choose from this list.'
- **Read it to her.** Say, 'Now, today we are going to soft play to meet Jordan and Leonie. What snack should we pack?'
- **Let her choose** and wrap it in tin foil and put it in her bag. Allow her to do this so that what she decides on sticks in her mind. Say, 'Now Jordan and Leonie will bring a snack and it won't be the same as yours. They will have different things. You will have (state item).' PAUSE. Say, 'No moaning and groaning. Do you understand?' You hope for a response, but it isn't vital. Say, 'Okay. Now let's find something to play with until we go.'

ACTION IT!

- **Now that you have made the Snack Menu** and your child has chosen her snack you have to go along with it.
- **When snacks are being handed out** say, 'Remember. Everyone is going to have a different snack.'
- **If a sulking occurs,** ignore it. If it builds up to shouting, you need to find a Shout Spot (tool) in the vicinity. Say, 'It is fine to shout. Do it here and when you have finished come back and have your snack.'

CARRY ON!

Remain consistent with the process and you will find that your child realises that the moaning gets no attention from you or your friends or from the other children. Neither does the moaning win her a different snack. Keep on asking your child to choose her own snack, then wrap it up and put it in the bag. This is the initial step to understanding not only that all snacks are different but that she has to 'own' her own decisions. Prepare her now, because the next issue on the list is 'lunchbox envy' at school! We all remember that one!

Why shouldn't my child have the same as others?

It is impossible to go through life without looking at what other people have and wishing, for a moment, that you had that item, figure, holiday, car – or whatever.

This is a normal emotion that we can all identify with. Children need to understand as soon as possible that you cannot always have the same as everyone else.

It's a hard life lesson, but one that needs to be learnt as early as possible.

Conclusion

By the time you read this you may have tried out – and found to be successful – perhaps one or two three-day processes, taking inspiration from the case studies and the scenarios in this book. I do hope so. Hopefully you will have found the process effective enough to carry on using for a whole range of family problems and now feel far more confident in your parenting skills in general.

As your child grows and changes you will experience many instances when you have to adapt and adjust – maybe new problems present themselves – and you have to rethink your strategies. Don't be put off by these unexpected things. Life is full of them and it is a challenge to keep on rising to the occasion and dealing with new problems. But remember, the key to success is communicating with each other, especially your child, listening to what he has to say, deciding what to do as a family and then being consistent when you apply your strategy and follow through with it. Always talk about everything with your child so that he knows what to expect in new situations and can see that you know what you're doing! That way he will feel confident and happy to go with the flow, feeling completely secure and reassured that you are

in charge of his life. He can rely on you! There will be times, such as holidays, trips to stay with grandparents and friends, plus a myriad other events that can throw even the most settled child off track. A new baby might arrive in the family or a relationship might break down. You might have to suspend your usual routine and get your child used to a different, though temporary, one – adapting and adjusting all the time. Don't despair or feel that all your hard work has gone to waste. Returning to the original routine is always challenging, but you will find that the three-day process can help you get your family back to normal in just three days – all with a large dose of your consistency and perseverence!

I hope you have found the ideas in this book fun and enjoyable, as well as creative, not to mention effective, and that you can keep on coming back to it if you need to remind yourself about what to do and to get inspiration. The most important thing is to enjoy your children and all of family life and I sincerely hope that this book has helped you fulfil yourself as a parent.

Testimonials

Sleeping problems

'I was getting a bit desperate because my daughter, aged nine months, kept waking at night a minimum of three times (when we were lucky) breastfeeding to re-fall asleep and sometimes ending up sleeping with me.

I read an article in the NCT magazine about this miraculous lady called "The Bespoke Nanny" and I thought, that's the one I need!

Kathryn lived with us for 72 hours and in this time she worked non-stop. When my daughter needed settling she would cuddle her, talk to her and smile. She did not take the approach of controlled crying. Kathryn did so much more than teach my daughter to sleep. She talked and guided me with her food, altered her routine and taught me ways to stimulate her during the day.

Before she arrived I dreaded the moment, but it all ended up with three days of holiday! Kathryn trained us as parents to wait, understand, listen and recognise our daughter's voice. The result: my child now sleeps on average from 19.30–07.15.'
Veronica

'I found Kathryn Mewes to be highly effective with her unique style and applications. She assessed our son in less than half a day and was able to focus on the sleep issue right away. Three days and nights later, he was on the path to better nights for everyone in our household!

Kathryn really does deliver on her three-day promise. She is intuitive, passionate, articulate and kind. She also worked with our twins and helped them navigate the screaming and tantrum phase with aplomb. I highly recommend Kathryn's effective and lasting approach.'
Lynn

'After two nights my son was well on the way to sleeping through the night. Both of my babies were weaned from the breast and new flavours and textures were being introduced. Our freezer was stocked with homemade food!

Kathryn has a great affinity with children and is excellent company and a very easy person to have around your home. She has high energy levels and a good sense of humour. I would recommend her to any parent.'

Mrs McNamara

'With a new baby number two and a terrible two life was reasonably stressful. Our nights were being broken by baby-feeding and by a toddler having never really established a night-time routine and demanding frequent comforting. Most nights felt as though the two were tag-teaming and we were a long way away from a full night's sleep.

When Kathryn arrived at our home she immediately fitted in. Within a very short space of time she had befriended our toddler and worked out the ways of our household.

By the time Kathryn left she had established a structured day and night-time routine for both of our girls. They were taking their day-time nap at the same time and for a lengthy time and going through the night.

The best money we ever spent!'

Emelye

'Kathryn has allowed us to have a much better understanding of our daughter and has left us with a clear direction for moving forward.

You cannot put a price on a good night's sleep and therefore Kathryn is, without a doubt, worth every penny!'

Mr and Mrs Butcher

Eating problems

'When I called Kathryn I was beside myself – all I seemed to do was cook all day and then throw the uneaten results in the bin. I'm a good cook, it's just that no one would eat it! Each meal brought on a feeling of dread. What can I give them? What won't I have to throw away? My cooking repertoire was getting smaller and smaller, and with it my will to carry on. I needed help and fast!

After a fantastically reassuring call with Kathryn, it was clear that she was right for us and we straight away made an appointment for a consultation. Kathryn met with my husband and I, and she very quickly understood where we needed help and guidance, and our three-day sessions were booked in.

I can honestly say I was really looking forward to her visit, I knew it would be challenging at times, but this was an opportunity to make a real difference for our family.

My brief to Kathryn was simple, I wanted to be able to make one meal for our family and then watch it being emptied into hungry little mouths rather than into the bin.

Within hours of being in our house, miracles happened. My younger son was spooning new tastes and textures into his mouth. And my eldest son was asking if it was the next mealtime, just so he could cook again!

The impact on our family has been enormous. My boys are eating well and are eating a fantastically rounded diet – and as such, are so much happier and healthier in-themselves. My mealtime dread has gone and been replaced by the contentment of full little tummies.'

Alison

'How lucky for us that we found Kathryn to help us. In 72 hours she had my four-year-old son settling himself to sleep and my seven-month-old daughter weaning onto solid foods, something I was very anxious about the first time round.

It has been a magical experience and I shall be saying to everyone that "just like Elvis.....she's alive....Mary Poppins is alive!... and she has visited our home".

Welcoming Kathryn into our home was the most pain-free method of smoothing out our family wrinkles!'

Emma

'Kathryn made ground-breaking progress with my son, aged seven, in terms of getting him eating, getting involved with cooking and communicating how he felt. She taught both him and me so much.

I realised we were in a rut when I contacted Kathryn, but only now do I realise quite how far we had sunk. An immense weight has been lifted off my shoulders and instead of dreading the weekly food shop I now look forward to it due to Kathryn's ideas and guidance.

Kathryn walked into our lives seamlessly. She is sensitive, supportive, encouraging, kind, professional and great fun. My only wish is that I had found her sooner!'

Emily

'We all loved having Kathryn in our home. She sat with Lucien and they created a weekend menu together and cooked all of the weekend food. She believes in children making their own choices rather than feeling food is forced upon them.

After eating the crunchy chicken Kathryn asked, "What did your taste buds tell you, Lucien?" "That was quite nice" he replied!

Our three days with Kathryn helped iron out Lucien's issues with mealtimes.'

Rosie Millard, Daily Telegraph Journalist

Behaviour problems

'I feel so lucky that we could ask for your help. You totally changed the way I viewed my son. There was a time when I dreaded him waking in the morning.

After three days with you and systems in place, our house is a calmer and happier place.'

Liz

'Our son, very intelligent, but struggling to engage at school. Kathryn got us, them and him to sing from the same hymn sheet. Tackling the problem before it got too big.

Kathryn was with us for three days, I would have happily let her move in!'

Mr Stevens

'I called Kathryn in when I feared that my one- and three-year-olds were moments away from being one step ahead of me rather than the other way around. And, in fact, almost as soon as Kathryn arrived, she observed that they were already there!

All was not lost and within hours, Kathryn had provided me with several clear strategies, which were both easy to grasp for me and exciting for the boys. Our initial problems of squabbling and fighting back were very quickly resolved, and although the boys found a shift back in power hard, they soon got used to the new ways of working and calm quickly returned to the house!

What has been most interesting to note is that once you are back in control and a clear reward/consequence programme is in place, the benefits spill over into all parts of behaviour. Both of my children now pride themselves in "being good" and love to receive their rewards and also understand clearly when they are fast approaching the boundaries of consequence.

We're still not perfect, that's life, but with practice we are a considerably happier and calmer household for Kathryn's recent visit.'

Mrs Harker

'My husband and I would like to thank you for the amazing advice you gave us to help with our son's communication and behaviour.

   He is thrilled about his reward charts and after two days this system is definitely helping. We were all, including Nanna and Grandad, completely "wowed" by you.'

Mrs Stevens

'I was feeling so frustrated with my son for not listening to me and I felt surprised by how angry I could feel towards him. I would shout really loud sometimes. We read through our new house rules at mealtimes and he is very clear about what is acceptable and not acceptable behaviour. Now after just one warning he will listen to me and stop the naughty behaviour. I don't have to get so angry with him. It's a huge relief.'

Esther

Index

Acknowledgements

Grateful thanks to Susanna Abbott and Catherine Knight for the opportunity to write this book.

To Jo Godfrey Wood and Peggy Sadler at Bookworx for editing and designing the book.

To all of the families I have helped with The Three-Day Plan.

Your input and suggestions for the book have been fundamental to the final product.